FLORENCE

Hints for using the guide

Following the tradition established by Karl Baedeker in 1846, buildings and works of art, places of natural beauty, and sights of particular interest, as well as hotels and restaurants of especially high quality, are distinguished by one ★ or two ★★.

To make it easier to locate the various places listed in the Sights from A to Z section of the guide, their coordinates are shown in red at the head of each entry: e.g. Palazzo Pitti H/J 6/7.

Only a selection of hotels, restaurants and shops can be given; no reflection is implied, therefore, on establishments not included.

In a time of rapid change it is difficult to ensure that all the information given is entirely accurate and up to date, and the possibility of error can never be entirely eliminated.

Although the publishers can accept no responsibility for inaccuracies and omissions, they are constantly endeavouring to improve the quality of their guides and are therefore always grateful for corrections and suggestions for improvement.

Preface

This guide to Florence is one of the new generation of Baedeker guides.

Baedeker guides, illustrated throughout in colour, are designed to meet the needs of the modern traveller. They are quick and easy to consult, with the principal features of interest described in alphabetical order and practical details about location, opening hours, etc., shown in the margin.

This city guide is divided into three parts. The first part gives a general account of the city, its population, culture, transport, economy, famous people, history, and history of art; in the second part the principal places of interest are described; the third part contains a variety of practical information designed to help visitors to find their way about and to make the most of their stay. Both the sights and the Practical Information are given in alphabetical order.

The picturesque Ponte Vecchio

Baedeker pocket guides, which are regularly updated, are noted for their concentration on essentials and their convenience of use. They contain many coloured illustrations and specially drawn plans, and at the back of the book will be found a large plan of the city. Each main entry in the Sights from A to Z section gives the coordinates of the square on the plan in which the particular feature can be located. Users of this guide, therefore, should have no difficulty in finding what they want to see.

Contents

Baedeker Specials

Cradle of the

Venus

from the famous painting by Botticelli

Florentia, a flowery name befitting a city boasting the lily in its coat of arms, probably derives from the campi fiorentini or flowering fields, the flower-covered meadows on the banks of the Arno which helped give Florence its sobriquet in Roman times.

The people of Florence are by tradition hard working and in the 15th c. some of its citizens achieved such prosperity through cloth manufacture and trade that they were able to devote themselves almost exclusively to the finer things of life. The call was to escape the cultural darkness of the Middle Ages and revive the spirit of Antiquity. The rinascità, the rebirth of Antiquity in the 15th c., is what gives this art-enlightened cloth town on the Arno its fascination; nowhere was the rediscovery of nature and humanity effected in so revolutionary a manner as in Florence. Sculptors such as Donatello and Michelangelo, casters of bronze such as Ghiberti and Verrocchio, architects and builders such as Brunelleschi and Michelozzo, and painters such as Masaccio and Ghirlandaio, all masters of their art, endowed their work with a hitherto unexplored dimension of significance by drawing upon nature.

The heyday of Florentine humanism in the 15th and 16th c. was founded on a solid craft tradition and wide-flung belief that money is the only form of wealth, combined with an instinctive understanding of art and spirit of

City Panorama

A wonderful view of Florence from the Piazzale Michaelangelo

Bobli

The beautiful gardens invite visitors to take a stroll

Renaissance

munificence. The civic authorities, guilds and wealthy patricians, the Medici among them, vied with each other in embellishing the city through art, not uninfluenced by a desire for self-glorification. The unrivalled cultural flowering which radiated throughout Europe from Florence is still powerfully conveyed today by the colourful frescoes and wonderfully expressive panel paintings and figures in marble and bronze.

Who could fail to delight in the rich panoply of paintings in the Uffizi, marvel at Michelangelo's David and pietà, gaze in wonder at the immensity

of the cathedral dome and bold interiors of San Lorenzo and Santo Spirito, find enchantment in the tranquillity of the monastic courtyard and fresco-clad cells of San Marco or enjoy a walk through the city's spacious squares or in the Boboli Gardens.

And when mind and body grow weary from this aesthetic cornucopia, who could resist a coffee in the Piazza, a glass of Chianti in one of a myriad bars, a snack in some cosy vault or a prosecco with antipasta in a noble Renaissance palazzo. Afterwards go up to the Piazzale Michelangelo or to the San Miniato al Monte steps; from here the eye is drawn down into the valley, to the silver-grey ribbon of the Arno with its bridges, to the towers and domes of the churches and to the palaces, while visible in the distance are cypress and pine-encircled villas and Fiesole on the slopes of the Apennines. Florence, in short, is a feast for the senses, but with a down-to-earthness that befits a proud merchant city.

Palazzo Vecchio
The Imposing building dominates the Piazza della Signoria

Santa Maria Novella
One of the best known churches in Florence

Nature, Culture
History

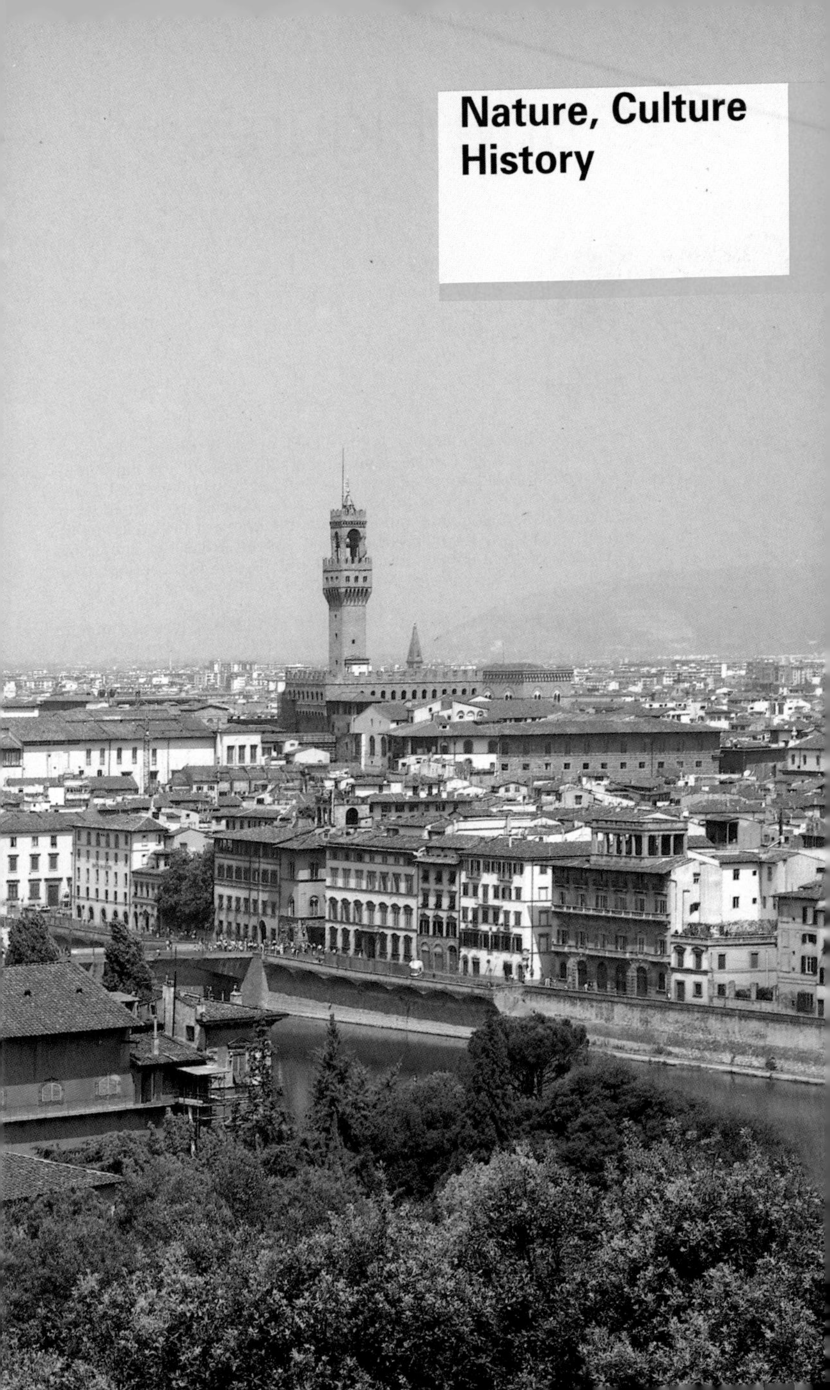

Facts and Figures

*Coat of arms of
the City of
Florence*

General

Florence – Firenze in Italian – is the capital of the Province of Florence
and the main city of Tuscany, one of Italy's 20 "regioni". In the Middle
Ages it superseded Rome as the mainspring of Italy's intellectual development, a role it has filled up to the present. Florence was the creative
source of Italian language and literature, the home of the great flowering of Italian art. Its marvellous wealth of art treasures and many
reminders of great times past, together with its delightful setting, make
Florence one of the cities of the world most worth visiting.

Located on latitude 43°46′N and longitude 11°16′E, Florence lies on both
banks of the Arno in a fertile basin encompassed by the Apennines and
the Tuscan hills (49 m/160 ft–70 m/230 ft).

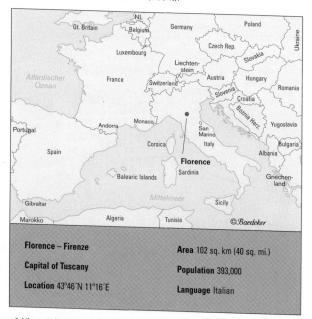

Florence – Firenze	**Area** 102 sq. km (40 sq. mi.)
Capital of Tuscany	**Population** 393,000
Location 43°46′N 11°16′E	**Language** Italian

◄ *View of Florence with the Ponte Vecchio and the Palazzo Vecchio*

Florence has hot dry summers and mild winters. July and August only have three days of rain each and daytime temperatures often exceed 30° (see table page 196).

Summer ends with sudden and heavy showers, and October and November have the highest rainfall of the year. In November in particular, Florence can get as much as 50 mm of rain in an hour, or 120 mm in ten hours, often with disastrous flooding as a result. Yet these autumn months also have long sunny periods, with temperatures in October often reaching about 20°C. In the winter months temperatures tend to range between 0° and 10°C. Occasionally it snows, but the snow does not lie. However, with 100 to 135 hours of sunlight a month from November to February, Florence gets twice as much winter sunshine as northern and central Europe. The spring weather is changeable with moderate showers, as temperatures start to climb from an average 14°C on March afternoons to 18°C in April and 23°C in May.

Florence covers an area of 102 sq. km (40 sq. mi.) and has a population of 393,000, making it Italy's eighth largest city.

The Roman settlement of Florentia, dating from 59 BC, was almost square in shape and stood on the right bank of the Arno, with the Forum where the Piazza della Repubblica is today. Its northern border was on a line with where the Cathedral now stands, while the south-west corner verged on the river. As the city boundaries gradually extended outwards under Byzantine rule in the 8th, 9th and 12th c. the left bank of the Arno also came to be part of the city, which was surrounded by a wall still visible today.

During the 18th and 19th c. the city spread beyond its ramparts into the surrounding hills, and now it is growing further upstream towards the east, although new industrial development is located principally in the north-west.

The historic centre of Florence has weathered the centuries largely

Throughout its history Florence has preserved its cityscape

unscathed. Apart from the destruction of the Arno bridges by German troops in late 1944 it has luckily been spared the ravages of war, and functional modern buildings have been kept out over recent years thanks to the wisdom of its city planners. Consequently the heart of Florence is still dominated by the Renaissance, followed by architectural evidence mainly of Romanesque and Gothic.

Districts

Florence in the Middle Ages was divided into four Quarters, or "Quartieri", named after the city gates – San Piero, Duomo or Vescovo, San Pancrazio, and Santa Maria. The four later became six, or "Sestieri" – San Piero, Duomo, San Pancrazio, San Piero a Scheraggio, Borgo, and Oltrama.

Today Florence has "Quartieri" again, mostly named after their churches, such as Santa Maria Novella, San Giovanni, Santa Croce, San Domenico, and Santo Spirito. There are also the suburbs lining the main trunk roads and on the hills, with San Miniato, Belvedere and Bellosguardo in the south, and Careggi, Montughi, Fiesole and Settignano in the north.

Administration

The Comune di Firenze is administered from the Palazzo Vecchio, the name chosen by the city authorities in preference to the more common Palazzo "della Signoria" or "Ducale". The most important local political organisation is the city council (consiglio comunale) for which elections are held every five years. It is responsible for the departments of traffic, health and schools; it chooses the Mayor (sindaco) who with the city councillors constitute the local authority (giunta comunale).

In 1990 five new administrative districts were created in Florence: Centro Storica, Campo di Marte, Gaviana-Galluzzo, Isolotto-Legnaia and Rifredi.

Population

The city's rise from the Colonia Florentia of the Roman veterans to the flourishing Florence of the Renaissance was a slow process. In about 1300 its population numbered about 30,000, but by 1348 this had grown to some 120,000, only for two-thirds to be wiped out by the dreadful plague of that year, leaving a figure of 40,000.

It was the middle of the 19th c. before the population reached 150,000, since when it has grown steadily, currently standing at around 393,000.

Religion

Florence has 99 per cent Roman Catholics, and is the seat of an Archbishop, who is traditionally made a Cardinal by the Pope. However, there are churches for other religious denominations in the city, as well as a synagogue.

Education

In addition to the State University, which dates from 1924 but was founded as a college in 1349, Florence has the colleges of the Università di Parigi, Università Europea (in Fiesole), Università Internazionale dell'Arte, and Università Libera per Attori, as well as nine public libraries open to scholars and the general public.

Institutions

With its buildings, churches, palaces and museums, Florence offers unique opportunities for artistic and historical studies. Consequently it has a great many scientific and cultural academies and institutes. These include the Italian language academy, the Accademia della Crusca per la Lingua Italiana, and various scientific institutes under the auspices of other nationalities.

Art

Ever since the Renaissance Florence has remained a centre for art and culture; more importantly, the cityscape is as it was in its heyday. We can still see today the churches and palaces, squares and bridges, frescoes and paintings that were created in its cultural golden age.

Twelve theatres, headed by the Teatro Comunale, satisfy the demand for modern plays, classic drama and opera. Florence has also won acclaim for its concerts, especially the offerings of the Maggio Musicale Fiorentina, the city's "musical month of May", which actually extends from May until the end of July, and has been staged, off and on, since 1933.

Florence has about 50 museums and collections open to the public. The Uffizi is world famous, but the Galleria dell'Accademia, Museu Nazionale del Bargello, Museo Archeologico, Palazzo Pitti and its collections, and many smaller museums also house art treasures of immeasurable value. Modern art, however, is virtually unrepresented, a fact barely altered by the recent opening of the Museo Marino Marini.

Much of the art of Florence is not in museums but is, or originally was, out in the open. To save sculpture and architectural features from environmental pollution many art works have been extensively restored and then put in museums. Replicas, some of them in artificial materials, have been put in their place. The fact that this course will have to be pursued in future with many art treasures is not in dispute – the argument is whether these copies should be in the original materials or a synthetic substitute.

The town undertook to make every effort to preserve the many valuable works of art. Everywhere they were restored, not only the paintings in the Uffizi, but also churches and their works of art as well as other buildings. This restoration work was financed jointly by the city and the state as well as by banks and industry.

Theatre/Music

Museums

Works of art

Transport

Florence's Amerigo Vespucci Airport is at Peretola, 5 km (3 mi.) northwest of the city centre. It is used on a regular basis by Alitalia, Meridiana and Lufthansa, but cannot take large aircraft. However, Galileo Galilie Airport at Pisa with a regular rail service to Florence can also be used.

Airports

Florence is an important junction for rail traffic in central Italy. All intercity trains converge on Santa Maria Novella, the main station. Public transport in and around the city is catered for by buses.

Rail and buses

Florence was already an important trading post on the Via Cassia during the Roman Empire and it built upon its position in the Middle Ages. Today the city enjoys excellent communications thanks to motorways, expressways and well-engineered trunk roads.

Roads

The Autostrada del Sole, the motorway from Milan to Reggio di Calabria, curves around the city, which is also connected by motorway with Siena, Lucca, Pisa, Livorno and Genoa.

There are trunk roads to Bologna, Pontassieve (Forli and Arezzo), Siena, Empoli and Prato (Pistoia and Bologna).

Florence has a street plan which is still largely medieval, and what is of

13

inestimable value from the art historian's point of view has become a nightmare for the road user. The narrow lanes of the old city, like the few main roads in and out, are permanently blocked. Some years ago it was decided to tackle the problem by partially banning the private car from the city centre. This means that specific areas, such as around the Piazza della Signoria, have been pedestrianised, while other parts of the inner city are residents' parking only.

This is enforced quite rigorously and, since it is still no pleasure driving in Florence, visitors would be well advised not to use their cars while they are there, and to leave them at their hotel or in a car park.

Economy

Since the Middle Ages the Florentines, as industrious craftsmen, astute businessmen and good civic administrators, have always made sure that they prosper. When the Florentine banks dominated Europe's money market their bankers influenced the course of European policy. The ruling family of Florence, the Medici, owed their rise to the success of their trading and banking enterprises.

Florence lost its economic standing when it failed to match the political power of such other Italian states as the Republic of Venice, Dukedom of Milan, the Vatican, and the Kingdom of Naples and Sicily.

Consequently nowadays it is not an outstanding international centre of commerce or banking.

Towards the end of the Middle Ages the Florentines owed their wealth to the textile industry (weaving, dyeing, garment-making and the silk trade), which, in its present form of the clothing industry, is still an important source of income. The artistic tradition has been carried on in the highly developed craft sector (earthenware, china, embroidery, leatherware and basketry). Most employment, however, is in chemicals and pharmaceuticals, precision engineering, the antiques trade, printing and publishing.

Also, much of Tuscany's agricultural produce is processed in Florence.

Of greatest importance to Florence today is the service sector which employs more than two thirds of the workforce. Many banks have their head offices here, its clothes shows (e.g. Alta Moda) are world famous, and its furs, antiques and book fairs (e.g. children's book fair) attract visitors from home and abroad.

Since it is also the seat of regional, provincial and local government, as the capital of Tuscany and the Province of Florence, the administration of these tiers of government together with the services sector as a whole also make a substantial contribution to the city's economy.

Florence's main industry, however, is tourism, with all the attendant advantages and disadvantages. About 6.5 million tourists a year – around 60 per cent of them from abroad – pass through this great Renaissance city. Although many of them are only there for the day, the city is in danger of being overwhelmed by crowds of visitors. In the peak holiday periods, such as Easter, Christmas and the summer, Florence is completely full and visitors must expect interminable queuing for museums, galleries, etc.

This has led to Florence becoming one of the most expensive cities in Italy. Not only do the hotel and restaurant prices tend to be higher than elsewhere, but admission to museums and other sights is also more expensive as well. However, as yet this does not seem to have deterred visitors – and it is still debatable whether making Florence accessible only to a "select" public is the right policy.

Famous People

The following prominent historical figures were born, lived, worked or died in Florence.

Prominent humanist, scholar and artist, Leon Battista Alberti was born in Genoa in 1404 during his family's exile. Like many Renaissance figures of the Florentine upper class, he was an "uomo universale", a versatile, well-educated and gifted writer, politician and architect. As a moral philosopher he wrote, among other things, the still topical book "Della Famiglia" (Of the Family) about marital problems, father-son conflict, bringing up children, love and friendship and much more. As an art theorist he wrote "Ten Books on Architecture", a book of standards of Renaissance architecture, in addition to "Three Books on Painting" and a treatise "On the Statue". His poetical works included Latin eclogues (pastoral poems), a comedy, poems and stories. As an architect he provided the plans for the Tempio Malatestiano in Rimini, for the Palazzo Rucellai and the façades of Santa Maria Novella in Florence, and San Andrea in Mantua. Alberti was also a diplomat, and in 1430/1431 he travelled to France, Flanders and Germany, and between 1432 and 1464 often stayed in Rome, as adviser to several Popes. He died in Rome in 1472, but was buried in the church of Santa Croce in his home town of Florence.

Leon Battista Alberti (1404–72)

The son of a wealthy landowner from the Mugello valley, Fra Angelico entered the Dominican convent at Fiesole at the age of twenty. There he spent many years as a monk, painting frescoes to adorn his home convent. His reputation as an excellent painter, largely a natural talent, spread rapidly and when the Dominican convent of San Marco in Florence was rebuilt in 1436, Fra Giovanni was commissioned to decorate the friars' cells with themes from the Passion of Christ. It is remarkable that the religious mural gains increasingly in significance compared with the customary crucifix in the friar's cell.

Despite drawing heavily on the flat Gothic style, Fra Giovanni's paintings possess surprising vividness and realism. In some cases, this realism is so effective, that his fellow friars fainted at the sight of his representations of the crucifixion, because of the copious amounts of blood. This kind of compassion, known as "compassio", was wholly intentional and gave painting a new emotional impetus. The painter-friar was also an important innovator in picture composition, making special use of the circle and semi-circle as constituent elements. His style of painting is characterised by brilliant colour, and the soulful expression and tender attitude of piety of the figures, especially in his altar-pieces. Subsequent generations glorified his way of life and his artistic achievement, by giving him the epithet "il beato Angelico" (the blessed angelic one). He died in 1455 during a stay in Rome where, years before, he had painted a cycle of frescoes with scenes from the lives of SS Stephen and Lawrence in the Cappella Niccolina for Pope Nicholas V; he was buried in Santa Maria sopra Minerva.

Fra Angelico (Fra Giovanni da Fiesole: c. 1387–1455)

Probably born in Paris, Boccaccio was the illegitimate son of an upper middle-class merchant from Certaldo. He grew up in Florence, and initially entered his father's occupation. In his early twenties he travelled on business to Naples, where he came into contact with courtly

Giovanni Boccaccio (1313–75)

15

Sandro Botticelli

Filippo Brunelleschi

Cosimo I de'Medici

circles, decided to study the classics, and subsequently remained for many years, as the author of literary works in Latin and Italian. Around 1340 he returned to Florence, where he met the humanist and scholar Petrarch, and they both attempted to revive the Latin and Greek languages and literature. During this time, Boccaccio produced, amongst other things, his psychological romance, "Fiammetta" (1343), which harks back to a personal love affair at the court of Naples.

Boccaccio survived the great plague of 1348, which carried off more than half the inhabitants of Florence, and the impression made on him by this disaster led him to write his famous cycle of tales "Il Decamerone" ("The Decameron", 1348–53), today regarded as the origin of Italian prose, and which had a decisive influence on world literature (Chaucer, Shakespeare, Rabelais, Lessing). The 100 tales, told by ten people in ten days, are concerned with questions of morality in love, with highly realistic representation of zest for living and joie de vivre, ranging from the high art of courtly love to sexual love, against the background of a plague which swept away the constraints of laws, religion and morality.

In addition to many further works in Italian and Latin, Boccaccio, as an admirer of Dante, also wrote an historically controversial "Vita di Dante" (c. 1360), and in 1373 received from the City of Florence the first public professorial chair for the interpretation of The Divine Comedy.

Sandro Botticelli
(Alessandro di
Mariano Filipepi:
1445–1510)

This painter, who was born in Florence and was nicknamed "Botticelli" (little barrel) in his youth, received an initial training as a goldsmith, and was then apprenticed to Filippo Lippi. He soon won favour with the Medici family who advanced his career with numerous commissions, and was even befriended by Lorenzo il Magnifico, who was about the same age. Botticelli was very much open to humanist ideas, which also influenced his paintings. He received inspiration from the Platonic Academy in Florence, but in later years inclined towards mysticism, finally even becoming a follower of Savonarola.

His most important works were produced in the period from 1470 to 1495 and an extensive exhibition of these, clearly showing their development, is to be seen in the Uffizi collection. There are also the frescoes in the Sistine Chapel in Rome, painted between 1481 and 1483.

Botticelli's pictorial representations unite the splendid lifestyle of the age of Lorenzo the Magnificent with sharpness of intellect, with their use of fine, elegant brush strokes and rhythmic colour tones. Notwithstanding a few nudes, Botticelli's method of painting is basically "neogothic", as he consciously dispenses with the graphic realism of

Renaissance art, instead conferring upon his pictures a transfiguring, mysterious magic.

After the death and expulsion of his Medici patrons in 1494, Botticelli suffered a personal and artistic crisis, which was partly turned to account in religious pictures, but without taking issue with the new painting of da Vinci, Michelangelo or Raphael. It is not surprising that towards the end of his life he produced over 90 pen-and-ink drawings for Dante's "Divine Comedy" and turned to mysticism and thoughts of salvation.

The architect and sculptor Brunelleschi, born in Florence, is the actual founder of Renaissance architecture. An intense interest in classical architecture was the pre-condition for architectural revival. Brunelleschi, together with his friend, the sculptor Donatello, even went to Rome, to study the classical remains on the spot. As a consequence of his measurements and calculations, he evolved geometric and stereometric shapes, which formed the basis for his buildings.

Filippo Brunelleschi (1377–1446)

Between 1410 and 1420, his study of Euclid's theory of optics finally led to his epoch-making discovery of central perspective projection, i.e. the scientifically exact representation of a three-dimensional space on a flat surface, which opened up undreamed-of possibilities, especially so far as painting was concerned. In addition, one of Brunelleschi's greatest feats of engineering is the colossal, self-supporting double-shelled construction of the dome of Florence Cathedral, executed between 1420 and 1436. He brought new emphases to secular building with his use of hanging domes in the Foundling Hospital. In church building, with San Lorenzo and Santo Spirito, he achieved success with revolutionary longitudinal buildings which made Gothic architecture appear to be completely outmoded. In a bold synthesis of early Christian basilical ideas of architecture with imitation of classical forms (column, pilaster, capital, entablature), Brunelleschi created a proportionally well-balanced structure, flooded with light, in which the interior as a whole is in constant interaction with the individual forms. For example, in San Lorenzo, the semi-circular arches of the arcades in the nave are repeated in the upper windows, in the archways leading into the chapels and in the arches of the hanging domes in the aisles. In Santo Spirito, the square formed by the crossing of the nave and transepts forms the unit of measurement for the whole building. Brunelleschi based the central area of the building on Byzantine models of dome-building. The Old Sacristy of San Lorenzo (cube in a dome), the Pazzi Chapel as chapter-house of the Franciscans of Santa Croce (combination of an over-domed rectangular and square ground plan) and the Oratorium of S. Maria deglia Angeli (octagonal dome space) offer interesting variants of the Renaissance central construction.

As a sculptor, Brunelleschi entered his relief "The Sacrifice of Isaac" in the competition for the second bronze door of the Baptistery in 1402, but his entry was beaten by Ghiberti's design. Both reliefs can today be seen in the Museo Nazionale del Bargello. In competition with his friend Donatello, he created a crucifix with a well-proportioned Christ-figure, representing an ideal of beauty, like the nude of classical antiquity (Santa Maria Novella). This great architect's final resting place is in Florence Cathedral.

The tombstone of this famous Florentine humanist, who was born in Arezzo, is to be found in Santa Croce, and bears the following inscription: "Since Leonardo departed this life, history mourns, eloquence is silent, and it is said that the Muses, Greek and Latin alike, cannot hold back their tears", written by his successor as Chancellor of Florence, the humanist Carlo Marsuppini.

Leonardo Bruni (1369–1444)

Throughout his life, Bruni devoted himself to the study of classical literature and philosophy. He translated works by Plato, Demosthenes, Plutarch and in particular Aristotle's "Politics" into Latin, making them accessible to the cultured class. He wrote biographies of Dante, Boccaccio and Petrarch in Italian. He also wrote an impressive history of the city of Florence, in which he observed: "It is extraordinary how the possibility for free citizens to enter government office stimulates their capabilities. Where people are given the chance of achieving state honours, this lends them wings, and they attain a higher level . . . As these preconditions are provided by our Republic, it is not surprising that talent and application have achieved so much."

Leonardi Bruni held various public offices; he was apostolic secretary from 1405 onwards, during the difficult period of schism, and was Chancellor of the City State of Florence from 1427 onwards. In this capacity he was responsible for all government correspondence, composing letters, documents and diplomatic communications. The remark by the arch-enemy of Florence, Gian Geleazzo Visconti, Duke of Milan, that the excellent epistolary style of Coluccio Salutati, Bruni's predecessor as Chancellor of Florence, had done him more harm than an army of mercenaries, can also be applied to Leonardi Bruni, who used his humanist education for the good of the Commune of Florence.

Benvenuto Cellini (1500–71)

The Florentine sculptor and goldsmith Benvenuto Cellini made an impact on his contemporaries through the artistic merit of his work no less than through his racy life which he described in his famous biography.

In Florence his ability as a sculptor can be admired in his "Perseus with the head of Medusa" (completed 1554) in the Loggia dei Lanzi and in the bust of Cosimo de' Medici in the Museo Nazionale del Bargello. The most famous example of his work as a goldsmith, and probably the only one still extant, is the salt-cellar made for François I of France in the Museum of Art in Vienna.

Cosimo il Vecchio de'Medici (Cosimo the Elder: 1389–1464)

Cosimo il Vecchio (Cosimo the Elder) was the first and the greatest of the Florentine Medici family to rule the city, serving the best interests of its citizens and contributing to its enhancement. Its people, inspired by ancient Rome, entitled him "Pater patriae", father of the fatherland. Jacopo da Pontormo's expressive painting of him in the Uffizi portrays Cosimo as an astute man, conscientious and a lover of the arts, by no means handsome but with an engaging expression.

The son of Giovanni Bicci, a successful banker and elected Gonfaloniere, Cosimo, together with his brother Giovanni, was already at the age of 31 acting on behalf of his family's diverse interests. He was banished in 1433 following one of the various power struggles among the noble families for the political reins of the city. He returned to Florence a year later, to the people's jubilation, and was elected Gonfaloniere, an office which he held until his death.

In addition to his political activities, Cosimo the Elder in his merchant capacity extended his banking business throughout Europe. As a patron he was generous in his advancement of artists, entrusting the building of the Palazzo Medici to the architects Michelozzo and Donatello, and transforming the convent of San Marco where he founded the library and set to work the painters Fra Angelico and Fra Filippo Lippi. He founded the Medici Library (Biblioteca Laurenziana) and the School of Philosophy (Platonic Academy) where Marsilio Ficino taught.

Cosimo lived at the time of the Council of Florence (1439–43) which gave him an insight into ecclesiastical and European politics. At his death he left behind a well-ordered city state and was deeply mourned by its people.

Cosimo I de'Medici (1519–74)

It was thanks to Cosimo I, Duke of Florence from 1537 and Grand Duke of Tuscany, upon his appointment by Pope Pius IV, from 1569, that the Medici family regained a position of political power in Florence.

Cosimo's father, Giovanni delle Bande Nere – so called because of the black armour he wore at the head of his Black Bands of mounted

Dante Alighieri   *Leonardo da Vinci*   *Lorenzo de'Medici*

soldiers – had squandered the whole of the Medicis' fortune with his constant military ventures. At 17 Cosimo made his entry into the political life of Florence and by tyrannical means brought the city under his rule. Once this was assured he set about revitalising its dormant economy and again made Florence a political power to be reckoned with.

As Duke of Florence he moved out of his family's townhouse, the Palazzo Medici, and into the Palazzo della Signoria which now became known as the Palazzo Ducale. Later he settled in the Palazzo Pitti, which became the political, artistic and intellectual hub of Florence, for Cosimo, a true Medici, was also patron to the artists of his time.

Successful though he may have been as a princely ruler, he did not enjoy the same measure of success in his private life. Seven of his eight children met with premature or cruel deaths.

Cosimo died in 1574, at the age of 55, after having handed over the affairs of state three years earlier to his son Francesco.

Dante was born in 1265, the son of a respected patrician Florentine family, and grew up in a quarter near the present-day cathedral, at a time when struggles were raging in the Northern cities between the Guelphs and the Ghibellines, the supporters of the Pope and the Emperor. These noble families were often not at all concerned with advancing the interests of the State or the Pope, but with their supremacy in their own cities. Dante's family sided with the Ghibellines, known as "white Guelphs" in Florence, and had to go into exile several times, when the Pope's supporters, the "black Guelphs" regained power.

Dante Alighieri (1265–1321)

This was the case when Dante was born, with part of his family having to live in exile. Dante received his schooling from the city's Dominicans and Franciscans. He then studied law in Bologna, and at about twenty he entered politics. In 1296 he was a member of the Council of the Hundred, and in 1297 of the Council of Podestà, finally, as Prior, being elected a Member of the Signoria in 1300, a year when bloody strife broke out again between the two noble camps in the city.

The Pope sent the French Prince Charles de Valois to Florence to restore order. The white Guelphs were charged with conspiracy and their leaders banished from the city. Dante, as one of their supporters, was also brought to trial, and in 1302 was sentenced to lifelong exile, which was five years later "commuted" to the death penalty in his absence. From then on, embittered and dependent upon the help of strangers, Dante lived in various towns in northern Italy – Verona, Treviso and Ravenna, where he finally entered the service of Signore Guido Novello della Polenta as an envoy, and died in 1321. He is buried in Ravenna, and is commemorated in Florence by a memorial in Santa Croce.

Dante wrote his most important works of political philosophy and literature during his years in exile. These include the treatises "Monarchia" and "De vulgari eloquentia", in Latin, and the "Commedia", written in the Tuscan dialect, the precursor of Italian, and which later received the epithet "Divina", an allegorical-didactic poem comprising 100 ($3 \times 33 + 1$) cantos, composed on a vast scale, its theme being the most important intellectual issues of the Middle Ages in theology and philosophy, Church and State, as well as the socio-political situation in the Italy of his day.

The figure of Beatrice appears time and again in his "Divine Comedy" and in a number of poems; a youthful encounter of Dante's, transformed, as he grew older, into the personification of redeeming love. This concept of courtly love shows Dante still very much in the thrall of medieval thought.

Donatello
(Donato
di Niccolò
di Betto Bardi;
c. 1386–1466)

Donatello, or to give him his full name Donato di Niccolò di Betto Bardi, ranks as the most influential single sculptor of the 15th c., unsurpassed in his time by any other in heroic expression, multiplicity of themes and richness of creativity.

Apprenticed to Ghiberti, he then worked with Nanni di Banco. In his native city of Florence he was responsible for the statues on the façade, outer walls and campanile of the cathedral, as well as for the church of Orsanmichele.

His study of the classical remains in Rome then led him far beyond the bounds of medieval artistic sensibilities and capacities. With his bronze David (c. 1430 in the Museo Nationale del Bargello) he created the first free-standing nude of the Renaissance, the bronze Gattamelata monument in Padua is its first equestrian statue, and Judith and Holofernes (1440), in front of the Palazzo Vecchio, its first free-standing monumental group. Also outstanding are the Tabernacle with the Annunciation (c. 1434) in the church of Santa Croce and the Cantoria with dancing children for the Cathedral (1433–40, in the Museo dell'Opera del Duomo). As a sculptor he was able to treat beauty and ugliness with equal realism, and influenced subsequent artists with the life-like presentation of his figures. The Medici honoured him by allowing his interment in the crypt of Cosimo il Vecchio in San Lorenzo.

Lorenzo Ghiberti
(1378–1455)

Lorenzo Ghiberti achieved undying fame through the two bronze doors which he made for the Baptistery (Battistero San Giovanni) in Florence. It was as a painter that he entered the competition for the North Door, which he won. He devoted 21 years' work, from 1403 to 1424, to these doors but his greatest masterpiece was to be the East pair of doors, the "Porta del Paradiso", which he rightly inscribed "mira arte fabricatum" – "made with admirable art".

The scenes on the doors from the Old and New Testament, framed by saints, fathers of the Church and ornamentation, display Ghiberti's expressive capability as an artist, and his technical craft as a sculptor. Distinguished by their harmony of form and balance of movement, they signify his ability to link the Gothic expression of piety with the antique ideal of beauty of the Renaissance.

His three figures for the church of Orsanmichele are the first large bronzes of the new era in art.

Ghiberti was also an architect (collaboration on Florence Cathedral), painter (glass window in the Cathedral), goldsmith (unfortunately no work extant), and author (commentaries on Italian art of the 13th c.).

In his workshops Ghiberti also employed other artists, including Michelozzo and Donatello.

Ghirlandaio
(Domenico di
Tommaso Bigordi;
1449–94)

Domenico Ghirlandaio is the most important member of a Florentine family of painters who in the second half of the 15th c. maintained a large studio and took their name as artists from the decorative garlands designed by the father, Tommaso Bigordi. His son Domenico was a popular social painter, who primarily depicted a host of local scenes and members of the Florentine upper class in his primarily religious paintings. Ghirlandaio's realistic, cheerfully sensual and rather superficial picture of Florence's bourgeoisie is on good view in his frescoes, in the Cappell Sassetti in Santa Trinita, funded by Francesco Sassetti, co-proprietor of the Medici Bank. The "Confirmation of the rule of the Franciscan Order by Pope Honorius III" (1485) shows Sassetti, his patron, with his son, but also Lorenzo il Magnifico, the humanist Angelo Poliziano with his two Medici pupils, and the Patrician Antonio de'Pucci, against the background of the Piazza della Signoria, a contradiction in historical terms. Domenico Ghirlandaio again demonstrates his great narrative talent in the chancel of Santa Maria Novella in his scenes from the lives of the Virgin and John the Baptist (1486–90), a magnificent commentary on the merry ways of late Quattrocento Florence.

Jean de Boulogne, a sculptor in marble and bronze, was born in Boulogne sur Mer, then went to Flanders, and came to Rome for two years in 1554/1555. He went to Bologna and Florence where from 1556 he was employed in the service of the Medicis.

Giambologna (Giovanni da Bologna; 1529–1608)

The statue of Duke Cosimo I on horseback (1587–94) in the Piazza della Signoria is the first equestrian monument of the age of absolutism. The Loggia dei Lanzi contains the marble group "Rape of the Sabines", a "figura serpentina" which, with its convoluted bodies, heralds the age of Baroque sculpture and its sense of movement. His bronze Mercury (1580) in the Museo Nationale del Bargello, which, poised on tip-toe, almost appears to be suspended in mid-air, provides a further example of the sculpture of the new era, free-standing, and to be viewed from all sides. A major work of early Baroque architecture, painting and sculpture is Giambologna's Chapel of St Antonino in San Marco, with six of his life-size statues in niches and as many bronze reliefs, together with the recumbent bronze figure of St Antonino in the sacristy of the convent church.

Giotto is generally described as the founder of modern European painting since his work around 1300 pioneered a breakaway from Byzantine and medieval traditions of painting, that were two-dimensional and insubstantial in nature. Based on direct observation of nature and reality, his frescoes and altar-pieces, still with religious themes, present a realistic picture of the world and the people in it. He painted figures whose corporal substance is emphasised, and who radiate human sensitivity, seeming to have an independent existence of their own. The realistic and monumental style of his figures, along with clear principles of (pyramidal) composition and brilliant colours, were instructive and inspirational for generations of painters.

Giotto di Bondone (c. 1266–1337)

Giotto was also active as an architect and sculptor, and in 1334 was appointed Florence's cathedral architect, and his final years were chiefly spent on progressing the construction of the Campanile.

He kept a large studio, and worked in Assisi, Padua, Rome, Rimini, Naples and Milan as well as Florence. His famous works include the 36 frescoes of the lives of the Virgin and Christ (c. 1305) in the Arena Chapel in Padua. Scholars now question whether he was responsible for the frescoes telling the story of St Francis in the Upper Church at Assisi, but the six frescoes of the life of St Francis (c. 1329) in the Cappella Bardi, and each of three scenes from the life of John the Evangelist and Baptist (c. 1325) in the Cappella Perruzzi, are believed to be genuine, as are the "Enthroned Madonna" in the Uffizi, and the "Crucifixion" in the sacristy of Santa Maria Novella, an early work dating from c. 1290.

The Italian Renaissance brought a host of versatile personalities to the fore but it was only the genius of Leonardo da Vinci that combined the skills of painter, sculptor, architect, natural scientist and engineer. He was comparable only with Michelangelo. He was the consummate artist

Leonardo da Vinci (1452–1519)

of the Renaissance; his findings and research in the technical sphere demonstrate his universality of spirit.

Leonardo da Vinci was a pupil of Verrocchio and in 1472, at the age of 20, was already a Master in the Florentine Guild of Painters (his first own large-scale work is "Adoration of the Magi" in the Uffizi). From 1482 to 1498 he worked at the court of Duke Lodovico Sforza in Milan ("Virgin of the Rocks" and "Last Supper" in the refectory of the convent of Santa Maria delle Grazie, badly damaged). He worked in Florence again from 1500 to 1506, then in Milan and finally, from 1513 to 1516, in Rome. In 1517 he moved to France at the invitation of François I.

The work carried out in the last twenty years of his life has almost all been lost or survives only in the form of copies by his pupils. The "Mona Lisa", probably his most famous painting, is in the Louvre in Paris, together with "Madonna and Child with St Anne". He started a wall-painting of the Battle of Anghiari for the Palazzo Vecchio in Florence but all except a section of the cartoon has been lost and nothing remains of the painting. The original scale model for a bronze equestrian monument of Duke Francesco Sforza was destroyed.

Leonardo was the architect of fortresses, devoted himself to intensely scientific projects, dissected corpses, wrote and illustrated an essay on the anatomy of the human body, carried out experiments in flight, made observations on the flight of birds, investigated the laws governing the movement of air and water and conducted botanical and geological studies. His many drawings, studies of movement of the human body, research into natural science, designs for buildings and technical projects attest to the catholicity of this Renaissance genius.

Lorenzo de'Medici (Lorenzo the Magnificent; 1449–92)

Lorenzo de'Medici, whom the people called "Il Magnifico" (the Magnificent), was the classic Renaissance prince in his style of government, way of life, philosophy, education and patronage.

Lorenzo made use of the Medici banking funds and the backing of the people of Florence to raise the city to a position of cultural and political prominence in Italy. His brother Giuliano fell victim to the Pazzi conspiracy in the Cathedral in 1478 when Lorenzo, wounded, managed to take refuge in the sacristy. After the Pazzi affair the constitution was changed so that power was concentrated in his hands. A patron of the Platonic Academy, he was himself a talented poet. In the Medici Garden near San Marco he assembled a collection of Classical sculpture, brought the sculptors of his time together and was responsible for the talented young men such as Michelangelo getting their training. Work was carried out on his behalf by Andrea del Verrocchio (Putto and Dolphin in the Cortile of the Palazzo Vecchio), Ghirlandaio and Sandro Botticelli. When Lorenzo died from a mysterious illness at the age of 43 Niccolò Macchiavelli wrote: "Never perished in Italy a man famed for such great astuteness nor was a man's death such a great sorrow for his fatherland. Every fellow citizen mourns his death, not one forebore to manifest his grief at this event". Lorenzo was originally interred in the old sacristy of San Lorenzo then subsequently laid to rest with his brother in Michelangelo's new sacristy.

Niccolò Machiavelli (1469–1527)

Niccolò Machiavelli, the great chronicler of the history of his native city, left behind an eight-volume history of Florence. As second chancellor to the Republic of Florence from 1498 until his dismissal in 1512, Machiavelli was a committed supporter of the Republican system, despite its internal political conflicts, as being where people could best achieve self-fulfilment. The Roman Republic seemed to Machiavelli to be an example of this, placing the common good of all citizens before self-interest, as he explained in his "Discourses" (Discorsi). He analysed his own times in various works and in "The Prince" in particular, arrived at penetrating but scarcely pleasant conclusions on the rules and conduct of politics, for, as he says, the ruler "who has known best how to employ the (nature of the) fox has succeeded best. But it is necessary to know

Niccolò Macchiavelli   *Michelangelo Buonarroti*   *Raphael*

well how to disguise this characteristic, and to be a great pretender and dissembler; and men are so simple, and so subject to present necessities, that he who seeks to deceive will always find someone who will allow himself to be deceived . . . A prince, so long as he keeps his subjects united and loyal, ought not to mind the reproach of cruelty; because with a few examples he will be more merciful than those who, through too much mercy, allow disorders to arise, from which follow murders or robberies; for these are wont to injure the whole people, whilst those executions which originate with a prince offend the individual only."

During his lifetime, Machiavelli's writings were known only to a small circle and it was their effect on subsequent generations that made him famous as an advocate of the art of government. In fact he was simply demystifying the medieval state with its veneer of religion, exposing the real power politics and saying that reason, will and instinct are what rule the world. It is less well known that Machiavelli also wrote poems, novels and highly original comedies.

Masaccio is regarded as the creator of Italian Renaissance painting. He evolved Giotto's early 14th c. style through precise and consistent application of the theory of perspective rediscovered by Brunelleschi between 1410 and 1420, to bring vividness and realism as never before to his people, places and landscapes. The spiritual intensity of his work is the ultimate expression of Renaissance man.

Masaccio (Tommasso di Giovanni di Simone Guidi; 1401–28)

Masaccio was a pupil of Masolino. He worked in Florence from 1422 and together with his teacher painted the series of frescoes of scenes from the life of St Peter in the Cappella Brancacci in S Maria del Carmine between 1424/1425 and 1427/1428. Those that he painted himself included: "Expulsion of Adam and Eve" – the first lifelike nude in Renaissance painting – "The Almsgiving", "St Peter healing with his shadow", "St Peter baptising the Neophytes" and his famous version of the "Tribute Money" with its emphatic and expressive gesture. His fresco of the "Trinity with Two Donors" (1426/1427) in S. Maria Novella, is a masterpiece of early Renaissance spatial perspective. His panel of the Madonna from S Giovenale a Cascia (1422) and the "Madonna and St Anne", on which he collaborated with Masolino, both in the Uffizi, are outstanding examples of religious panel paintings using tempera, with their powerful, realistic representations of the saints.

Michelangelo Buonarroti, painter, sculptor, architect and poet, brought the art of the Renaissance to the peak of perfection. In 1488, at the age of 13, Michelangelo was apprenticed to the Florentine painter Domenico Ghirlandaio. Besides his aptitude for painting he increasingly developed

Michelangelo Buonarroti (1475–1564)

his passionate interest in sculpture. In 1489 the young Michelangelo transferred to the school for sculptors set up in the Medici Gardens. He left Florence in 1494 (before the expulsion of the Medici and the ensuing political upheaval when the Dominican monk Savonarola seized power). He returned to Florence (1495–96) then journeyed to Rome where he stayed from 1496 until 1501. His "Bacchus" (Museo Nazionale del Bargello) and the Pietà for St Peter's in Rome date from this period.

Michelangelo was back in Florence from 1501 to 1505, when he created his "David" (Galleria dell'Accademia), the Bruges Madonna, the "Madonna Pitti" tondo (Bargello) and the painting "The Holy Family" (Galleria degli Uffizi). Because of his restless spirit, the years between 1505 and 1534 were spent wandering between Florence, Rome and Bologna to work on commissions. During these years his achievements included the frescoes on the ceiling of the Sistine Chapel in the Vatican, the funerary chapel for the Medici in San Lorenzo in Florence, "Moses" for the tomb of Julius in Rome, the "Boboli Slaves" (Accademia), "Apollo" (Bargello) and the "Vittoria" (Palazzo Vecchio), with many drawings. From 1534 until his death in 1564, apart from brief interludes, Michelangelo lived in Rome ("Last Judgment" on the altar wall of the Sistine Chapel in the Vatican, bust of Brutus in the Bargello, figures for the tomb of Julius in Rome, projects for the Biblioteca Laurenziano at San Lorenzo in Florence, and in Rome, the Piazza del Campidoglio and, his greatest architectural achievement, the dome of St Peter's). The work of his old age, the marble group of the Pietà in Florence Cathedral (Opera Del Duomo), and a few lines of his verse manifest the suffering of this great artist:

"Released of the burden that I groaning bore,
At last set free from all earthly desires,
A frail barque, to Thee, O Lord, I steer my course
From storm-tossed seas to Thy calm still waters."

Michelangelo's body was brought from Rome and laid to rest in the church of Santa Croce.

Giovanni Pico della Mirandola (1463–94)

Count Mirandola was born in 1463 in the village of the same name near Modena, and showed great gifts as a humanist whilst still a young man. He learnt Greek, Hebrew and Arabic, and made a thorough study of Plato and Aristotle, but showed himself to be equally interested in medieval mysticism and the Jewish Cabala. As a pupil of Marsilio Ficino, he was accepted into the circle of humanists at the Platonic Academy in Florence, and was a companion of Lorenzo il Magnifico and his brother Giuliano de'Medici. Among Pico della Mirandola's writings, "De dignitate hominis" (Of human worth) is of particular significance. At the beginning of his treatise, he has God speak to Man as follows: "I have placed you in the centre of the world, so that you may, the more easily, look around you and see everything which it contains. I have not created you as a heavenly being, nor as an earthly being, neither mortal nor immortal, so that you can be your own free instructor and master and give yourself your own form. You can sink to the level of the beasts, or you can freely choose to raise yourself up to the divine . . . you alone have an evolution which depends on your will, and you alone bear the germ of all life within you."

On the basis of the Christian view of the world, Pico della Mirandola attempts to redefine Man's worth and freedom, to extend them through knowledge and education and at the same time to preserve them.

He is interred in San Marco.

Raphael (Raffaello Santi; 1483–1520)

Raphael, whose real name was Raffaello Santi or Sanzio, was the artist whose paintings most clearly and comprehensively represented the High Renaissance at its apogee, especially his Madonnas and his frescoes for the Vatican "The School of Athens" and the "Disputà".

Born in Urbino, the son of the painter Giovanni Santi, he became a pupil of Perugino in Perugia at the age of 17. In 1504 he moved to

Florence where he set about learning all he could from the works of past and contemporary artists. After 1508 he lived in Rome where he succeeded Bramante (d. 1514) as architect of the new St Peters. His twelve years in Rome were marked by his greatest artistic achievement, the Stanze de Raffaello frescoes in the Vatican.

Raphael's numerous paintings to be seen in Florence include "Pope Leo X with two Cardinals", "Pope Julius II", "Madonna with the Goldfinch" and "Portrait of Perugino" in the Uffizi (Galleria degli Uffizi) and "La Donna Velata", "La Donna Gravida", "Madonna del Granduca", and many others.

Raphael died at the age of 37 and was the only artist to be accorded the honour of burial in the Pantheon in Rome.

History

59 BC	The hills around Florence have long been farmed and populated, with the Etruscans settling in nearby Fiesole around the 7th or 6th c. BC Florence itself was probably first founded in 59 BC under Julius Caesar as the veterans' colony. Given the name "Florentia", it lies in the fertile valley of the Arno at the junction of three roads: the Cassia from Rome to Fiesole, the Via Pisana from Pisa to Spina, and the Volterrana from Volterra to Fiesole. Finds from this period yield up an approximate picture of Florentia: it has a forum – on the space now occupied by the Piazza della Repubblica – with a temple, two thermal baths and an amphitheatre near the present Palazzo Vecchio. The rectangular pattern of streets surrounding the insulae, the residential quarters, are still recognisable in the centre today.
2–4 c. AD	From the 2nd c. merchants from the eastern Mediterranean region, particularly Syria, bring Christianity to Florentia where, in about 250, Saint Minias (San Miniato) is martyred. Later the church of San Miniato al Monte is built over his grave. In the 4th c. a bishopric is established and the church of San Lorenzo assumes the status of a cathedral.
5th/6th c. Folk migrations	At the time of the folk migrations Florentia experiences a period of decline. Its unprotected valley location leaves it more vulnerable to attack than the Etruscan cities. Plundered and sacked mainly by the Goths and Byzantines, in the 6th c. it is only about a third the size of the Roman settlement, with a population of only about 1000. From 568, with the establishment of Lombard rule, the chaos of war ends; the Duchy of Tuscia is created. In Florence ten new churches are built; but the city forfeits its position of pre-eminence to Lucca and Pisa where the Lombard dukes reside.
Part of the Holy Roman Empire From 774	Charlemagne overthrows the Lombard king Desiderius and makes Tuscia a Frankish margravate. Florence acquires new, more extensive walls stretching to the Arno. The economy gradually improves and the population rises to 15,000.
854	The Emperor Lothar I unifies the counties of Florence and Fiesole thereby increasing the city's economic power.
c. 1000	In about 1000 Count Hugo transfers his residence to Florence. His heraldic colours, white and red, become those of the city. In subsequent years the Baptistry and the churches of San Miniato and Santi Apostoli are built.
1077–1155	Matilda, Countess of Tuscia, mediates at Canossa in 1077 in the Investiture dispute between the Emperor Henry IV and Pope Gregory VII. Some years later, forsaking her role as intermediary, she makes a will bequeathing all her estates apart from Florence, Lucca and Siena to the Pope (the Matildan inheritance). Florence, on Matilda's side, becomes one of the Pope's chief allies in the struggle against anti-ecclesiastical forces. In 1115 Matilda grants Florence autonomous status as a city.
1125–1200	Little by little Florence subjugates the surrounding countryside and also Fiesole. Under the rule of the nobility the city rises to become the dominant power in Tuscany.
Till 1250	The 13th c. sees Florence experiencing a massive economic boom. There are frequent outbreaks of hostilities between the Ghibellines,

who support the Emperor, and the Guelphs, loyal to the Pope. In 1238 the city's ruler, a Guelph, is driven out of Florence. Besides this conflict between Guelphs and Ghibellines, Florence is also riven by deep social divisions. On the one hand there are the nobility, who side with the Ghibellines, and on the other the merchant and craft guilds, the majority of whom support the Guelph faction. Eventually the Guelphs gain the upper hand. Imperial appointees are dismissed

and in 1250 the Florentine guilds promulgate their own constitution (primo popolo) diminishing the power of the nobility. Control over civic affairs now lies with the Capitano del popolo ("city captain"). Among other measures the nobles are required to reduce the height of their towers to below a certain

1250:
First constitution

mark. In 1252 Florence begins minting a gold ducat which becomes accepted as a currency throughout Europe (hence the name "florin" for the Dutch guilder and the old British two-shilling piece).

1252

The new constitution of 1282 strengthens the "greater guilds" at the expense of the "lesser guilds" (artisans). Most of the Guelph-supporting heads of guilds (priori), having become wealthy through banking and commerce, acquire considerable political influence. Despite its democratic stamp, under the new constitution only male guild members enjoy political rights. Within a few years serfdom is abolished. In 1293 the Gonfaloniere (banner-bearer of Justice) replaces the Podestà (city ruler). His role is to safeguard the interests of the citizens against the nobility. The Signoria, headed by the Gonfaloniere, is the prime authority.

The guilds
1282–1293

   This period also witnesses a substantial amount of building, including a new city wall five-times more extensive than before. Intended as a defensive ring, it serves principally as a demonstration of political power. Among the most important buildings of this architectural explosion are the Cathedral and the Palazzo Vecchio.

In the 14th c. Florence suffers a series of political defeats, natural disasters and economic catastrophes: battles against Pisa and Lucca are lost; an Arno flood in 1333 destroys many bridges and buildings; famine, and two epidemics of plague (1340/48), reduce the population by two-thirds; several large banking houses fail.

14th c.

In 1378 economic problems, the weakening of the Guelph upper middle class, and dissatisfaction over lack of a voice in political decision making, provoke the ciompi (textile workers) uprising, resulting in a brief period of democratisation. The rising is eventually put down by the other guilds. The political supremacy of the greater guilds is enshrined once again in the new constitution of 1382. The Albizzi, Peruzzi, Capponi, Soderini, Rucellai and Strozzi families now control the city.

1378–1402

Through the purchase of Pisa in 1405 and its subjection the following year, Florence enhances its supremacy within Tuscany.

1405/1406

At the time of the Great Schism during which two rival popes hold office, the Florentines ally themselves with a third pope, Alexander V, waging war against Ladislaus, King of Naples. Ladislaus lays Tuscany to waste but any further threat is averted by his death.

1409–1414

By acquiring the ports of Livorno and Portopisano Florence gains access to the sea and secures for itself a prominent position in European trade. However the introduction of silk contributes to a decline in wool production.

1421

Giovanni, known as Bicci de'Medici, who had become the Gonfaloniere, opposes an Albizzi plan to disband the lesser guilds. In 1433, following

The Medici
1426–1433

defeat in the war against Lucca, the Albizzi-led oligarchy places Cosimo the Elder under arrest; he is banished from the city for ten years.

1433–1464:
Rule of Cosimo
the Elder

In 1434 Cosimo de'Medici, who enjoys papal protection, is recalled by the oligarchs to succeed Rinaldo degli Albizzi who has fallen from office. Outwardly appearing to respect republican institutions, Cosimo in fact rules as a dictator. Those opposed to him are exiled while supporters are rewarded with office.

The Albizzi incite the Milanese to wage war against Florence, but in 1440 the campaign ends in victory for the Florentines at the Battle of Anghiari. Subsequently Venice emerges as a new political and economic rival. When Venice shows interest in Milan, Cosimo supports the claim to Milan of the mercenary leader Francesco Sforza. The ensuing war ends in the Peace of Lodi (1454) which awards Milan to Sforza.

In 1444 Cosimo commissions the Palazzo Medici and establishes the Medici Library (now the Biblioteca Laurenziana).

1464–1468:
Rule of Piero
de'Medici

Seeking to revenge their loss of power under Cosimo, patricians of the Poggio faction form an alliance against his son, the weak Piero de'Medici. With the aid of his own son Lorenzo, and help from Milan, Piero succeeds in defeating the alliance in 1466. Supported by Venice, the Poggio faction regroups, leading two years later to the inconclusive Battle of Imola.

1469–1492:
Rule of Lorenzo
the Magnificent

Under Lorenzo the Magnificent (il Magnifico), Florence enjoys its heyday. However Lorenzo's talents lie in areas other than business and commerce; mismanagement and lack of direction weaken the Medici bank. Two members of the de'Pazzi banking family, backed by the Pope, make an attempt on the lives of Giuliano and Lorenzo de'Medici. Lorenzo is wounded but survives. The conspirators are hanged. Florence's constitution takes on aspects characteristic of a monarchy. The glorification of his family is as important to Lorenzo as that of the city. By skilful diplomacy he succeeds in resolving peacefully conflicts between rival Italian states.

1492–1498:
Piero de'Medici,
Savonarola

By concentrating power in too few hands Lorenzo's son, Piero de'Medici, antagonises the nobility. Stability is further undermined by the arrival in Florence of the Dominican Fra Girolamo Savonarola. Preaching asceticism and repentance and calling for religious and political reform, Savonarola wins converts among the middle and lower classes. In 1494 Charles VIII of France invades Italy. When, without consulting the Signoria, Piero de'Medici surrenders to Charles at Pisa, he is driven out of Florence in a popular uprising. A republican constitution is reintroduced. The following year Savonarola declares a theocratic democracy. In a puritanical fervour, symbols of luxury and extravagance and are publicly burned. In 1498, at the instigation of the notorious Pope Alexander VI, Savonarola is hanged and his body burned.

1502–1512

Under the constitution of 1502, the office of gonfaloniere becomes an appointment for life. During his period of incumbency Gonfaloniere Piero Soderini enjoys popular support; his reforms prompt opposition in the Signoria which allies itself anew with the Medici.

1512:
Return of the
Medici

In 1512 the Medici return to the city and with the aid of troops occupy the Palazzo della Signoria. The republican constitution is annulled. Under the guardianship of his uncle Giulio de'Medici, appointed bishop of Florence, the young Lorenzo de'Medici assumes power. Following Lorenzo's early death, Guilo himself takes over, so averting a revolt against the ruling families provoked by Lorenzo's political machinations. Even after becoming Pope Clement VII in 1523, Giulio maintains his moderate rule over Florence, implemented by his representative Cardinal Passerini. But when opposition turns to revolt in 1527 Passerini is forced to leave the city.

In 1498 the body of the preacher Savonarola was burned in the Piazza della Signoria

The newly established republican government enters into an alliance with France, but when Francis I forsakes his Italian allies, Florence is left isolated. Beset by the Emperor's troops in 1529, the city is forced to capitulate the following year.

1527–1530

The nobility, having suffered materially as a result of the war and subsequent exile, now willingly places itself under the Medici. Famine and pestilence reduce the population of the city by half. The Emperor Charles V endorses Alessandro de'Medici as ruler and in 1532 makes him Duke of Florence. Alessandro is hated for his tyrannical rule. In 1537 his advisor Lorenzino de'Medici has him murdered.

1531–1537: Rule of Alessandro de'Medici

The city makes Cosimo de'Medici its ruler. He suppresses a revolt by republican-minded immigrants. Cosimo governs in absolutist fashion, taking up residence in the Palazzo della Signoria. The arts are harnessed to provide visible expression of his power. Construction of the Uffizi begins. Cosimo's wife, Eleonora of Toledo, turns the Palazzo Pitti into a magnificent palace. In 1554 and 1555 Cosimo conquers Siena. Following the death of his daughter, two of his sons, and his wife, Cosimo hands over the regency to his son Francesco whom he succeeds in marrying to Johanna of Austria, daughter of the Emperor Ferdinand (1565). This leads to the Palazzo Vecchio being embellished and the Vasari corridor being built. Cosimo's greatest triumph however comes in 1569 when Pope Pius V makes him Grand Duke, an event celebrated with great splendour the following year in St Peter's in Rome. Francesco, though interested in art and science, is a weak ruler. After the death of his wife he marries his mistress Bianca Cappello, having first murdered her husband.

1537–1587: Rule of Cosimo I de'Medici and Francesco I de'Medici

29

History

1587–1609: Rule of Ferdinand I de'Medici	With the death of Francesco in 1587, power passes to his brother Ferdinando I. Known hitherto only as a scholar and patron of the arts, when the city is ravaged by flood (1589) and successive famines Ferdinando acts decisively, importing grain. He also allows religious freedom. He constructs the Fortezza de Belvedere to secure the power of the Medici, and the chapel of the Medici princes in San Lorenzo.
1609–1737	Ferdinando is followed by a number of weak and undistinguished rulers from the House of Medici: Cosimo II (1609–20), Ferdinando II (1620–70), Cosimo III (1670–1723) and Gian Gastone (1723–37). The economic situation becomes increasingly bad in Florence. The wool and silk industries come to a standstill. The nobility live off their country estates while the people become ever poorer. With the death of Gastone in 1737 the male line of the Medici expires. Anna Maria Ludovica, the last of the Medici, decrees that the Medici art treasures should remain in the city, thus forming the nucleus of the Florentine collections. The Grand Duchy passes to the Austrian House of Lorraine.
Lorraine 1765–1790: Rule of Peter Leopold	During the reign of the enlightened Grand Duke Peter Leopold, reforms are implemented: the guilds, ecclesiastical privileges and the death penalty are all abolished; the large estates are broken up and land redistributed among small landholders.
1790–1860	Liberal government continues under Ferdinand III (1790–1824) – interrupted by the Napoleonic Interlude (1799–1815) – and Leopold II (from 1824). In 1860 Florence secedes from the Habsburg-Lorraines to join the newly-formed kingdom of Italy.
Kingdom of Italy 1865–1871: Capital	Florence becomes the capital of Italy. A building boom ensues, changing the face of the city. The city wall is demolished and the great ring roads built in its stead.
1817–1922	After Rome replaces Florence as Italian capital, the economic situation in Florence deteriorates. Liberal, democratic and socialist ideas spread. Florence becomes an intellectual centre to which *literati* and on occasion futurists are drawn. In the 1913 elections the socialists achieve an outright majority. Social tensions are further heightened by the First World War after which street battles erupt between leftists and Fascists.
1922–1938	The Fascists come to power in 1922. Many Florentines are party members but few are politically active. In 1938 Mussolini and Hitler meet in the city.
1943–1944	During the Second World War, following Mussolini's removal from office in 1943 and the new government's agreeing a ceasefire with the Allies, German troops occupy Florence (on September 11th 1943). As a result the city is bombed by the Americans. The following August the Germans destroy all the Arno bridges with the exception of the Ponte Vecchio, as well as parts of the city along the river.
Post-war period	In the post-war period there is rapid social and economic change. With the upturn in the economy large sections of the population enjoy prosperity. After Italy is proclaimed a republic in 1946, Florence is governed until 1951 by a coalition of Communists and Socialists. In the years to 1964 local politics are dominated by Giorgio La Pira, the populist Christian Socialist mayor who champions groups on the fringes of society. Then come a succession of centre-left and from 1975 again mostly Communist-Socialist administrations.
1966	Catastrophe strikes Florence when the Arno bursts its banks, inundating streets, houses, museums and libraries a depth of up to 6 m (20 ft). Many people are killed and many more made homeless; considerable damage is caused to the historic fabric of the city and its artistic heritage.

The student riots of 1968 foment political unrest; in Florence traditional values are called into question. Feminism also plays an important role. The protest movement loses support however when some adherents embrace the drug culture and terrorism.

The eighties are dominated by a renewed economic boom. Florence is chosen European Culture Capital 1986.

In an effort to control noise and traffic pollution in the city centre, restrictions are introduced on the use of private cars.
   In October a museum dedicated to the work of Tuscan sculptor, painter and graphic artist Marino Marini is opened.

Fierce debate accompanies a city council decision to substitute replicas made from the same materials for original works of art in open-air locations.

On May 27th six people are killed and about 30 injured when a terrorist bomb explodes at the Uffizi. The gallery is badly damaged and numerous works of art damaged or destroyed.

After years of reconstruction following the bomb attack on the Uffizi in 1993, many of the new rooms are opened.

Commerce, Art and Church

Although many noble Florentine families had already acquired riches and influence in the 14th c., it was the Medici whose star was most ascendant in the 15th c. The foundations of the family's vast wealth were laid originally by Giovanni di Bicci de'Medici. He made credit available to the papacy in Rome at the time of the Great Schism beginning in 1378. When the schism finally ended in 1417 and the city on the Tiber began its transformation under Pope Martin V into the papal seat, the Medici were already installed as papal bankers, an opportunity which Cosimo the Elder ably exploited to the full.

At that time the branch of the family banking house in Rome accounted for more than half of all the Medici profits from banking. This was achieved without much capital of their own. So much money was deposited by the curial offices that the Medici were able to realise returns of 20 per cent on the incoming capital, while being taxed at only about 3 per cent. Apart from Rome there were other, independently managed, branches of the banking house in Venice (principally financing trade with the Orient), Bruges (North European trade) and Geneva (the main commercial centre for Central Europe), as well as in London (serving the English court and wool trade) and Milan and Naples (both the seats of bishops and princes). This network of branches contributed significantly to the economic influence of the Medici family enterprise, further enhanced by diversification into raw materials (including a monopoly in alum), textiles (in particular wool and silk) and luxury commodities. Cosimo, generous with his gifts but cautious with his loans, always looked for creditworthiness in his clients. Most were clergy or members of the princely houses, which enormously enhanced the political influence of the Medici. A talented financier, Cosimo appointed only the most capable people to manage the

various branches of the business, and reinvested the bulk of the profits. His grandson Lorenzo il Magnifico on the other hand was little concerned with the business and elected to live above his means, as a result of which, when he died in 1492, the banking house had been reduced almost to bankruptcy. By this time however the political dominance of the Medici was such that, notwithstanding a short period of expulsion, from 1513 onwards, with the support of the papacy, they held the political fate of Florence in their hands and were in time elevated to the rank of princes.

Like others among the Florentine upper middle-class, the Medici expended a considerable proportion of their immense wealth on public and private endowments. In this, piety, the spirit of commerce, patronage of the arts and portrayal of self were closely interwoven. The extent of the Medici family's commitment to the public prosperity was noted by Lorenzo the Magnificent whose calculations, based on the Medici accounts for the period 1434 to 1471, showed that a total of 664,000 gold florins was dispensed in the form of alms, endowments and taxes. This was at a time when a medium-sized household such as that of a craftsman managed comfortably on two to three gold florins a month. Why then such vast expenditure? One reason was to salve the family conscience, dealing in credit being considered disreputable and frowned on by the Church. Such pious patronage allowed the Church to benefit from the profits, acceptance of the endowments bestowing tacit approval on the business practices which generated them. In their choice of projects and artists for support the wealthy patrons showed themselves men of taste and virtuous persuasion, at the same time demonstrating the cultural utility of their wealth – not least to set themselves apart from the nouveaux riches. Their beneficence also served a political purpose. The numerous substantial private commissions created employment, were visible proof of the economic power of the families, and brought votes for those aspiring to public office. Another important consideration lay in the notion that, in contrast to people, buildings, sculptures and paintings endure to bear lasting witness to the greatness of families.

The fact that by the mid 15th c. the bourgeois Medici had attained princely rank and were surrounding themselves with courtly splendour is clear from the "Procession of the Three Holy Kings" in the private chapel of the Medici Palace. Painted by Benozzo Gozzoli in 1459/60, it elevates the members of the House of Medici to the rank of kings. Clearly intended to emphasise their position of power, the huge mural also makes allusion to three glorious Florentine occasions in each of which the Medici played a substantial role – the 1439 Council for the Union of the Eastern and Western Churches, the great celebration for Pope Pius II and

Galeazzo Sforza, Duke of Milan, and the magnificent annual processions of the Brotherhood of the Three Holy Kings in which the Medici participated directly. Sandro Botticelli's altar panel "Adoration of the Kings" (circa 1475) in the Uffizi bears further witness to the kingly-aristocratic pretensions of the Medici family, immortalising the Florentine upper class. The three kings, portrayals of Cosimo the Elder and his sons Giovanni and Piero, are of course subordinate to the Holy Family; but they are central to the picture and positioned accordingly. To one side, making up their retinue, are the younger members of the Medici family – Cosimo's grandson the reflective Lorenzo the Magnificent, with black hair and dark clothes, and, in brightly coloured garb, Giuliano, his proud brother, with a notable zest for life, who was murdered in the course of the Pazzi Conspiracy. They are depicted encircled by a group of humanists, artists and friends against the backdrop of a Classical landscape. The supposedly religious theme recedes into the background, little more than a pretext for an imposing group portrait of the Medici.

Altar panel by Botticelli "Adoration of the Kings"

Culture

Florence is a capital for art and culture of the highest order. In the period from the 14th to the 16th century, particularly during the Renaissance, its artists' achievements had a lasting impact on the history of European art and culture. Its abundance of major works of art is such that we can only give a very general account here of its architecture and figurative art.

Antiquity

There were ancient settlements in the hills around Florence but it was not until 59 BC that the city itself was founded by Julius Caesar as the veterans' colony of Florentia. During the Etruscan period and the Roman Republic art and culture were concentrated in Faesulae, now Fiesole, higher up the Arno valley.

Florence did not come into its own culturally until the time of the Roman emperors in the 1st and 2nd c. BC when marble temples, colonnades and baths were built around the Forum (Piazza della Repubblica), with, outside the city walls, a theatre on the site of today's Palazzo Vecchio, and a large amphitheatre west of the church of Santa Croce. Since the 19th c. city works have uncovered many Roman remains, including mosaics, fragments of statues, parts of temples and houses, and coins today on display in Florence's Archaeological Museum, together with Etruscan art from central Italy. The many classical statues in the Uffizi, Palazzo Pitti, and Boboli Gardens are not originally from Florence but arrived here from Rome and southern Italy because they were collected by the Medici.

Early Middle Ages

Early Christian buildings existed here in the late 4th and early 5th c. as predecessors to Santa Felicità, San Lorenzo and Sant'Ambrogio. Excavations in the catacombs of Santa Felicità uncovered gravestones with Greek inscriptions dating from 418. Much was destroyed, however, when the Lombards invaded in the 6th c.

Thereafter Florence failed to produce anything of cultural or artistic importance until the 11th c.

Romanesque

Architecture

Around the middle of the 11th c., Florence developed into a centre of ecclesiastical reformation, when Gerhard, a Burgundian by birth, became Bishop of Florence in 1045, bringing with him from Cluny reforming ideas that also found expression in church architecture. As Pope Nicholas II he laid the foundation stone in 1059 for the Battistero San Giovanni. Probably in the same year, Legate Hildebrand, later Pope Gregory VII ordered a start to be made on the renovation of San Miniato, a Benedictine convent which had implemented the Cluniac reforms. As both these buildings have survived unchanged up to the present day, they count as outstanding examples of Romanesque

Michelangelo: "David", in the Galleria dell'Accademia ▶

architecture of the 11th and 12th c. in the Florentine Tuscan style, as strikingly illustrated by the closeness to Roman classical architecture of their interior and exterior. The façade of San Miniato, covered with an impressive tracery of green and white revetment, whereby brick-work is clad with different-coloured, thin marble panels, an ancient Roman building technique revived in Florence and Tuscany in the 11th c. Geometrical patterns, triangles, squares, rectangles, inserted into the great Romanesque arches – also reminiscent of Roman architecture – make up the three layers forming the façade of the church. The three-aisled interior has no transept, but with its raised choir over the early 11th c. crypt, containing the grave of St. Minias, has the appearance of an early Christian colonnaded basilica of unusually harmonious proportions. Notable late Romanesque works include the magnificent marble choir screen and pulpit and the intarsia floor of the nave (1207).

The 11th c. Battistero San Giovanni, which was considered in the Renaissance, on account of its proportions and revetment, to be a classical work of architecture and thus particularly worthy of imitation (cf. Duomo and façade of Santa Maria Novella; 15th c.), in its octagonal shape harks back to early Christian baptisteries (e.g. the Baptistery of San Giovanni in Laterano, Rome), but surpasses them in its monumental scale. Its three storeys are covered with a geometric pattern of green and white marble. In its harmoniousness and regularity of forms, the Baptistery, by applying classical Roman models (Pantheon), in many respects already resembles the art of the Renaissance, which is why this is termed Proto-Renaissance, since it heralds the features of the actual Renaissance three hundred years before its time.

The interior walls are also geometrically faced with multi-coloured marble, but the spatial effect is sombre and medieval in character, with the narrow windows admitting little light. The interior is divided up by massive granite pillars in eight sections braced against each other. The famous 13th c. mosaics of the vault depict, inter alia, the Creation, the legend of Joseph, the life of Christ and the story of John the Baptist. These mosaics were by the Venetian artists who worked in Florence from *c.* 1230 onwards, and who brought with them the Byzantine art of mosaic so masterfully replicated in Venice and Ravenna.

The Church of Santi Apostoli, first mentioned in 1075, was roughly contemporary with the Baptistery. Its interior still has the appearance of an early Christian basilica with its nave and two aisles, its timbered roof and narrow clerestory windows. Structural and decorative components such as columns with entasis, composite capitals, two of them from the nearby Roman baths, and graduated arcade arches are informed by classical design, and give the antique Roman stamp to the Florentine Renaissance.

Art

Florence has retained little of note from this period when it comes to painted works of art. Byzantine iconic representations generally predominated in the painting of religious panels. One early Florentine painting is the Crucifixion (1225–35) by the Maestro del Bigallo (Museo del Bigallo), an unknown painter who was also responsible for the antependium of St Zenobius (Cathedral Museum).

Sculpture

Sculpture was largely shaped by carving in ivory. An example of this is the ivory cover of a Florentine Gospel (11th c.) showing the Whitsuntide miracle (now in the Vatican Library).

Gothic

Architecture

Gothic architecture did not arrive in Florence until the late 13th c. After much internal political strife, the formidable Palazzo del

Palazzo del Bargello

The Cathedral dome: an architectural masterpiece by Brunelleschi

Podestà was built between 1254 and 1261, and later renamed Bargello as the seat of the Bargello or Chief Constable whose neutral authority, allied with strict laws, was to take care of law and order in the city. The imposing, fortress-like building with its high tower, constructed of ashlars, originally had wooden galleries on the outside. Inside there is an impressive courtyard with broad arcades, several stone-vaulted halls and a chapel decorated with frescoes. When the Signoria finally emerged as the Executive in 1292, a new seat of government was required, and in 1299 work started on the Palazzo dei Priori, later to be known as the Palazzo Vecchio, and the main building was completed in 1314. This city hall still looks very much the medieval fortress, the building's massive façade faced simply with dressed stone. The "Palace of the Commune" is crowned by a battlemented gallery atop two storeys with rows of Gothic two-arched windows. The gallery is marked by a row of coats-of-arms reflecting the eventful history of the rulers of Florence as a city state in the Middle Ages. To the left of the Palazzo Vecchio, set back slightly, is a small Palazzo, the former commercial court from *c.* 1359, with a Gothic façade also decorated with a series of coats-of-arms of seven large guilds or *arti maggiori* and of fourteen small ones, or *arti minori*.

In the 13th c. family towers were still predominant in domestic architecture, but these were demolished following the consolidation of the commune, since the tower of the Palazzo Vecchio was to stand out above all other buildings as an expression of communal power and civic pride. However, the 14th c. loggia-crowned Palazzo Davanzati and battlemented Palazzo Spini-Ferroni survive as examples of Gothic palazzo architecture.

In ecclesiastical building, Santa Maria Novella from around 1300 (foundation stone laid 1246, nave from 1279, façade 1458–70) was the first Gothic church of the Dominican mendicant order in the form of a spacious, pillared basilica, having a nave and two aisles, with rib vaults and transept choir chapels. The monumental Gothic edifice of the Cathedral of Santa Maria del Fiore was begun in 1296, but, because of interruptions, not consecrated until 1436 and the façade completed in the 19th c. in the Gothic style. In all of Florence's Gothic churches, there is hardly a sign of the finely articulated construction traditionally associated with Gothic architecture, virtually none of the usual flying buttresses, tracery or sculptured façades. The interiors also demonstrate Florentine characteristics. The interior of the Cathedral reveals itself to be a pillared basilica with a nave and two aisles on the ground plan of a Latin cross. The nave, with its four widely spaced pillars, appears airy but austere. This effect of compact spaciousness is also reinforced by the cross-ribbed vaulting directly supported on the vast arcades with no triforium. There is scarcely anything resembling the slender, soaring forms that are characteristic of Gothic architecture in Germany and France. In Florence the architects were concerned with achieving a balance between the vertical and the horizontal.

Art

Cimabue (c. 1240/1245-post 1302) was one of the first of the painters to edge slowly away from the rigidity of the standard forms of Byzantine iconography that had held sway for centuries, and achieve greater realism and heightened colour differentiation. His "Madonna in Majesty" (c. 1275, Uffizi) and Crucifixion (c. 1287, Santa Croce) testify to this.

But it was Giotto di Bondone (c. 1267–1337) who first made a complete break with the incorporeal and two-dimensional representational method of Byzantine-medieval art. His frescoes (Santa Croce) and altarpieces ("Madonna in Majesty", Uffizi), works from the first three decades of the 14th c., make him the founder of European Renaissance painting, since his picture of people and the world around him was based on observation of nature and the real world.

During the 14th c. a number of painters worked partly on the lines of Giotto and partly in the international Gothic style. Important Florentine works include the frescoes of the Last Judgment, Paradise and Hell (c. 1357) by Nardo di Cione (Santa Maria Novella), stylistically conservative works imbued with medieval spirituality. Somewhat more cheerful in basic mood is the important cycle of frescoes by Andrea Bonaiuto da Firenze (died 1377) in the Spanish chapel (Santa Maria Novella) with a magnificent series of images (1365–67) of Dominican theology, showing Mankind's road to salvation.

The Franciscan church of Santa Croce, the scene of some of Giotto's pioneering work, also has a series of frescoes by his immediate successor and pupil Taddeo Gaddi. These are in the Cappella Baroncelli and are of scenes from the life of Christ and the Virgin (c. 1357). The apse of Santa Croce became the setting between 1380 and 1390 for Agnolo Gaddi's significant frescoes of the Legend of the Holy Cross. Both painters largely adopted Giotto's monumental style of figures and his depth of perspective, without arriving at any new solutions for composition.

Sculpture

The outstanding achievements in Gothic sculpture include Arnolfo di Cambio's reliefs, Pisano's first bronze door of the Baptistery and Orcagna's marble tabernacle in Orsanmichele. Arnolfo di Cambio (c. 1245–1302) became Florence's Cathedral architect in 1296. The small number of works attributed to him (e.g. "St Reparata", "Madonna with Christ-child blessing", "Boniface VIII"; Cathedral Museum), show a close-blocked outline of the monumental figure, with some classical traits in pose and gesture. Another epoch-making sculptor and goldsmith, Andrea Pisano (c. 1295–before 1358) came to the fore in c. 1330. His major work, and the only one that can be attributed to him with certainty, is the oldest bronze door of the Baptistery (1330–36) with its 28 relief panels. The reliefs of scenes from the life of John the Baptist are composed with spatial clarity and a balanced distribution of the figures, images of calm movement and expressive gesture, some modelled as well-rounded bodies and others in folds of drapery, stylistically recalling both Giotto and the reliefs from Roman sarcophagi.

Andrea Orcagna (first mentioned in Florence 1343/1344; died 1368) was not only a sculptor but also a painter and architect. Few of his works are extant, but one of his most accomplished is the marble tabernacle with scenes from the life of the Virgin (1352–59) in Orsanmichele.

Early Renaissance

Architecture's most pressing task at the start of the 15th c. was to complete the Cathedral and above all to erect the dome over the crossing. Filippo Brunelleschi (1377–1446) achieved this by means of a self-supporting double-shelled, parabolic structure built between 1420 and 1436, and which pointed the way for dome-building in the Baroque period. Brunelleschi was essentially the first Renaissance architect and its founder in that he more than anyone else was responsible for formulating the laws of linear perspective, an art he rediscovered between 1410 and 1420. This resulted in secular and religious buildings that were less concerned with the revival of antiquity than with practical construction and management of space. The Foundling Hospital (Ospedale degli Innocenti), begun in 1419, is often claimed to be the first Renaissance building with its revolutionary arcades of Corinthian columns like a classical temple, instead of medieval buttresses. The vaulting of this loggia also consists of a series of suspended cupolas that replace the medieval cross-groined and cross-ribbed vaulting. In church building,

Architecture

Fresco by the narrative painter Ghirlandaio

with the Old Sacristy of San Lorenzo (c. 1420), Brunelleschi introduced a new style of architecture over the central area by having a cube roofed by a dome. He also brought important innovations to the construction of the nave area. Examples of this are San Lorenzo (begun c. 1420) and Santo Spirito (begun 1436) as basilicas developed not from Imperial Rome so much as the Tuscan Romanesque or Proto-Renaissance, on a Latin cross ground plan and with clearly articulated and extremely harmonious interiors.

Michelozzo (1396–1472) in particular was another important Florentine architect and sculptor, alongside Brunelleschi whom he succeeded as Cathedral architect (1444–60). With the Palazzo Medici-Riccardi (1444–60) Michelozzo created the first Renaissance palace and the prototype of the Florentine city palace, with its fortress-like rusticated façade, reminiscent of the Palazzo Vecchio, its windows a further development of Gothic biforia, its cornice, and arcaded *cortile*. Also commissioned by the Medici, between 1437 and 1452 he was responsible for the monastery buildings of San Marco. Individualism, which penetrated even 15th c. monastic life, finds expression here in the fact that there is no dormitorium, but small individual barrel-vaulted cells grouped around an inner court, under a common timbered roof. The church of Santissima Annunziata (nowadays Baroque) was originally built between 1444 and 1453 under Michelozzo's direction and was the first centralised building to be erected in the Renaissance, comprising a single nave with side chapels, a layout subsequently to be employed in many Baroque churches.

Leon Battista Alberti (1404–51), the archetypal Renaissance man, an architect and a humanist, designed the façade of the Palazzo Rucellai (1446–51), its rusticated walls articulated by the superimposed orders of pilasters. The façade of Santa Maria Novella (1458–70) was also built to plans by Alberti, adopting the coloured Romanesque inlay used in the Baptistery and San Miniato. Not only is this the first instance of the use of harmonic proportions in the Renaissance, but it has other innovations such as the pedimented temple front linked to the sides by great scrolls, and the softly curved swags between the two storeys, that even accept large round Gothic windows as an ornamental motif.

Other Renaissance architects worthy of mention include Antonio Manetti, a pupil of Brunelleschi, who collaborated on the building of San Lorenzo and Santissima Annunziata, and whose chief work was the Chapel of the Cardinal of Portugal (1461–66) in San Miniato al Monte, and Bernardo Rossellino (1409–64), who was involved in building the Palazzo Ruccellai and the cloisters of Santa Croce. The two-storeyed Chiostro degli Aranci in the Badia Fiorentina (1435/36) is also attributed to him.

Art

Art at the start of the Quattrocento (15th c.) was still dominated by the traditional forms of standard international Gothic. Lorenzo Monaco (1370–1423), born in Siena, in his "Adoration of the Magi" (c. 1420, Uffizi) was using fine lineation and subdued colours. Another painter in the late Gothic style was Gentile da Fabriano (c. 1370–1427), also from the marches, who was a master of detail in his splendid portrayals of courtly life, as in his "Adoration of the Magi" (1422, Uffizi).

It is Masaccio (1401–28) who is actually considered the founder of Italian Renaissance painting. With the aid of the linear perspective rediscovered by Brunelleschi, he succeeded in giving his figures, interiors and landscapes a three-dimensional, true-to-life quality never achieved before, as can be seen in his altarpiece "Madonna and Child with St Anne" (1424/1425, Uffizi), with its powerful, naked Christchild, his frescoes of the life of St Peter in the Brancacci Chapel in Santa Maria del Carmine, and the fresco of the Trinity (1426/1427), a masterpiece of perspective. Paolo Uccello (c. 1397–1475) carried on from Masaccio and in 1436, with his huge fresco in Florence Cathedral of the equestrian statue of the English condottiere Sir John Hawkwood, demonstrated the fascination with perspective that was central to his style. His fresco of the Flood (c. 1448; Chiostro verde, Santa Maria Novella) and the panel from the Battle of San Romano (c. 1435, Uffizi), show his passion for perspective that he took to extraordinary lengths, resulting occasionally in unnatural, almost abstract compositions.

Andrea del Castagno (1421–57), on the other hand, was concerned with painterly reproduction of the three-dimensional figure and showed himself strongly influenced by early Renaissance sculpture. His Sant'Apollonia frescoes (1445–50; Cenacolo di Sant'Apollonia) includes scenes of the Passion and a Last Supper with life-size voluminous figures, communicating with each other by every sort of look and lively gesture. In his "Uomini famosi" (c. 1450) for the Villa Pandolfini in Legnaia (now in the Uffizi and Sant'Apollonia), personalities from Florentine history, mythology and the Old Testament are depicted life-size and statuesque, with amazing powers of illusion. The Dominican monk Fra Angelico (c. 1387–1455) made sparing use of perspective and articulated little in body language in his altarpieces and frescoes (San Marco and Uffizi). His images of serene devotion, of figures clad in magnificently coloured, richly folded garments against an ornamented golden background nevertheless, through the circular and semi-circular arrangement of those figures, achieved a convincing composition and a unity of dimension.

Fra Filippo Lippi (1406–69), on the other hand, also both monk and artist, inclined more towards the three-dimensional figures of Masaccio. His major works are the frescoes in Prato Cathedral, but there is also a series of paintings of the Virgin and Child (Uffizi, Palazzo Pitti), showing the wistful delicacy that marks his work.

Benozzo Gozzoli (1420–97) owes his place in history to the frescoes with which, between 1458 and 1460, he decorated the chapel of the Palazzo Medici.

Sandro Botticelli (1445–1510) was another painter who was in the service of the Medici. In his "Adoration of the Magi" (1475, Uffizi), three generations of Medici appear as kings and members of their train, among other men of letters, humanists and the painter himself. More famous, however, are Botticelli's allegorical pictures, "Primavera" and "The Birth of Venus" (both in the Uffizi), which reveal the painter grappling with humanist ideas around 1480 as a daring synthesis of neo-Platonic and Christian ideas. Despite the representation of a few nudes, Botticelli's painting is essentially neo-Gothic with its emphasis on the traditional, sinuous curve of the figure and its draperies, and the radiance of the face, instead of the realistic human figure of the Renaissance, based on anatomical studies.

In Domenico Ghirlandaio (1449–94), the Florentine upper classes found one of its best chroniclers. His frescoes in the apse of Santa Maria Novella of scenes from the life of the Virgin and John the Baptist (1486–90) are a tribute to the wealthy Florentine burghers of his time, portraying many famous contemporaries and local scenes, with glimpses of noble homes, of panoramic landscapes, of banquets and merrymaking, all of them reflecting the sensuous pleasures of life in the second half of the Quattrocento, the era of Lorenzo the Magnificent.

Sculpture

If there was a date for fixing the Florentine impetus for the revival of western sculpture, it could only be the public competition for the best sculptor in bronze for the second door of the Baptistery in 1401. The competition entries, including the Sacrifice of Isaac (1402) by Ghiberti and Brunelleschi, can still be seen (Bargello) and exemplify, in

Brunelleschi's expressive realism, and Ghiberti's decorative illusion, the key lines of early Renaissance sculpture. With his fine bronze doors that took him from 1403 to 1424, Lorenzo Ghiberti (1378–1455) had already completed a masterpiece. Directly these were completed, Ghiberti was also commissioned to make the third set of Baptistery doors, the East portal, later named the "Gate of Paradise". Once again, Ghiberti was to spend over twenty years working on these doors (1425–52). Their completion was delayed mainly for technical reasons since casting the bronze and doing the gilding involved much experimentation, and this craft, which had been lost since Roman times, had to be relearnt. Ghiberti's ten gilded bronze panels of Old Testament scenes combined three-dimensional reliefs in the foreground with bas-relief in the background, to achieve a hitherto unattained effect of artistic illusion.

Another outstanding project for the sculptors of Florence was the sculptural adornment of the Cathedral of Santa Maria del Fiore. In about 1403 Nanni di Banco (c. 1370/75–1421) was working on the Porta della Mandorla, the cathedral's most richly decorated portal and in 1414 or thereabouts he was responsible for the high relief on the gable depicting the Virgin Mary presenting her girdle to St Thomas. In 1408 he sculpted the marble figure of St Luke for the façade, an exemplary seated figure showing complete mastery of anatomy and with an eloquent facial expression. This was followed by his Four Crowned Saints for the niches of Orsanmichele. All these sculptures use classical *contrapposto* for the first time, as well as a modelling of the head influenced by Roman portrait busts.

"Mary Magdalene" by Donatello

Excitingly divergent from Nanni in his work, Donatello (1382/1386–1466) scored achievements that made him the greatest European sculptor of the 15th c. and for some the true creator of Renaissance sculpture. His free-standing "David" (1408/1409, Bargello) and his "St George" (c. 1415–1517, Bargello) bear witness to his dramatic concept of *contrapposto*, the asymmetrical pose characteristic of much Greek and Roman sculpture, in which the body's weight is borne mainly on one leg, so the hip of that leg rises relative to the other, creating a sense of movement within the stone. He excelled in emotional force, and his revolutionary concept of sculpture is exemplified in the figures in niches of the cathedral: Prophet with scroll, Habakkuk, Jeremiah (1425–35; all in the Cathedral Museum), in which he combines classical anatomy with the Gothic standing figure and drapery, lending the statues passion and prophetic vigour. In contrast to these there is the bronze David (c. 1435, Bargello), gentler and more classical, credited with being the first free-standing nude since antiquity. In his famous "Cantoria" (singing gallery, 1433–39, Cathedral Museum), Donatello illustrates the praise of God in the 150th Psalm, and makes a lavish show of freely interpreted classical motifs with his frolicsome putti. Donatello shows his great talent for sculpting in wood in the Crucifix (1412–20) in Santa Croce, its expressive naturalness underlining the humanity of the Son of God, and in his late work (post 1453) "Mary Magdalene" (Cathedral Museum), harrowingly tragic as an aged and emaciated figure that, set against the immaculate beauty of the bronze "David" of 1435, clearly shows Donatello's versatility as an artist.

His colleague Lorenzo Ghiberti was primarily a goldsmith and a sculptor in bronze who, in addition to the Baptistery doors, created the monumental bronzes of "John the Baptist" (1414), "St Matthew" (1419–22) and "St Stephen" (1429) for Orsanmichele.

Although Luca della Robbia (1400–82) created in his Cantoria (1431–38, Cathedral Museum), a companion singing gallery to

Donatello's, a remarkable marble relief of considerable originality, and in his north door of the Cathedral sacristy, was responsible for an important work in bronze, he was best known for his development of coloured, glazed terracotta as a sculptural medium. He founded an important 15th and 16th c. family workshop, to which Andrea (1435–1525) and his sons Giovanni and Giuliano della Robbia also belonged, and which produced enamelled or lead-glazed reliefs, initially in blue and white, and then in other colours, which are to be found in many of Florence's churches (Cathedral) and public buildings (Foundling Hospital).

Desiderio da Settignano (c. 1430–64), another Florentine sculptor, was influenced by Donatello, but his artistic personality was more delicate. His tomb of the humanist and statesman Gregorio Marsuppini (c. 1453) in San Croce, the sacramental tabernacle (c. 1461) in San Lorenzo and his busts (e.g. "Young Woman", Bargello) are characteristic of his predilection for ornamental detail, his sensitive modelling and the refinement of handling reminiscent of drawing techniques.

His contemporary was the architect and sculptor Bernardo Rossellino (1409–64) whose tomb (c. 1450) in Santa Croce for Leonardo Bruni, the great humanist and Chancellor of the Florentine Republic, became the model for the niche tomb for the rest of the century. His brother Antonio (1427–75) was responsible for the tomb of the Cardinal Prince of Portugal (1461–66) in San Miniato del Monte and excellent lifelike portrait busts, including that of Matteo Palmieri (1468, Bargello).

Benedetto da Maiano (1442–97) also made an important contribution to Florentine sculpture with his outstandingly realistic portrait bust of Pietro Mellini (1474, Bargello) and the pictorial relief on the marble pulpit of Santa Croce, dating from around the same time, depicting the virtues and the legend of St Francis, together with his unfinished later works "Madonna and Child" and "Saint Sebastian" (Misericordia Chapel), in a style already heralding the High Renaissance.

However, the outstanding sculptor of the second half of the 15th c. was Andrea del Verrocchio (1436–88) who was also a noted painter ("Baptism of Christ", Uffizi). His tomb for Piero and Giovanni de'Medici (completed 1472) consists of pure ornamentation in bronze and multi-coloured marble. His bronze "David" (1472–75, Bargello) is the finely modelled, naturalistic figure of a shepherd boy, his stance self-confident in his own space. Even more concerned with presenting an all-round view is his powerfully realistic "Putto and Dolphin" (Palazzo Vecchio), heralding the twist to the figures of the fountains of the Baroque. The marble bust of a "Lady with Flowers" (Bargello) shows such refined treatment of the marble that not only head and hands, but also the various layers of material are shown to advantage. His major large bronzes include "Christ and Doubting Thomas" (1466–83, Orsanmichele), where the way in which the niche figures dominate their space provided important inspiration to Baroque sculpture.

High Renaissance

Within a few decades, the classical style had fully asserted itself in Italy, so that the period from the turn of the century to the death of Raphael (1520) is termed the High Renaissance.

The buildings that led the way for High Renaissance architecture in Florence were those of Giuliano da Sangallo (1445–1516), who carried further the building concepts of Brunelleschi and thus helped Florentine architecture to its fullest flowering. He supervised the

Architecture

building of the Villa Medici in Poggio da Caiono (1480–85) and in Florence was responsible for the octagonal sacristy of Santo Spirito, with a double-shelled dome (1488–92) and a barrel-vaulted vestibule with classical decoration, particularly in the richly adorned capitals. From 1480 to 1500 Sangallo also supervised the conversion of Santa Maria Maddalena dei Pazzi, adding side chapels to the nave, thus reinforcing the impression of a single-naved church interior. His contemporary, the architect Cronaca, (1457–1508) used the same principle in the construction of San Salvatore al Monte, but introduced new internal highlights with the two-storey wall articulation like a palace façade.

Da Sangallo's Palazzo Gondi (1490–1508) was already developing ideas of an urban palazzo as a precursor to the Roman architecture of the High Renaissance. Only a year previously, work had begun on building the Palazzo Strozzi, which between 1489 and 1500 was to be supervised in turn by Sangallo the Elder, Benedetto da Maiano and Cronaca. In contrast to the Palazzo Gondi, where the rustication of the three storeys gradually decreases towards the top, making it appear structurally lighter the further it rises above the ground, the façade of the stylistically more conservative Palazzo Strozzi shows uniform rustication with even spacing of the arched windows and painstakingly worked cornices separating the three storeys. Both Palazzi have very beautiful inner courtyards. A third example of a High Renaissance palazzo worth mentioning is the Palazzo Pandolfini (1517–29), whose tabernacle windows (with half columns), alternating segmental and triangular pediments and rusticated portal in the centre of the grey stone façade clearly point to the style of the Roman High Renaissance. It is said to have been designed by Raphael, and carried out by members of the Sangallo family of architects.

Art

The work of Filippino Lippi (1457–1504) signifies the threshold of the High Renaissance. After completing Masaccio's fresco cycle in the Brancacci Chapel of Santa Maria del Carmine between 1481 and 1483 he painted his most famous altarpiece, the "Vision of St Bernard" (1486, Badia), in which he revived early Renaissance concepts for one last time, and integrated the portrait of the founder, the landscape, architecture and still life to produce a single unity, by means of warm tonal colour and balanced composition. In contrast, the "Adoration of the Magi" (1496, Uffizi), is a dramatic piece, full of movement and picturesque effect, and the same motifs are to be found in the frescoes in the

"The Annunciation" an early work by Leonardo da Vinci

Cappella Strozzi in Santa Maria Novella, of scenes from the lives of St Philip and St John which Lippi completed in 1502. These are dominated by a robust use of line, the architecture is monumental and laden with ornamentation, the figures are gesturing dramatically, all of these aspects that already herald Mannerism.

Leonardo da Vinci (1452–1519), painter, sculptor, architect, engineer and scientist, studied painting under Andrea del Verrocchio, and demonstrated his exceptional talent in two of his youthful works, the "Baptism of Christ" and the "Annunciation" (1472–75, both in the Uffizi), which he produced in collaboration with Verrocchio. The "Adoration of the Magi" (Uffizi) is regarded as being executed by his own hand, but remained unfinished when Leonardo entered the service of the Duke of Milan in 1482. What had been a simple tale of Christmas acquires a new dimension of world redemption in Leonardo's turbulently expressive version of a disjointed world. Leonardo laid the basis for the High Renaissance style with his heroic figures, balanced compositions and the subtle modelling through light and shade that lent a highly atmospheric quality to his paintings.

The Florentine painter Fra Bartolommeo (1472–1519) was a Dominican monk whose real name was Baccio della Porta. He had a strongly developed sense of colour, probably the result of his journey to Venice in 1508. His "St Mark" (1514–16) and "Risen Christ" (1516, both Palazzo Pitti) indicate the influence of Michelangelo, but also the solemn restraint and monumentality so representative of the High Renaissance.

Raphael (Raffaello Santi; 1483–1520) was born in Urbino, and apprenticed to Perugino. His major works are in Rome but he spent some four years working in Florence between 1504 and 1508 during which time he painted sharply observed portraits of Agnolo Doni and his bride Maddalena Strozzi (1505/1506, Palazzo Pitti), the "Virgin Mary with the Goldfinch" (c. 1506, Uffizi) and the "Madonna del Granduca" (1505/1506, Palazzo Pitti), both charming representations of a slightly melancholic mood, resulting in a highly biased image of Raphael which was to last for centuries. The high art of portraiture exercised by Raphael is demonstrated by the portraits painted in Rome of Pope Leo X (1517/1518, Uffizi), the beautiful "Donna Velata" (c. 1514, Palazzo Pitti), and Cardinal Inghirami (c. 1516, Palazzo Pitti). Raphael was the artist in whose work the ideals of the Renaissance found their most complete expression, as well as their conclusion, with a consistently optimistic attitude towards life, despite the time of crisis (Reformation) and where the human image is determined by harmony and beauty, pride and dignity.

Andrea del Sarto, whose real name was Andrea d'Agnolo (1486–1539), was influenced by Raphael, Leonardo and Michelangelo, but worked almost exclusively in Florence. A series of his frescoes can be seen in the church of Santissima Annunziata, including the "Birth of the Virgin" (1514), a picture of highly geometric composition, but richly alive with striding figures. Del Sarto's change in style can be clearly followed in the grisailles of scenes from the life of John the Baptist in the Chiostro dello Scalzo, that he worked on, with interruptions, from 1510 to 1526. The Palazzo Pitti contains his powerfully heroic John the Baptist, probably based on a classical torso, and his Assumption of the Virgin (c. 1527), a deeply religious work of atmospheric intensity achieved by impressive chiaroscuro technique.

It was Michelangelo Buonarroti (1475–1564) who brought High Renaissance sculpture to the pinnacle of its success with his early work in Florence before his first period in Rome (1496–1501). Having studied classical examples and been apprenticed to Ghirlandaio and Bertoldo, Michelangelo's first works (all in the Casa Buonarroti) – the "Madonna

Sculpture

and Child" (1491), the "Battle of the Centaurs" (1492) and the wooden crucifix for Santo Spirito (1494) – were already showing his receptiveness to, and at the same time his pioneering revival of classical art, with bold foreshortening and modelling full of contrast.

The "Drunken Bacchus" (begun 1496, Bargello) is at first glance merely an imitation of the classical, but is perplexing in that the shoulder above the right, free, leg is turned not backwards, but forwards, giving the figure a lack of stability which would have been as alien to classical sculpture, as the expressive naturalism of the slightly potbellied, vulgar figure with its drunkard's mouth. Michelangelo was less interested in the balanced classical concept of figures that are harmonious in every respect, than in the tension created by having parts of the body twisted in opposite directions. This is expressed in his colossal statue of "David" (1501–04, Accademia), a classical *contrapposto* figure, strongly opposing movement and repose, tension and relaxation. Michelangelo's "David", originally planned for the façade of the Cathedral, then sited in front of the Palazzo Vecchio, concludes a whole series, begun around 1400, of representations of Old Testament heroes in Florence, which in addition to their religious significance also served as models of gallant valour and hence moral courage. In the early 16th c. his fight for right and freedom could be seen as portraying the Republic of Florence fighting for civic autonomy against the absolute rule of princes. That is why Michelangelo's "David" was on display in front of the Palazzo Vecchio, where he joined Donatello's "Judith and Holofernes" and the City Lion, as one of a series of republican monuments.

Mannerism

Mannerism has come to designate the era in Italian art between the High Renaissance and the Baroque from about 1520 to 1600. It is derived from *maniera* meaning style or stylishness, and describes the anti-classical style which instead of an idealised natural form, seeks dynamism in all forms of expression, and thus permits distortions of reality to the extent of a delight in the unusual and the bizarre.

Architecture

The most important legacy of Mannerism in the architecture of Florence is the Biblioteca Laurenziana. It was begun in 1524, to plans by Michelangelo, but not put to its intended use until 1571, after his death. The vestibule, much more than the main hall of the library, is among the most individualistic architectural works of Michelangelo or of his time, and has been called one of the most dramatic architectural conceptions ever realised, and this high and narrow, yet monumentally articulated triumphal entry up into the library is unique in architectural history. At first the visitor is not sure exactly where he is – on a main floor or on a mezzanine, actually inside or outside the library. The articulation is by means of double columns, and the walls hold recesses that are half window, half niche. Everywhere the architectural rules appear to be reversed: the niches are too shallow to take figures, the pilasters at their sides get narrower towards the bottom and not wider, the delicate volutes of the lowest storey are much too weak to support the columns. The columns in their turn are there only to decorate the walls. The architrave runs above the wall, so that the columns lose their support function. The staircase has a peculiar effect, having to get over a large difference in height in a very small space. The central flight of stairs flows broad and rounded from the portal, and climbing the side stairs, which have no banisters, brings with it a feeling of insecurity, and this sense of insecurity through the reversal of architectural forces is typical of Mannerism.

Buontalenti Grotto in the Boboli Garden

Giorgio Vasari (1511–74), painter, architect, and artists' biographer followed very much in the footsteps of Michelangelo. When he built the Uffizi (1560–74) as the seat of government for the Grand Duchy of Tuscany he gave it an extremely foreshortened court-like prospect, with the movement not focusing on a central section, but leading out through the open loggia into the distance. His *Studiolo* (little study), built for Grand Duke Francesco I (1540), is Vasari's showpiece of Mannerism, a philosophically inspired creation, jumbling together architecture, art and sculpture, so as completely to dispel any boundaries between art and reality.

For Bartolomeo Ammanati (1511–92), a Mannerist architect and sculptor, his masterpiece was the courtyard of the Palazzo Pitti (1660–70), based on Vignaola's Palazzo Farnese in Rome. Whilst he retained the three-storied structure with classical columns (Doric, Ionic, Corinthian), he re-divided the vertical columns by bands of rustication varying in size over the three storeys, thus re-integrating the protruding columns in the face of the wall. The courtyard façade therefore appears a charming interplay of projecting three-dimensional forms and retreating two-dimensional forms.

Probably the most versatile Mannerist architect was Bernardo Buontalenti (1536–1608), who was also a painter and sculptor as well as a prolific designer of gardens, as well as masques, fireworks and other court entertainments. His works for the diversion of princes included the Tribuna (*c.* 1581), a magnificently elaborate octagonal room in the Uffizi, the grottoes in the Boboli gardens (*c.* 1585, plans by Vasari), and the interior decoration of the Palazzo Vecchio (1588). Other important pieces of architecture by Buontalenti include the Palazzo Nonfinito (1593), the Forte di Belvedere (1590–95) and the Baroque façade of Santa Trinità (1593).

Art

Giovanni Battista Rosso (1494–1549), known as Rosso Fiorentino, was one of the leading figures in the early development of Mannerism. The fresco of "The Assumption of the Virgin" (1517, Santissima Annunziata) and the panel "Madonna with four saints" (1518, Uffizi) are the earliest works demonstrating his skill, which was probably acquired under Andrea del Sarto. The altar panels "Madonna with four saints" (1522, Palazzo Pitti) and the "Marriage of the Virgin" (1523, San Lorenzo) are distinguished by their refined elegance in the asymmetrical composition of robed figures and iridescent colour. His "Moses defending the daughters of Jethro" (1523, Uffizi) is an unusual work with its sharp contrasts of colour and line, imbued with violent energy. After 1530 Rosso worked at the court of François I in Fontainebleau, and had a considerable influence on French painting of the 16th c.

Jacopo da Pontormo, or Jacopo Carrucci (1494–1557), in his early fresco "The Visitation" (1514–16, Santissima Annunziata) was still drawing on the monumental style of his teacher, Andrea del Sarto, and on Raphael's "School of Athens" in Rome. His distinctive style put him in the vanguard of Mannerism, and his "Entombment" in Santa Felicità, together with a fresco of the Annunciation (1526–28), is one of the keyworks of the movement, with its vivid colours and poignant emotion. He was also an outstanding portraitist and his posthumous portraits of the Medicis, Cosimo the Elder and Lorenzo the Magnificent are of great refinement and sensitivity.

His pupil and adopted son Agnolo Bronzino (1503–72) was also a portraitist at the court of the Medicis as well as a poet, but he lacked the emotional intensity of his master and the ten portraits in the Uffizi Tribuna, which include Eleonora of Toledo with her son (c. 1546) and Lucrezia Panciatichi (c. 1540), are in a style that is cold and unemotionally analytical.

Sculpture

Typical works of Mannerist sculpture are Michelangelo's "Slaves", intended for the tomb of Pope Julius II (1519, Accademia), and the Medici tombs (1520–34) in the New Sacristy (San Lorenzo), in which a hitherto unknown complexity of movement and intensification of expression give visible form to spiritual tension and emotions. As all the works are unfinished, they simply provide an insight into Michelangelo's creative process. But even in their unfinished state, they appear to be ahead of their time, fundamentally illustrating an existential struggle between freedom and constraint, between mind and matter. Although Michelangelo was an adherent of neo-Platonic philosophy, in the central theme of the Pietà he repeatedly took issue (four times in all) with the Christian doctrine of salvation. The Cathedral Pietà (Cathedral Museum) and the Pietà Rondanini (Accademia) are unfinished late works of harrowing tragedy.

Michelangelo's Florentine contemporary Baccio Bandinelli (1493–1560) was only mediocre by comparison. His colossal marble group "Hercules and Cacus" (1533/1534, Piazza della Signoria) was commissioned by Alessandro de'Medici, who saw himself in the role of Hercules, defeating the fire-breathing, man-eating monster Cacus, and thus demonstrating to the Florentines his power and strength as Duke.

Benvenuto Cellini (1500–71), sculptor, goldsmith and metal-worker, was one of the most important Mannerist sculptors. His bronze bust of Cosimo I (1545, Bargello), with its lavishly detailed armour ornamentation, is as much a masterpiece as his lifesize "Perseus" (1545–54, Piazza della Signoria), one of the glories of Florentine art. His style is characterised by impulsive theatrical movement of the figure, which is always well-balanced and finely modelled.

Bartolomeo Ammanati's (1511–75) colossal statue of Neptune (1571–92), on the other hand, crowning the fountain in the Piazza della Signoria, and commissioned for the marriage of Francesco de'Medici to

Johanna of Austria, appears quite off-balance. Mockingly nicknamed by the Florentines *biancone* (great white thing), this figure of Neptune as god of the sea symbolises the Medici princes' new title of Grand Duke and claims to naval supremacy as the political consequence of this marriage.

"Mercury" by Giovanni da Bologna

Sculpture in Florence reached a final highpoint at the end of the 16th c. with the work of Giambologna, or Giovanni di Bologna (1529–1608), a Fleming from Boulogne sur Mer, and the greatest sculptor of the age of Mannerism. His essential contribution to the development of sculpture, not least to that of the Baroque, was the *figura serpentinata*, figures in complex twisting poses and designed to be viewed from all sides, their convolutions forcing the viewer to walk around them. Outstanding examples of this are his "Florence Triumphant over Pisa" (1570, Bargello), and "The Rape of the Sabine" (1583, Loggia dei Lanzi). His bronze statuettes, particularly of animals, were enormously popular (Bargello), while his "Winged Mercury" (*c.* 1580, Bargello), also in bronze, seems to defy gravity and be virtually about to hover in space.

His monument to Grand Duke Cosimo I de Medici (*c.* 1594) on the Piazza della Signoria was the first equestrian statue made in Florence and an immensely influential design. It also counts as the first of the epoch of Absolutism. As a public monument to a ruler, posed like an Emperor, on horseback, raised up above the heads of the people, it represents the height of the glorification of princely power, and glaringly illustrates the political situation in Florence. With the approaching end of the 16th century the republican-spirited citizens, who compared themselves with freedom-fighters such as David, have become subjects paying homage to the Prince.

Baroque

Florence was of minor importance as a showplace for Baroque art. Since the beginning of the 17th c. economic decline and a rigid political system had also led to a falling-off in Florentine artistic endeavour; henceforth the Establishment was to dedicate itself to maintaining and preserving the art and culture of the previous centuries.

Architecture

The greatest building project in Florence in the 17th and 18th c. was the Princes' Chapel, the Capella dei Principi (commenced 1608), an enormous domed octagon adjoining the choir of San Lorenzo and a magnificent mausoleum for the Medici Grand Dukes. After many changes of plan and much delay the chapel was completed in 1737, although the dome took until the 19th c. and the interior until 1939 (altar and inlay).

Other building works included the extension of the Palazzo Pitti as a ducal residence when the façade was lengthened (1620–40) by Giulio and Alfonso Parigi, and the terrace wings were added between 1764 and 1783 on the lines of the layout of French Baroque palaces. The Palazzo Corsini (1648–56) by Gherardo Silvano is a good example of a Baroque city palace with a monumental internal staircase.

In church architecture the new design for the choir of Santa Maria dei Pazzi occasioned an important collaboration between Pier Francesco Silvani (architecture) and Ciro Ferri (art). Pier Francesco Silvani, with Gherardo, was essentially responsible for the rebuilding of the Baroque

Art

church of San Gaetano. In the 18th c. there was also the reconstruction of Santa Felicità by Ferdinando Ruggieri (1736–39), who previously incorporated classical elements.

Art in Florence around 1600 was still under the influence of the aftermath of Mannerism. Alessandro Allori (1535–1607) was the pupil and adopted son of Bronzino, and one of his major influences was his master's Mannerism. Another influence, Michelangelo, is evident in his fresco of the Last Judgment in Santissima Annunziata (1560). He first made his name as a painter of portraits, but around 1570 he adopted the images of Counter Reformation, and then themes from mythology and classical history. "The Pearl Fishers" (c. 1570, Palazzo Vecchio) is held to be his masterpiece, combining nude figures with stylish colouring. Other major works in Florence include "The Sacrifice of Isaac" (1589, Uffizi) and "Madonna and Child" (c. 1590, Palazzo Pitti), reminiscent of the realism of the Quattrocento.

His son and pupil, Christofano Allori (1577–1621), preferred a richer use of colour and more natural, unconstrained movement in his figures, making effective use of chiaroscuro. The "Adoration of the Kings" (Palazzo Pitti) and "Judith with the head of Holofernes" (Uffizi) are good examples of his work.

Ludovico Cigoli (1559–1613) was painter, architect, and poet, as well as a pupil of Allessandro Allori, whose skills were frequently drawn on for the Grand Dukes' court entertainments. His work was subject to many influences, from Correggio to Carracci, in the complex process of transition from Mannerism to Baroque. He has some important works in the Palazzo Pitti. These include the early work "Madonna and Child", "Maria Magdalena", and the "Trinity" (1592), and the "Ecce Homo" (c. 1606), testifying to the influence of Caravaggio.

Exhibition hall in the Gallery of Modern Art in the Palazzo Pitti

Pietro da Cortona (1596-1669) was commissioned by the Medicis to paint some of the walls and ceilings in the Palazzo Pitti. These influential examples of "Illusionism", sensual and vigorous, which were painted between 1637 and 1647, can be seen in the Palace in the Venus, Apollo, Mars and Jupiter Rooms, and in the Sala della Stufa.

The most significant sculptor of the Baroque in Florence around 1700 was Giovanni Battista Foggini, who also worked as an architect, and he was responsible for a series of sculptures in Santissima Annunziata, as well as the refurbishment of Sant'Ambrogio in the Baroque style. However, none of his work had the impact of Roman Baroque.

Pietra dura, mosaic work, often using precious stones, was an important craft in Florence during the Baroque period. A good place to see it is the Medici vault in San Lorenzo. In 1588 Grand Duke Francesco I de'Medici founded the workshops which were soon famous throughout Europe and which still exist today (Opificio delle Pietre Dure).

Sculpture

Modern (19th–20th c.)

Classicism and Historicism have left some traces mainly in residential and town-house architecture, but often the architectural creations, such as the Palazzo delle Assicurazioni Generali di Venezia (1871) on the Piazza della Signoria, were rather unfortunate. Around 1890 the medieval quarter with the Mercato Vecchio and the Ghetto was demolished to make way for the Piazza della Repubblica as a promenade for the upper middle classes, with a triumphal arch, the "Arconte" (1895), surrounded by a number of administration buildings in classical formats reminiscent of the Roman forum that once stood on this site.

Architecture

In church architecture, the marble façade of Santa Croce (1853–60) was completed by Niccolò Matas, supposedly according to Cronaca's (15th c.) ideas. Between 1875 and 1887 the façade of the Cathedral of Santa Maria del Fiore was built in the neo-Gothic style by the Florentine architect Emilio de Fabris.

Twentieth-century buildings worth mentioning include the station, the Stazione di Santa Maria Novella (1933), by the architects Baroni, Berardi, Gamberini, Guarnieri, Lusanna and Micheluzzi, and the Savings Bank Building (1958) by G. Micheluzzi.

A group of mainly Florentine painters emerged in the mid-19th c. known as the "Macchiaioli" for their use of blots or patches (macchie) of colour.

Art

Turning away from academic conventions, they were influenced by Impressionism and the Barbizon School, in their landscapes, loose brushstrokes, natural colours and realistic subjects.

The works of Boldini, Fattori, Lega, etc. can be seen in the Galleria d'Arte Moderna in the Palazzo Pitti. Futurism also had its followers in Florence in the early 20th c. Under Mussolini abstract art was frowned upon, if not banned, so it was the end of the Second World War before Italy rejoined the modern art movements.

The best-known Classicist sculptor in Florence in the 19th c. was Pio Fedi (1816–92), whose "Rape of Polyxena" (1866) has a place of honour among the statuary in the Loggia dei Lanzi.

Sculpture

Around the turn of the century Florence also had a series of imitators of the Rodin style. Under Fascism sculpture was all heroism and pathos. After the Second World War the boundaries between painting and sculpture were increasingly being swept aside so that contemporary art now abounds in installations and environments and the like, thus also giving sculpture a whole new dimension.

Quotations

The city is very fair and rightly bears the name of Florence the Fair, the flower of Italy. There one sees magnificent buildings, some dedicated to God, some for the use of its citizens.

One's gaze first falls upon the wondrous temple of Santa Maria del Fiore, all clad with marble, with the sublime cupola created by that most excellent Florentine, the architect Brunelleschi.

Leondro Alberti
1568

Of the Florentines, though most courteous, yet sparing, other Italians jeast, saying, that when they meete a man about dinner time, they aske Vos' Signoria ha desinato, Sir, have you dined? and if he answer, I, they replie, as if they would have invited him to dinner: but if he answere no, they reply Andate Signor, ch'e otta, Goe Sir, for it is high time to dine. They thinke it best to cherish and increase friendship by metings in Market places and Gardens, but hold the table and bed unfit for conversation, where men should come to eate quickly, and sleepe soundly.

Fynes Moryson
1566 to c. 1617
English traveller

"An Itinerary", 1617

The diversions of a Florentine Lent are composed of a sermon in the morning, full of hell and the devil; a dinner at noon, full of fish and meager diet; and, in the evening, what is called a Conversazione, a sort of assembly at the principal people's houses, full of I cannot tell what.

Thomas Gray
1716–71

Letter to his mother, 1740

Yesterday, with violent rains, there came flouncing down from the mountains such a flood, that it floated the whole city. The jewellers on the Old Bridge removed their commodities, and in two hours after the bridge was cracked. The torrent broke down the quays, and drowned several coach horses, which are kept here in stables underground. We were moated into our house all day, which is near the Arno, and had the miserable spectacles of the ruins that were washed along with the hurricane. There was a cart with two oxen not quite dead, and four men in it drowned; but what was ridiculous, there came tiding along a fat haycock, with a hen and her eggs, and a cat.

Horace Walpole
1717–97

Letter to Richard West, 1740

Apart from such Dutch cities, Florence is probably the cleanest city in the world and certainly one of the most elegant. Its neo-Gothic architecture possesses all the purity and perfection of a lovely miniature. Fortunately for the beauty of the city, its citizens, when they lost their freedom, also lost the energy to embark on large buildings. In consequence nowhere here is the eye affronted by an ignoble façade and there is nothing to disturb the fair harmony of these streets which are imbued with the medieval ideal of beauty.

Stendhal
1783–1842
French writer

The Cathedral, together with Campanile and Baptistery, is the most magnificent building in the city and I first turned my step in its direction after I had gazed my fill upon the Piazza del Gran Duca with its impressive Loggia dei Lanzi and many colossal statues, including those by Giovanni da Bologna of which I had become particularly fond. The Campanile adorned with fine multi-colored marble exerts an immediate charm and surpasses in reality any image of it that I have ever seen. It is clear from

Max Nohl
1805

the very first glimpse that its creator was an artist rather than a builder for it is color that predominates among the elements brought together to such charming effect."

"Italian Sketchbook"

Elizabeth Barrett
Browning
1806–61

Florence is beautiful, as I have said before, and must say again and again, most beautiful. The river rushes through the midst of its palaces like a crystal arrow, and it is hard to tell, when you see all by the clear sunset, whether those churches, and houses, and windows, and bridges, and people walking, in the water or out of the water, are the real walls and windows, and bridges, and people, and churches.

Letter to Mr Boyd, 1847

Charles Dickens
1812–70

How much beauty is here, when, on a fair clear morning, we look, from the summit of a hill, on Florence! See where it lies before us in a sun-lighted valley, bright with the winding Arno, and shut in by swelling hills; its domes, and towers, and palaces, rising from the rich country in a glittering heap, and shining in the sun like gold!

Magnificently stern and sombre are the streets of beautiful Florence; and the strong old piles of building make such heaps of shadow, on the ground and in the river, that there is another and a different city of rich forms and fancies, always lying at our feet.

"Pictures from Italy", 1846

Jacob Burckhardt
1818–97
Swiss art
historian

One finds united in the history of Florence the highest degree of politi-cal awareness and the greatest wealth of cultural forms, and in this sense the city may well have earned the title of the world's first modern state. Here it is an entire populace that engages in what is in the princely states a family affair. The wonderful Florentine spirit, at the same time artistic and acutely reasoning, unremittingly reshapes the political and social condition and describes and judges that same condition just as unremittingly. Thus Florence became the home of pol-itical doctrines and theories, of experiments and advances, but together with Venice the home of statistics and solely and above all other states in the world the home of historical image-making in the modern sense.

Matthew Arnold
1822–88

Florence is the most enchanating place I know in the world. . . . The Cathedral outside (not inside) is to my feeling the most beautiful church in the world, and it always looks to me like a hen gathering its chickens under its wings, it stands in such a soft, lovely way, with Florence round it.

Letter to his sister, 1879

Eckart Peterich
1900–68
German author

The Italians say 'Firenze'. Compared with the English and French 'Florence' this has a hard, almost harsh sound. That is why d'Annunzio wanted people to use the old name, Fiorenza, which is what Dante called his native city. D'Annunzio's suggestion was not taken up, however. The sober, austere Florentines found the old name too rich, and, to a certain degree, too extravagant.

Max Frisch
1911–91
Swiss author

In the chamber of Savonarola: the man is fascinating, the profile, next to it the small picture of his funeral pyre, the black face of the right-thinking, yet one must allow these judges something: they will soon be witnessing the execution, everything is ready on time, in its place, a wooden walkway leads from the court to the red flames. Here I sense something akin to my recent feelings at the Fishmarket: all the circumstances are public, on view in a human dimension, not anonymous.

Florence is a manly town, and the cities of art that appeal to the current sensibility are feminine, like Venice and Siena. What irritates the modern tourist about Florence is that it makes no concession to the pleasure principle. It stands four-square and direct, with no air of mystery, no blandishments, no furbelows – no Gothic lace or baroque swirls . . . The great sculptors and architects who stamped the outward city with its permanent image or style – Brunelleschi, Donatello, Michelangelo – were all bachelors. Monks, soldier-saints, prophets, hermits were the city's heroes. Saint John the Baptist, in his shaggy skins, feeding on locusts and honey, is the patron, and, except for the Madonna with her baby boy, women saints count for little in the Florentine iconography.

Mary McCarthy
1912–89
American author

"The Stones of Florence"

Suggested Walks

These suggestions are intended to help first-time visitors to Florence make the most of their stay. Places with a separate entry in the "A to Z" section of this Guide are shown in **bold** type.

Flying visits

Anyone with only a few hours to spend in Florence and keen to see the major sights is best advised to join one of the organised bus tours (see Practical Information, Sightseeing Programme).

Those who prefer to explore the city for themselves though can still gain an impression of the principal sights, these being situated close together and easily accessible on foot. Start by visiting the magnificent ★★**Duomo Santa Maria del Fiore** and adjacent ★★**Battistero San Giovanni**, the latter with the extraordinarily fascinating and beautiful Gate of Paradise. From here it is only a short distance to the ★**Piazza della Signoria**, encircled by famous buildings, among the most imposing of which is the ★★**Palazzo Vecchio**, of exceptional historical interest. The lovely Gothic ★**Loggia dei Lanzi** houses notable statues. Next proceed to the Uffizi, the internationally famous art gallery for a visit to which some time should certainly be allocated, before rounding off the mini-tour with a brief look at the picturesque ★**Ponte Vecchio** and its many jewellers shops.

Walk 1

Walk 1 covers the Piazza del Duomo and the Piazza della Signoria, two squares close together in the very heart of Florence. This small area boasts an incomparable collection of world-renowned works of art.

Start:
Cathedral Square

Start from the **Piazza del Duomo** on which is located the magnificent ★★**Duomo del Santa Maria del Fiore** with its majestic dome and harmonious free-standing Campanile. The adjacent ★★**Battistero San Giovanni** delights above all on account of its marvellously beautiful east portal, known as the Gate of Paradise. After exploring the cathedral complex be sure to visit the ★★**Museo del Opera del Duomo** in which major items of furnishing from the Cathedral are displayed. Among the exhibits is the famous pietà by Michelangelo, acknowledged one of his finest masterpieces. Next go southwards along the Via Calzaiuoli, a well-known shopping street, to the church of ★★**Orsanmichele** which houses important sculptures. Continue along the Via Calzaiuoli, soon reaching the ★**Piazza della Signoria**, a square rich in history where many buildings of great interest are to be found. Of these the most noteworthy is the massively-constructed ★★**Palazzo Vecchio**, occupying a leading place in the city's history. The lovely ★**Loggia dei Lanzi** contains further important sculptures. Before concentrating on the neighbouring **Palazzo degli Uffizi**, home to one of the world's premier ★★art galleries for which several hours should be set aside, sightseers can rest tired limbs in the Café Rivoire and try the famous chocolate. Near by, and next stop after the Uffizi, is the picturesque ★**Ponte Vecchio**; taken over almost exclusively by goldsmiths, this has become one of Florence's great tourist attractions. After crossing the bridge it is only a short distance to the ★★**Palazzo Pitti**, another art gallery ranking among the world's best.

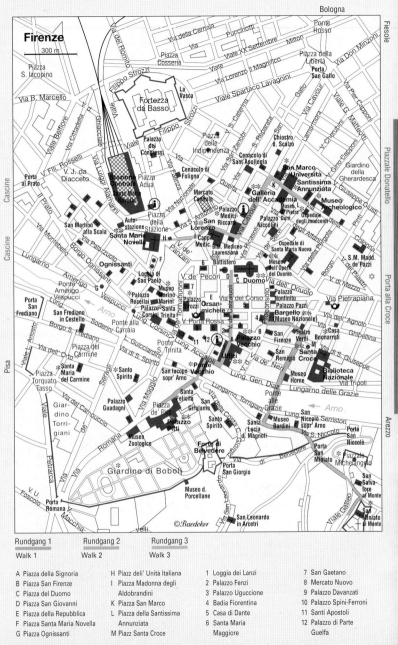

Firenze

300 m

Rundgang 1 | **Rundgang 2** | **Rundgang 3**
Walk 1 | Walk 2 | Walk 3

A Piazza della Signoria
B Piazza San Firenze
C Piazza del Duomo
D Piazza San Giovanni
E Piazza della Repubblica
F Piazza Santa Maria Novella
G Piazza Ognissanti

H Piaz deli' Unità Italiana
I Piazza Madonna degli
   Aldobrandini
K Piazza San Marco
L Piazza della Santissima
   Annunziata
M Piaz Santa Croce

1 Loggia dei Lanzi
2 Palazzo Fenzi
3 Palazzo Uguccione
4 Badia Fiorentina
5 Casa di Dante
6 Santa Maria
   Maggiore

7 San Gaetano
8 Mercato Nuovo
9 Palazzo Davanzati
10 Palazzo Spini-Ferroni
11 Santi Apostoli
12 Palazzo di Parte
   Guelfa

Having sampled the Pitti's many exceptional art treasures, the walk concludes delightfully with a stroll through the lovely ★Giardino di Boboli.

Walk 2

Walk 2 starts at ★★Santa Maria Novella, one of Florence's foremost churches. Situated further to the east, and of even greater art historical significance, lies the church of ★★San Lorenzo, known especially for its world-famous Sagrestia Nuova by Michelangelo. The ★Palazzo Medici Riccardi opposite is vivid testimony to the power of the family which once ruled the city, the Medici. Next follow the Via Cavour northwards to the monastery of ★San Marco, with particularly beautiful frescoes by Fra Angelico. Also not to be missed only a short distance away is the ★★Galeria dell'Accademia, its chief attraction being the again world-famous statue of David by Michelangelo. Afterwards proceed in a south-easterly direction to the imposing ★Piazza della Santissima Annunziata where stand the church of ★Santissima Annunziata, an architectural masterpiece, and the ★Ospedale degli Innocenti with its beautiful loggia.

Start: Santa Maria Novella

Walk 3

Start this third walk at the ★★Museo Nazionale del Bargello, which contains some exceptionally fine 14th–16th c. sculptures. Then head south-eastwards to the wide Piazza Santa Croce, dominated by the church of that name. With its tombs and memorials and important artworks ★★Santa Croce is one of the most impressive ecclesiastical buildings in Italy. Having explored the church interior go up to the ★Piazzale Michelangelo on the south side of the Arno for a splendid view of the city and its imposing buildings. From the square it is just a short walk to yet another magnificent church, ★San Miniato al Monte, from where more lovely views of Florence can be enjoyed.

Start: Bargello

◀ *Statue of Neptune in the Piazza della Signoria*

**Sights
from A to Z**

Sights from A to Z

Arcispedale di Santa Maria Nuova   K5

Location
Piazza Santa
Maria Nuova

Buses
13, 23, B

Early in the 14th c. Florence's old **hospital** was considerably enlarged
and renamed Santa Maria Nuova (St Mary the New). Most of the present
spacious building between Via degli Alfani, Via della Pergola, Via
Bufalini and Via Sant'Egidio dates from the 17th c.
    An interesting feature is the clearcut articulation of the loggias over-
looking Piazza Santa Maria Nuova.

★Badia Fiorentina   K6

Location
Via del
Proconsolo
(access also from
Via Dante
Alighieri)

Buses
14, 23

Open Mon.–Sat.
5–7pm; Sun.
7.30–11.30pm

The spire of the Badia opposite the Palazzo del Bargello (see entry) is
an unmistakable feature of the skyline of Florence. This **church** and
its Benedictine abbey was founded in 978 by Willa, the mother of
Ugo, Margrave of Tuscany (commemorated here every year on
December 21st, the anniversary of his death). The church was subsequently enlarged by Arnolfo di Cambio in the 13th c. and then
internally virtually rebuilt by Matteo Segaloni in the 17th c.
Interesting features of the Gothic façade are the portal by Benedetto
da Rovezzano (1495) with a "Madonna and Child" (early 16th c.) in
glazed terracotta by Benedetto Buglioni in the lunette. A walk round
the church should take in Filippino Lippi's masterpiece (1485) "The
Madonna appearing to St Bernard" (left of the entrance), the tomb of
Ugo, Margrave of Tuscany (d. 1001), built between 1469 and 1481 by
Mino da Fiesole (in the left transept), and, entered from the Choir of
the church, the beautiful 15th c. cloister, popularly known as the
"Chiostro degli Aranci" because of its orange trees, with a fresco of
scenes from the life of St Benedict dating from the completion of the
cloister (c. 1436–39).

★★Battistero San Giovanni   J5

Location
Piazza S. Giovanni

Buses
1, 6, 7, 11, 17, 33

Open Mon.–Sat.
1.30–6.30pm;
Sun., pub. hols.
9am–1pm

The "**Baptistry of St John**" or, in Dante's words, "il bel San Giovanni",
was completed about 1128 after 70 years of building. It is famous for the
three massive bronze doors on the south, north and east sides and for
the magnificent mosaics in its octagonal interior.
    A number of builders were responsible for the construction of what,
after 1128, was to serve as a baptistry. Its pleasing proportions and
green and white marble scheme of decoration made it an architectural
masterpiece that was to serve as a model for other European buildings.
The three bronze portals – works of sculpture unsurpassed in the
Western world – were added in the 15th c.

The **south portal** is the oldest and was designed by Andrea Pisano
(1318–30) and cast by Leonardo d'Avanzano (1330–38). It is divided into

◀ *View of the Palazzo Pitti from the Boboli Gardens*

28 square Gothic panels. With workmanship reminiscent of the art of the goldsmith, the reliefs on 20 of the panels depict scenes from the life of John the Baptist, patron saint of the church; the other eight panels are allegorical representations of the theological and cardinal virtues. Every figure stands out in clear relief, each one a unique work of art in the modelling of the face, of the folds of the garments and the expressive posture of the body.

The decorations of the framing are by Vittorio Ghiberti, son of Lorenzo, and their foliage, creatures and fruit are an early indication of the wealth of form that characterised the Renaissance.

In 1401 Lorenzo Ghiberti beat six others (including Brunelleschi and Jacopo della Quercia) to win the competition for the **north portal**. From 1403 to 1424 Ghiberti worked on the bronze doors with his assistants (Masolino, Donatello, Paolo Uccello, Bernardo Ciuffagni, Bernardo Cennini) and in doing so adhered closely to Andrea Pisano's design for the south portal: 28 square panels each with a Gothic relief, twenty of them scenes of the Life of Christ and eight of them the figures of the four Evangelists and four Early Fathers of the Latin Church. His work, however, far excels that of Pisano in the grace of the figures and the liveliness of expression.

Ghiberti's difference of approach, while still keeping to the traditional forms, is particularly evident in the vivid scenes of the "Resurrection" (right-hand door, top row, left), the "Baptism" and the "Temptation of Jesus" (left-hand door, 4th row down, left and right), the "Nativity" (left-hand door, 5th row down, right) and "Christ among the Doctors" (right-hand door, 5th row down, right).

Ghiberti also designed the bronze framing of the portal from which small heads protrude at every intersection.

Ghiberti adopted an entirely new approach when he came to design his greatest work, the **east portal**. Michelangelo considered it worthy to serve as the Gate of Paradise – hence "Porta del Paradiso" – and Ghiberti himself sang its praises by adding "mira arte fabricatum" (made with admirable art) on the right-hand door next to his signature. In 1990 the original door was replaced by a replica and can now be admired in the Museo dell'Opera del Duomo (see entry).

Nowhere else has a sculptor expressed himself in bronze as perfectly as in this door, created between 1425 and 1452. The ten separate panels contain reliefs of scriptural subjects. The framing incorporates figures of prophets and sibyls and portrait medallions, including one of Ghiberti

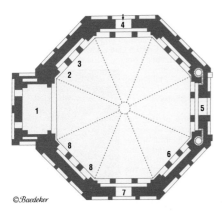

Battistero San Giovanni

1 Tribuna (Hauptaltar)
  mit Mosaiken
  des Jacopo
2 Steinsarg des
  Bischofs Ranieri
3 Grabmal des
  Antipapstes
  Johannes XXIII.
4 Nordportal (Eingang)
5 Ostportal
  (Porta del Paradiso)
6 Marmorner Taufstein
7 Südportal
8 Römische
  Sarkophage

©Baedeker

Baptistry of San Giovanni

himself (4th from the top in the middle row on the left). The beauty and mastery of the finely delineated perspectives, the three-dimensional levels of representation, the individual characterisation of the figures, the meaningful composition of the groupings, all combine in the consummate perfection of the whole.

From top left to bottom right the panels depict:

Adam and Eve: creation, fall, expulsion from Paradise;

Cain and Abel: sacrifice by Cain and Abel, death of Abel, punishment of Cain;

Noah: his sacrifice, departure from the Ark, his drunkenness;

Abraham and Isaac: angel appearing to Abraham, Isaac's sacrifice;

Jacob and Esau: birth of Esau and Jacob, selling the birthright, Esau hunting, Rebecca, Isaac's betrayal;

Joseph: selling of Joseph, Benjamin, Joseph and his brothers;

Moses: Moses receiving the Tablets of the Law on Mount Sinai;

Joshua: the Jews before Jericho, encampment, the walls come tumbling down when the trumpets sound;

Saul and David: battle with the Philistines, slaying of Goliath;

Solomon and the Queen of Sheba.

The sombre, mystical nature of the dim **interior** of the Baptistry comes as something of a surprise after the clearcut articulation of the exterior. It is dominated by the octagonal dome (diameter 25.6 m (84 ft)) which is completely lined with mosaics, the work of Florentine artists (Jacopo da Torrita, Cimabue, Andrea di Riccio, Gaddo Gaddi) in the 13th c. or possibly about 1300

Panel on the Paradise Door

and therefore at the time of Dante. One of the greatest mosaics in the Western world, it is as outstanding for its treatment of its subject matter as for the richness of its ornamentation.

Above the choir chapel is the gigantic figure of Christ – the face alone measures 8 m (26 ft) – as Judge of the World at the Last Judgment. Grouped around him, in different sections, are the figures of the Resurrected and the Damned, of angels, apostles, prophets and saints, with Mary and John the Baptist ranged against the realm of the Devil, devourer of men. (It is worth remembering that Dante, Italy's greatest poet, who described Heaven, Purgatory and Hell in his "Divine Comedy", hailed from Florence.) Other vivid mosaics depict the Creation, scenes from the life of Joseph and the lives of Jesus Christ, Mary and John the Baptist.

Also of interest are one of Donatello's masterpieces, the tomb of the Antipope John XXIII (deposed by the Council of Constance), and the niello decoration of the marble floor (zodiac and metallic ornamentation), the marble font, the sarcophagus of Bishop Ranieri and the high altar with a candlestick in the form of an angel.

Another of Donatello's masterpieces used to stand in the Baptistry – his wooden statue of Mary Magdalene – but this is now in the Museo dell'Opera del Duomo (see entry).

Biblioteca Nazionale Centrale   K6

The large building of the **National Library** (built 1911–35) on Corso dei Tintori, Via Magliabechi and Piazza dei Cavalleggeri, near the Santa Croce complex (see entry) contains 24,721 manuscripts, 723,138 letters and documents, 3780 incunabula, over four million books, 5855 volumes and 4451 sheets of music, 630 atlases and 14,754 geographical and topographical maps.

Of especial value are an early 14th c. copy of Dante's "Divine Comedy" (probably the oldest in existence), manuscripts by Galileo, and missals and bibles dating from before the invention of printing. The library goes as far back as the 13th c. and preserves manuscripts by all the famous Florentines.

Location
Piazza dei
Cavalleggeri

Buses
13, B

Open Mon.–Fri,.
9am–7pm,
Sat. 9am–1pm

Casa di Bianca Cappello   H6

Bianca Cappello was the daughter of a noble Venetian family and the sweetheart and later wife of Grand Duke Francesco I. Her house, **(formerly the house of the Corbinelli)**, which was completely rebuilt by Bernardo Buontalenti in 1567, is a fine example of the mansions lived in by the nobility of that time. It has an unusual feature in the grotesque representations of bats below the windows.

Location
Via Maggio 26

Bus
B

★Casa Buonarroti   K/L6

Michelangelo's house that he bought for his nephew Leonardo di Buonarroti but never lived in it himself. Leonardo's son, Michelangelo, decorated it and turned it into a memorial to the great artist. After a long period of dilapidation it was completely restored in 1964.

Two original sculptures by Michelangelo merit special attention: "Battle of the Centaurs and Lapiths", a marble relief which, although Michelangelo was only 17 when he created it, presages in the sense of movement and substantial nature of the figures, much of his later

Location
Via Ghibellina 70

Bus
14

Open Mon.,
Wed.–Sun.
9.30am–1.30pm

mastery; and "Madonna and Child" (or "Madonna della Scala"), Michelangelo's earliest work, completed at the age of sixteen. The signs of genius are already clearly marked in the sense of space, the flow and counterflow on the steps on the left (hence the name "Madonna of the Steps"), the rich expression of the profile, the fall of the mantle.

The wooden crucifix (1494) from Santo Spirito (see entry), supposedly Michelangelo's earliest work for a church, is also interesting. Christ is depicted not as a man of sorrows but as a gentle handsome youth.

Other items on display are models or copies of the works of Michelangelo or mementoes of the artist's life. There are also sculptures and paintings by other masters.

Casa di Dante   J/K6

Location
Via Santa
Margherita 1

Buses
14, 23

Open Mon.–Sat.
10am–6pm;
Sun. 10am–2pm

The houses that belonged to the Alighieri family are in Via Dante Alighieri. According to Florentine tradition one of them was the birthplace in 1265 of Florence's greatest poet, Dante Alighieri (see Famous People), who did not exactly find favour with his native city. Dante opposed the attempts by Pope Boniface VII to incorporate Florence and the whole of Tuscany into the Papal States. When Charles de Valois was summoned to Florence by the Pope to treat for peace, Dante, as leader of the Ghibellines, was exiled from the city.

The building was rather haphazardly renovated in the 19th c. Some rooms contain photographs, editions of the "Divine Comedy", reproductions of Boticelli's drawings for Dante's work and portraits of Italy's greatest poet.

Cascine   A3–F5

Location
Arno north bank

Buses
1, 9, 26, 27, 80

West of the city the Cascine park extends more than two miles along the Arno. Formerly the estate farms of the Medici and then the Lorena family, the park was opened to the public by the Grand Dukes of Lorraine in the second half of the 18th c.

Its woodland and meadows make it a favourite picnic place for many Florentines at the weekend, and the large race-course is another major attraction.

Casino di San Marco   K4

Location
Via Cavour 57

Buses
1, 6, 7, 11, 17, 33

The **palace** on the site of the former Medici gardens was built by Bernardo Buontalenti between 1568 and 1574 for Grand Duke Francesco I de'Medici who had his artist's studios and alchemist laboratories here.

Today the building houses the **Court of Appeal**, the Corte d'Appello.

Cenacolo di Foligno   J5

Location
Via Faenza 42

·Buses
4, 10, 13, 14, 23, 25,
28, 31, 32, 33, 80

The **refectory** of the former convent of St Onuphrius, which belonged to the Franciscan nuns of Foligno, contains Perugino's "Last Supper". It was seriously damaged in the 1966 floods. With this work Perugino proved that he was the equal in Florence of Andrea del Castagno and Ghirlandaio. His "Last Supper" can be viewed by appointment only (tel. 23885).

Cenacolo di San Salvi   O6

Andrea del Sarto's masterpiece, his version of the "Last Supper" in the Cenacolo di San Salvi (San Salvi refectory), is well worth seeing. It is one of the finest early 16th c. frescoes in Florence.

The gallery in front of the refectory and the refectory itself contain copies of lost works by Andrea del Sarto, as well as other works by Florentine masters. The monastery kitchen with its huge fireplace is also worth a visit.

Location
Via di S. Salvi 16

Buses 3, 6, 20

Open Tue.–Sun.
9am–2pm

★Cenacolo di Sant'Apollonia   J/K4/5

The former convent of Sant'Apollonia (refectory of Sant'Apollonia), which was secularised in 1808, then used as a military storehouse and which now houses part of the university, is worth visiting on account of its interesting church and the beautiful cloister with its graceful 15th c. columns. The Coenaculum of St Apollonia, the convent's refectory, is now a museum. Previously inaccessible because of the nuns' seclusion, the Benedictine convent's refectory holds Andrea del Castagno's "Last Supper" (c. 1457). This fresco has an important place in Renaissance painting: the accuracy of its perspective and the realistic physical vigour of the figures (especially Jesus and the figure of Judas sitting apart from the others) makes the picture intensely dramatic.

Also interesting are, above it, Castagno's "Crucifixion", "Entombment" and "Resurrection" and his two lunettes "Pietà" and "Christ crucified with the Virgin, St John and Saints".

Location
Via XXVII Aprile 1

Buses
1, 6, 7, 10, 11, 17,
20, 25, 31, 32, 33

Open 8.30am–
1.50pm
Closed 2nd, 3rd
Mon., 1st, 3rd, 5th
Sun. in the month

★Certosa del Galluzzo

The former Carthusian monastery of Galluzzo is equally famed for its architecture and its works of art. It is reached by taking the Siena road from Florence, then turning right at the end of Galluzzo following the signs to the monastery. The last Carthusian left in 1956 when the monastery passed to the Cistercians. The Benedictine monks who have the monastery today will gladly take visitors round – the tour is usually in Italian – for a voluntary contribution.

Niccolò Acciaiuoli, an important Florentine statesman and a friend of Petrarch and Boccaccio, had the monastery built in 1341 for the Carthusians, an anchorite order founded by St Bruno of Cologne. It contained blocks of individual cells for the monks and common areas for prayers and services. In the centuries that followed it was much extended and rebuilt. This hilltop monastery complex still bears the imprint of the Carthusian way, which trod an austere path between monastic community and the life of the hermit.

In earlier days the monastery was richly endowed with art treasures, but Napoleon robbed the order of about 500 works of art and only a few were ever returned.

In the late 18th and early 19th c. Popes Pius VI and Pius VII spent long periods in the Foresteria, the monastery's guest-house.

The church of San Lorenzo, which is worth seeing, is reached by crossing a large square. The Cappella di San Tobia (left of the high altar) contains the tomb of Niccolò Acciaiuoli and the tombstones of three other members of the Acciaiuoli family (including that of Lorenzo di Niccolò).

Excursion
5 km (3 mi.) S

Bus
37

Open Tue.–Sun.
9am–noon,
3–6pm; in winter
3–5pm

Great Cloister in the Certosa del Galluzzo

In the Cappella di Sant'Andrea is the famous tomb of Cardinal Agnolo II Acciaiuoli, formerly ascribed to Donatello but now thought to be by Francesco da Sangallo. The other chapels also contain valuable fitments.

The tour carries on through the **monastery buildings** which include a parlatory, a "Medium" cloister, the chapter house, the "Great" cloister (1498–1516), the refectory, and the "Small" cloister. Unlike other orders, the monastery buildings were not where the monks lived – their cells were in separate blocks – but where they assembled for communal activities. It is possible to visit one of these cell blocks, consisting of three rooms, a loggia and a little garden.

Two rooms of the art gallery show examples of the once immense collection of art treasures, including four lunette frescoes of Christ's Passion by Pontormo (based on drawings by Dürer) and a "Madonna and Child" by Lucas Cranach.

At the end of the tour there is a chance to visit the old pharmacy where the monastery's souvenirs, liqueurs, etc. are on sale.

Chiostro dello Scalzo   K4

Location
Via Cavour 69

Buses
1, 7, 25, 33

Open Mon., Thu.
9am–1pm

The Chiostro dello Scalzo, a graceful **cloister** with slender columns, was decorated by Andrea del Sarto between 1514 and 1526 for the "Confraternity of St John the Baptist", whose crossbearers used to walk barefoot (scalzo) in processions.

The famous **frescoes** depicting scenes from the life of John the Baptist have been restored several times.

The most important frescoes, all monochrome, are the Birth of John the Baptist (1526), the Sermon of St John (1515) and the Dance of Salome (1522).

Colonna della Croce al Trebbio   J5

This granite **column**, which stands in a narrow square at the junction of Via del Moro, Via delle Belle Donne and Via del Trebbio, was erected in 1338.

It has a fine Gothic capital, decorated with the symbols of the Evangelists, and a cross of the Pisan school.

Location
Via del Moro

Bus
37

Conservatorio Musicale Luigi Cherubini   K5

The Conservatorio, founded in the early 19th c., houses a comprehensive music library and a **collection of old musical instruments**, (Museo degli Strumenti Antichi), including early pianos by the inventor of the pianoforte, Bartolomeo Cristofori, violins by the famous Italian violinmakers Stradivarius and Amati, and musical instruments from ancient Egypt and the Orient.

The collection was founded in the early 18th c. by Ferdinando, the son of Cosimo III. Cristofori was its curator and was also responsible for the most important acquisitions.

Location
Via degli Alfani 80

Buses
1, 6, 7, 10, 11, 17, 20, 25, 31, 32, 33

Closed for renovation

★★Duomo Santa Maria del Fiore   J/K5

Florence's **cathedral** is more than the symbol of the city. Together with the Campanile and the Baptistry (see Battistero) it forms one of the most magnificent works of art in the world. Florentines could not live without a glimpse of the dome of their cathedral. It would seem that when Michelangelo created the dome of St Peter's he was seeking to transplant Brunelleschi's masterpiece from his native city of Florence to Rome.

At the end of the 13th c. the citizens of Florence, conscious of the growing importance of their city, wanted to erect a great new edifice on the site of the church of Santa Reparata that would surpass the other churches in the city in its beauty and its dimensions.

Famous architects, first Arnolfo di Cambio (from 1294), then Giotto, Andrea Pisano, Francesco Talenti and Giovanni Ghini made such progress with the building work despite numerous interruptions that between 1420 and 1434 Filippo Brunelleschi was able to crown it with the dome – that sensational feat of architectural bravura. In 1436 the cathedral was dedicated to St Mary the Virgin and acquired the epithet "del Fiore" from the lily on Florence's coat of arms.

The present ornate façade, designed by Emilo de Fabris', was not added until 1875–87. (The old façade, which had never been completed, was demolished in 1587.)

The cathedral has some impressive dimensions. It is 160.45 m (527 ft) long; the nave is 43 m (141 ft) wide; the transept 91 m (298 ft) wide; the façade is 50 m (164 ft) high; the dome is 114.36 m (375 ft) high and 45.52 m (150 ft) in diameter. The church's 8300 sq.m (89,308 sq.ft) of floor space can accommodate about 25,000 people. Santa Maria del Fiore is Italy's third largest church after St Peter's in Rome and Milan Cathedral.

The main feature of the **exterior** is the rich articulation with coloured

Location
Piazza del Duomo

Buses
1, 6, 7, 11, 13, 17, 33

Open Mon.–Sat.
10am–5pm; Sun.
1–5pm; 1st. Sat.
of the month
10am–3.30pm;
Dome (access to
stairs) Mon.–Sat.
9.30am–5.30pm

marble – white from Carrara, green from Prato and red from the Maremma. There is marble everywhere – on the façade built in the medieval Gothic style, on the sides of the aisles leading to the nave, on the buttresses, the small side domes and the massive main dome. The alternating colours show rectitude and beauty, the two basic principles of Florentine art.

The exterior has an abundance of sculpted figures: on the top spandrel of the façade "God the Father", with, immediately below, busts of famous Florentine artists; below a huge rose window "Virgin and Child" and statues of the apostles; below that in the niches of the four pillars are bishops of Florence and Pope Eugene IV who consecrated the church in 1436. The bronze doors have reliefs of Mary and allegorical figures of the Christian virtues.

A walk round the cathedral should include a look at the four portals. On the right-hand side near the Campanile is the Porta del Campanile, with "Christ giving a Blessing" in the gable and "Madonna and Child" in the lunette, both in the style of Andrea Pisano. Next comes the Porta dei Canonici with, above the "Porch of the Canons", a "Virgin and Child" by Lorenzo di Giovanni d'Ambrogio. Nearby are the memorials to the architects Arnolfo di Cambio and Brunelleschi and a stone with the inscription "Sasso di Dante" marking the spot where the poet is supposed to have watched the cathedral being built.

On the left side the "Porta della Balla" (late 14th c.) has a polychrome "Madonna and Child and two Angels". The twisted columns at the sides are supported by lions. Also on the left, the "Porta della Mandorla", the finest portal in the church, was designed by Giovanni d'Ambrogio and Nanni and completed by various artists (Donatello, Niccolò di Pietro Lamberti and Ghirlandaio). Above the door in the *almond* can be seen the Virgin borne up by angels (1421, by Nanni di Banco); in the lunette is a mosaic of the "Annunciation" by Domenico and Davide Ghirlandaio (1491).

In his building of the **dome** Brunelleschi gambled on creating a structural masterpiece (with modest wisdom he commended it to the protection of the Virgin) which is both powerful and aesthetically pleasing. The white ribs that meet at the lantern clearly outline the contours of the red covering of the dome.

The streets behind the apse offer an impressive view of the marble mount that is the cathedral, with Brunelleschi's dome. At this point there is a gallery on the drum of the dome. This was built at the time of Michelangelo who was intensely critical of it, voicing the opinion that it looked like a "cricket cage".

In the pavement in front

The Cathedral with its dome is the symbol of Florence

Duomo
Santa Maria del Fiore

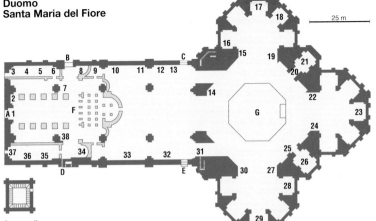

Campanile

©Baedeker

A Portale Maggiore with relief "Maria in Gloria" by A. Passaglia

B Porta dei Cornacchini

C Porta dell Mandoria, by Giovanni d'Ambrogio and Nanni. Above the portal Nanni di Banco's "Virgin borne up by Angels"

D Porta dei Campanile with an "Annunciation"

E Porta dei Canonici, above "Madonna col Bambino" by d'Ambrogio

F Crypt of Santa Reparata, remains of old cathedral

G Brunelleschi's dome with fresco of the Last Judgement by Vasari and valuable stained-glass windows

I "L'Assunta" window, designed by Ghiberti Incoronazione di Maria, mosaic by G. Gaddi

2 Tomb of Antonio D'Orso

3 Window "St Stephano e Due Angeli" by Ghiberti

4 Bust of Emilio de Fabis, designer of the façade, by V. Consani (1887)

5 Statue of Joshua (head by Donatello)

6 Bust of Arnolfo di Cambio, by U. Cambi (1843)

7 Recess with St Zanobius, by G. del Biondo 14th c.

8 Bust of the organist Squarcialupi, by Benedeto da Maiano (1490)

9 Equestrian figure of Niccolò da Tolentino, painted by A. del Castagno (1456)

10 Equestrian figure of Giovanni Acuto (John Hawkwood) painted by P. Uccello (1436)

11 Window dated 1395. Below in the marble recess a statue of King David (B. Ciuffagni, 1434)

12 "Santi Cosma de Damiano" by Bicci di Lorenzo (15th c.)

13 14th c. window, below, "Dante and the Divine Comedy" by D. di Michelino 1445)

14 "S. Giacomo Maggiore" by J. Sansovino, 16th c. statue

15 "S. Tommaso" by De'Rossi, 16th c. statue

16 "G. Giuseppe", painting by Lorenzo di Credi

17 Marble altar (Buggiano)

18 "Madonna with Saints", altar-cloth in the style of P. Bonaguida

19 "S. Andrea", by A. Ferrucci, statue (16th c.)

20 In the door lunette, "Risurrezione", terracotta by Luca della Robbia (1444). Bronze door, also by della Robbia, assisted by Michelozzo and Maso di Bartolemeo

21 Sagrestia nuova o delle Messe

22 "S. Pietro", by B. Bandinelli, statue (16th c.)

23 Above the altar, two angels carrying candles (Luca della Robbia, 1450). Below the altar, reliquary of St Zenobius Ghiberti, 1432–42)

24 "S. Giovanni", by B. da Rovezzano, statue (16th c.)

25 In the lunette, "Resurrection" in enamelled terracotta by Luca della Robbia (1450)

26 Sagrestia vecchia o dei canonici

27 "S. Giacomo Minore", by G. Bandini, 16th c. statue

28 Fragment of a fresco in the style of Giotto, "Madonna del Popolo"

29 Altar by Michelozzo

30 "S. Filippo", by G. Bandini, 16th c. statue

31 Entrance to the dome

32 Bust of the philosopher Marsilio Ficino, by A. Ferrucci (1521)

33 In the marble recess, a statue of Isaiah, by B. Ciuffagni (1427)

34 "S. Bartolomeo in Trono", by R. di Jacopo Franchi

35 Roundel, by B. da Maiano, showing Giotto at work

36 Bust of Brunelleschi, by A. Cavalcanti

37 Window, "S. Lorenzo e Angeli", after Ghiberti

38 Stairs to the Cripta di Santa Reparata

of the apse can be seen a marble slab marking the spot where on January 17th 1600 the gilded ball from the dome hit the ground and shattered after it had been struck by lightning. It was replaced by a larger one below the cross.

The lantern, too, was often a victim of lightning but was constantly repaired. Today it is protected by a modern lightning conductor. (Visitors may climb up inside the dome as far as the lantern; the stairs start from the left aisle.)

Rectitude and beauty are also the theme of the **interior** of the cathedral which makes its impact through its Gothic forms, its soaring arches and pillars, untrammelled by gaudy ornamentation to detract from the feeling of spaciousness (later additions were removed during restoration), while the sense of severity is heightened by the earthy hue of the stonework.

The ground plan of the cathedral (see p. 62) is a Latin cross with a nave and two aisles; the space beneath the dome is enlarged by its extension into the three surrounding apses.

Despite its altogether austere decor, the interior has some rich and precious figures.

Front The three stained-glass windows above the main portals depicting St Stephen (left), the Assumption of the Virgin (centre) and St Laurence (right) were designed by Lorenzo Ghiberti and executed by Niccolò di Piero.

Above the central door is a mosaic depicting the Coronation of the Virgin (c. 1300, by Gaddo Gaddi) together with the famous clock with hands that move anticlockwise. The heads of prophets in the corners were painted in by Paolo Uccello in 1443.

Right of the main portal is the Gothic tomb of Bishop Antonio d'Orso (d. 1321) by Tino da Camaino (incomplete; various parts in the Museo Nazionale del Bargello, see Palazzo del Bargello).

North aisle In the first marble recess stands a statue of Joshua (early 15th c.) by Bernardo Ciuffagni, Donatello and Nanni di Bartoli. Opposite the second pillar is a fresco transferred on to canvas by Niccolò da Tolentina (1456). To the right of this is the equestrian figure of John Hawkwood (Giovanni Acuto in Italian), commander of the Florentine mercenary army, painted by Paolo Uccello (1436) to imitate sculpture. The next marble recess contains the statue of King David made for the façade by Bernardo Ciuffagni (1434).

Below the window is a painting by Domenico di Michelino glorifying Dante (1465), a late rehabilitation of the poet by the city that once sent him into exile.

The staircase that leads up to the dome starts from the point where the aisle joins the apse. There is a marvellous panoramic view from the lantern.

The **north apse**, or tribune, is divided into five chapels. The stained-glass windows were designed by Ghiberti. In the fourth chapel is an interesting double-sided retable in the style of Pacino di Bonguida depicting the "Madonna and Saints" and "Annunciation and Saints".

In the pavement is Toscanelli's gnomon which since 1468 has been used for astronomical calculations such as the summer solstice, indicated by the sun's rays which, on June 21st, shine down through a conical hole in the lantern of the dome precisely on to this metal plate.

On the inner surface of the **dome** is the great fresco of the Last Judgment by Giorgio Vasari (begun in 1572 and completed by Frederico Zuccari in 1579). The stained glass in the round windows of the drum was executed from designs by Ghiberti, Paolo Uccello and Andrea del Castagno.

At the foot of the pillars supporting the drum are eight **statues of apostles**. Against the first pillar on the left stand St James the Greater by Jacopo Sansovino and St Thomas by Vincenco de Rossi, and against the second pillar on the left stand St Andrew by Andrea Ferrucci and St Peter by Baccio Bandinelli. On the opposite side the third pillar on the right has St John by Benedetto da Rovezzano and St James the Less by Giovanni Bandini, and against the fourth pillar on the right are St Philip, also by Giovanni Bandini, and Vincenzo de Rossi's St Matthew.

Under the dome is the **choir** with the high altar. The octagonal marble balustrade is based on a design by Baccio d'Agnolo; the 88 reliefs decorating it are by Baccio and Giovanni Bandinelli. The high altar (by Baccio Bandinelli) and the crucifix (by Benedetto da Maiano; 1495–97) are also of interest.

The sacristies are also especially interesting. In the lunette above the door of the **new Sacristy** can be seen a glazed terracotta "Resurrection of Christ" by Luca della Robbia (1444). The fine bronze door is also by della Robbia (with Michelozzo). Its ten panels depict Mary with the Infant Jesus, John the Baptist, Evangelists and early Fathers. The sacristy is decked out with wooden cupboards and a drinking fountain.

This sacristy is where Lorenzo the Magnificent took refuge in 1478 when he and his brother were attacked during a service in the cathedral on the day of the Pazzi conspiracy. Lorenzo managed to escape but his brother Giuliano perished.

A fine bronze urn by Lorenzo Ghiberti in the Cappella di San Zenobio (chapel of St Zenobius) in the **central apse** contains the relics of the saint.

Above the door of the **Old Sacristy** ("dei Canonici", "of the canons") is a terracotta relief of the "Ascension of Christ" by Luca della Robbia. In the sacristy can be found a piscina by Buggiano, Lorenzo di Credi's "Archangel Michael", and two terracotta candlesticks in the form of angels, also by Luca della Robbia.

The **south apse**, or tribune, is also divided into five chapels. The first chapel (after the Old Sacristy) contains an interesting fresco by Giotto – "Madonna del Popolo".

The details of the statues against the pillars supporting the drum are given in their own section on the statues of the apostles.

South aisle Interesting features here include a bust below the window of Marsilio Ficino (1521), the great Renaissance philosopher, and a medallion depicting Giotto by Benedetto da Maiano (1490; opposite the last pillar).

Next to it in a wooden recess is the statue of the prophet Isaiah by Nanni di Banco (1408) and a medallion of Brunelleschi. This is the work of Andrea Cavalcanti, known as Buggiano, who was the heir and favourite pupil of Brunelleschi.

From the cathedral porch stairs lead down to the tomb of Brunelleschi, first discovered in 1972, and into what is left of the earlier church of Santa Reparata, first built in the 4th/5th c. then extended in the 8th and 11th c. The cathedral was originally built around the older church which was finally demolished in 1375, apart from part of the **crypt of Santa Reparata** which was excavated in 1965 and today serves as a museum (closed Sun.).

Campanile

One of the great landmarks of Florence, the Campanile, the cathedral belfry, 82 m (269 ft) high and 14.5 m (48 ft) wide, was begun in 1334 by Giotto (di Bordone). After his death in 1337, Andrea Pisano continued

Open Apr.–Sep.
9am–7.30pm;
Oct.–Mar.
9am–5.30pm

the building of the belfry in accordance with Giotto's plans but his successor, Francesco Talenti, deviated from the original design. The tower was completed in 1387.

The building is characterised by the harmony of its dimensions, the strength of the octagonal pillars, the delicate articulation of the intervening walls and the intricate alternation of the colours of the marble. It is decorated on the lowest storey by two rows of panels containing allegorical bas-reliefs. Most of the hexagonal panels are by Andrea Pisano, who worked to Giotto's designs, and Luca della Robbia. They depict the life of Man, his work and his art.

The lozenge-shaped panels in the second row contain allegories of planets, virtues, liberal arts and sacraments.

The harmonious lines of the Campanile dominate the skyline

The niches in the second storey above these lozenges used to contain statues of saints, prophets and sibyls sculpted between 1300 and 1400 by Florentine artists (including Donatello). Today these are kept in the Museo dell'Opera del Duomo (see entry). There are copies in some of the niches. It is well worth while climbing the 414 steps of the Campanile for the splendid view of the city from the top.

★ Fiesole

Excursion
8 km (5 mi.) NE

Bus 7

The little town of Fiesole, 295 m (968 ft) above the Arno, is an Etruscan foundation of 7th–6th c. BC Towards the end of the 1st c. BC the Roman town of Faesulae arose; it had a capitol, a forum, a temple, a theatre and baths. However, during the time of the migration of the peoples the town declined and was later completely overshadowed by its neighbour Florence. Since 492 Fiesole has been the seat of a bishop.

Fiesole is worth a visit, not just for the beautiful panoramic views of Florence from the hilltops of San Francesco or Sant'Apollinare, but also for the sights of the town itself.

Piazza Mino da Fiesole

In the centre of the town lies the broad Piazza Mino da Fiesole (named after the sculptor Mino da Fiesole, c. 1430–84); this was the ancient forum, and on the north side stands the **Duomo**, the cathedral begun in 1028, extended in the 13th and 14th c. and considerably altered in the 19th c. The Duomo San Romolo has been an episcopal church since the 11th c.; its predecessor stood on the site of the present Badia Fiesolana. The battlemented campanile, more than 42 m (138 ft) high, dates from the 12th c. The interior is notable for its frescoes and pictures, especially

Spedale degli Innocenti
The Founding Hospital and its Museum

PINACOTECA DELLO SPEDALE

0033

Biarritz Tourist Office   05 59 22 37 10

night Tues 26 May P

Biarritz Camping SA 43 74 67 →

23 00 12

0033 05 59 05 35 99

Pont L'ogere   Wed 29 Mai

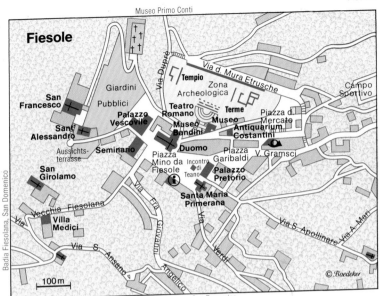

Badia Fiesolana, San Domenico

in the Cappella Salutati where the monument of Bishop Leonardo Salutati was the work of Mino da Fiesole around 1465.

To the north of the cathedral is the **Museo Bandini**, containing a collection of religious works of art, including many pictures of saints, which Canon Angiolo Maria Bandini, librarian of the Biblioteca Mediceo-Laurenziana (see San Lorenzo) and scientist, had been assembling since 1795. After his death the collection passed to the Cathedral Chapter of Fiesole and is now in this museum.

Open in summer Mon., Wed.–Sun. 9.30am–1pm and 3–7pm; in winter: Mon., Wed.–Sun. 10am–1pm and 3–6pm.

On the narrower north-west side of Piazza Mino da Fiesole stand the stately building of the **Seminario**, dating from 1697, and the **Bishop's Palace** (Palazzo Vescovile) which was an 11th c. foundation.

On the south-west side of the square are two interesting buildings, the **Palazzo Pretorio** (14th and 15th c.), which is decorated with coats of arms, and the medieval **Oratorio Santa Maria Primerana**, with a 16th c. portico.

The monument in the square is called **"Incontro di Teano"** (1906). The bronze equestrian statues represent Victor Emanuel II and Garibaldi.

The excavation site, the Zona Archeologica, extends to the north-east behind the cathedral. The highlight is the Roman theatre, not discovered until the early 19th c.; it was built at the beginning of the imperial age (1st c. BC) and was extended under the emperors Claudius and Septimius Severus. The semi-circular amphitheatre has a diameter of 34 m (111 ft), and has room for about 3000 spectators in 24 rows; the stage area measures 26.4 m (87 ft) by 6.4 m (21 ft). In summer the theatre is used for the occasional classical or pop concert.

Zona Archeologica

Open summer 9am–7pm; winter Mon., Wed.–Sun. 9am–6pm

The excavation site in Fiesole

Not far from the theatre are the ruins of Roman baths which were also built at the start of the imperial age and enlarged under the Emperor Hadrian. Although the arches, supported by huge pillars, were still visible, it was not realised that these were Roman baths until the end of the 19th c., when the whole complex was excavated.

The north-west corner of the site holds the remains of a Roman temple (1st c. BC) and an Etruscan temple (3rd c. BC).

On the north the archeological site is bordered by part of the huge Etruscan town wall.

The little **archeological museum** to the south of the Roman theatre contains artefacts from the Roman and Etruscan periods; these include a funeral stele (470–460 BC, with representations of a funeral meal, dancing and animal contests), the head of the Emperor Claudius (AD 41–54) and a statue of Dionysus, a Roman copy of a Greek original.

The **Antiquarium Costantini**, east of the entrance to the Zona Archeologica, can be visited on the same ticket as the one for the excavations, and contains a collection of Greek, Etruscan and Italian ceramics.

Museo Primo Conti Open Tue.–Fri. 9am–3.30pm, Sat. 9am–1.30pm	In Via Duprè 18 north-west of the archeological site is a small museum and foundation for the Tuscan artist Primo Conti (1900–88). Initially a subscriber to Futurism and Cubism, after the Second World War Conti developed an individual style of hectic colour. There are documents on Italian Futurism in addition to Conti's own works.
Sant'Alessandro	Between the Bishop's Palace and seminary buildings a steep track climbs up to two small churches and a tree-shaded terrace with a magnificent view out over Florence. The little park contains monuments to

the Fallen of the First World War, and to three Carabinieri killed by the National Socialists in 1944.

Above the terrace stands the Church of Sant'Alessandro, probably founded as early as the 3rd c. Originally San Pietro in Gerusalemme, it is dedicated to Bishop Alexander of Fiesole. It occupies the site of an old Etruscan temple which was later replaced by a Roman temple of Bacchus. At the beginning of the 6th c. Theodoric the Great is said to have converted the building into a Christian church which in the course of time was refashioned on several occasions.

Church of
Sant'Alessandro

Diagonally opposite the Church of Sant'Alessandro stands the monastic Church of San Francesco. It was built in the 14th c. and given over to the Franciscans in 1407. In 1905 the church was extensively restored.
    The interior, with valuable art treasures, the mission museum and the idyllic cloisters are all worth seeing.

Church of San
Francesco

Open 9am–
12.30pm, 3–7pm
(in winter until
6pm)

From the church a path leads to the public gardens, the Giardini Pubblici, from where it is possible to return to the centre of Fiesole.

Giardini Pubblici

Taking the Strada Vecchia Fiesolana which runs south-west downhill from Fiesole we reach the Villa Medici, also known as "Belcanto" or "il Palagio di Fiesole"; it was built by the architect Michelozzo between 1458 and 1461 for Cosimo the Elder. This is where the Pazzi conspirators originally planned to murder the Medici brothers, Lorenzo and Giulano, until they decided in 1478 that the Duomo Santa Maria (see entry) was a more convenient meeting place.
    (The Villa can only be visited by prior arrangement as part of a guided tour; consult tourist information.)

Villa Medici

The little hamlet of San Domenico di Fiesole (148 m (486 ft)) above sea level is only about half a mile south-west of Fiesole and right on the boundary of Florence, with a panoramic view of the city. Its San Domenico Church (1406–35; rebuilt in the 17th c.) is worth seeing; it has a richly furnished interior, with a beautiful altarpiece by Fra Angelico (*c.* 1430) in the first chapel on the left.

**San Domenico di
Fiesole**

To the north-west below San Domenico, at an elevation of 123 m (404 ft), lies Badia Fiesolana. Until 1026 this was the site of the cathedral church of Fiesole, now replaced by the present cathedral. After Camaldolese monks had rebuilt the church and monastery (badia=abbey), the buildings passed to the Benedictines. During the Renaissance the monastery and the church were again rebuilt; on the façade of the church can be seen Romanesque features, dating from the 12th c. The international college, the "Università Europea", has been here since 1976.

Badia Fiesolana

Forte di Belvedere   J7

The best way to get to the Forte (Fortezza) di Belvedere (Forte di San Giorgio), above Florence on the left bank of the Arno, is on foot through the Giardino di Boboli (see entry).
    The massive **fortress** was the work of the architect Buontalenti (1590–95), probably based on plans drawn up by Giovanni de'Medici. It was commissioned by Grand Duke Ferdinando I who intended it to serve as a strong-hold where he could safeguard his family and all their riches. Inside is a small palace, also designed by Buontalenti, which today is used for temporary exhibitions. The ramparts of the star-shaped bastion near St George's Gate, the Porta San Giorgio (see entry), afford a splendid view of the city.

Location
Costa di S.
Giorgio

Buses
B, C

Open 9am–8pm
(6pm in winter)

Fortezza da Basso   H/J4

Location
Viale Filippo
Strozzi

Buses 4, 10, 13,
14, 23, 25, 28, 31,
32, 33

The vast five-sided **fortress** (San Giovanni Battista) near the main station, today used as a barracks and exhibition building, was designed in 1534 by Antonio Sangallo the Younger and built under the direction of Pier Francesco da Viterbo and Alessandro Vitelli (1534/1535). With this bastion Alessandro de'Medici sought to manifest and consolidate his power after his return to the city.

★★Galleria dell'Accademia   K5

Location
Via Ricasoli 60

Buses
1, 6, 7, 10, 11, 17,
20, 25, 31, 32, 33

Open Tue.–Sat.
8.30am–10pm;
Sun., pub. hols.
8.30am–1.50pm.
Closed 1 May

Ground Floor

The spacious rooms of the hospital of St Matthew near the former church of San Matteo house the "Academy" **art gallery**, the Galleria dell'Accademia, founded in 1784 as a school for artists by Grand Duke Pietro Leopoldo I of Lorraine.

Together with Florence's other famous art galleries (see Palazzo degli Uffizi and Palazzo Pitti) it contains important works of the Florentine school from the 13th to the 16th c. The Gallery's main claim to fame, however, is its outstanding collection of **works by Michelangelo** that came into the Academy's possession in the late 19th and early 20th c.

Salone del Colosso Florentine works of art of the early 16th c. by, amongst others, Perugino, Filippino Lippi and Fra Bartolomeo della Porta, as well as an original plaster version of Giambologna's "Rape of the Sabine".

Galleria del David in the Academy Museum of Art

The Accademia is the one place, above all others, where it is possible closely to follow Michelangelo's creative process as a sculptor. In the **Galleria del David** can be found the four unfinished figures of the Slaves that Michelangelo planned for the tomb of Pope Julius II in Rome. Between 1519 and 1536 he worked on six statues in all but was unable to complete them. After his death they were set up in the Giardino di Boboli (see entry), which is why they are also known as the Boboli Slaves. In 1909 four of these figures came to the Accademia, the "waking slave", the "bearded slave", "boy" and "Atlas": the other two are in Paris in the Louvre.

Also unfinished is the figure of St Matthew, sculpted by Michelangelo in 1505/1506. With eleven other statues of apostles, which were not even begun, it was intended for Florence Cathedral. The block of marble is distinctly flatter than those of the Slaves, as the statue was intended to be viewed from the front.

A certain lack of balance in the Pietà di Palestrina in this hall has of late caused doubt to be cast on whether this piece is actually by Michelangelo. It may possibly have been carried out by one of his followers under his direction.

Michaelangelo: "The Captive"

Tribuna del David Of all Michelangelo's sculpture his "David" (see Baedeker Special, pp 80/81) takes pride of place. In 1873 the Florentines installed it here after removing it from its original setting in the Piazza della Signoria (see entry) to protect him from the ravages of the weather (traces of which are still visible), and putting a copy in its place. After a

PIANO TERRA

Tribuna del David

Salone delle Toscane

Sale Bizantine

© *Baedeker*

Sale Fiorentine

Galleria del David

Salone del Colosso

PRIMO PIANO

Sala III

Sala IV

Sala II

Sala I

Sala dell' Anticolosso

Entrance

Galleria dell'Accademia

Religious warrior, historical hero and nude figure

As a personification of ideal manhood, Michelangelo's larger than life-size figure of David has fascinated the countless visitors to the city for almost five hundred years. Since 1887 the original has been housed in the Galleria dell'Accademia. Copies can be seen in front of the Palazzo Vecchio, on the Piazzale Michelangelo and in every souvenir shop. Now reduced to little more than an Eros-figure serving as an advertisement for Florence, it was as the portrayal of a champion of faith and righteousness and symbol of the Florentine Republic that this David first acquired fame.

In the 15th c. the city state of Florence had to gather all its strength to defend itself against power-hungry princes from Milan and Naples. It was after 1402 that, granted temporary breathing space by the sudden death just outside the city of their great adversary the Duke of Milan, the people of Florence began to draw fresh courage by identifying with a biblical hero who famously displayed strength from a position of weakness, namely the little shepherd-boy David who, armed with an unshakeable faith in God, slew the mighty giant Goliath and was eventually made king. In this way did right's cause easily cloak itself in the trimmings of religion and politics.

The artist and art historian Giorgio Vasari enunciated this very clearly in the 16th c. at a time when the free commune was already in decline: "As David defended his people and ruled them with justice, so shall this city be ruled with justice and defended with courage."

Art, too, gave of itself in the service of freedom and civic autonomy. Between 1410 and 1416 Donatello sculpted his marble of David (Bargello), a not quite life-size, Late Gothic, robed figure, originally commissioned by the stonemasons' guild. Afterwards sold to the Signoria, it stood from then on in the Palazzo Vecchio. Twenty years later Donatello produced another not quite life-size figure of David (circa 1435; Bargello), this time in bronze and, even more revolutionary, in the form of a nude, the first to be sculpted since antiquity. The rather dreamy-looking, naked, delicate-limbed shepherd-boy, with his jaunty hat and long sword, stands in victory pose, his foot on the severed head of Goliath.

More than a generation later Andrea del Verrocchio likewise cast his David (pre 1476; Bargello) in bronze. Self-assured with drawn sword, his arm resting on his hip and with an arrogant smile, the victorious hero is garbed in shirt and tunic, the head of the tyrannical giant at his feet. It was into this tradition that Michelangelo's David was to fit when the stonemasons' guild gave the young sculptor his commission.

For the 26-year old Michelangelo this was no simple undertaking, complicated by the fact that the 5.5 m (18 ft) block of marble he was to use had originally been acquired in 1464 by Agostino di Duccio, a pupil of Donatello, for a statue intended for a buttress on the Cathedral. Duccio had made little progress with the work, only the space between the legs having been chiselled out. The shallowness of the block meant however that Michelangelo was limited to producing a figure designed to be seen primarily from the front. In truth the monumental statue executed between 1501 and 1504 was never intended as a free-standing figure but for display high up in a niche. Taking this into account, Michelangelo's inspired solution seems all the more extraordinary.

To begin with he must be credited with creating the first larger than life-size nude figure of the modern period, drawing closely on the example of classical art. What most distinguishes this marble David is the contrapposto arrangement of the figure, the positioning of the free leg in advance of the supporting leg introducing asymmetry and a slight shift in the axis of the body. Correspondingly the shoulders, one dropped and drawn back, the other raised and thrust forward, suggest a harmonious balance between rest and movement, relaxation and tension. The taut muscles are clearly carved, implying a considerable knowledge of anatomy on the part of the sculptor. And indeed Michelangelo did immerse himself in anatomical studies from an early age, seeking out mortuaries where he could observe post mortems.

The face, on the other hand, shows little originality, though the eyes under the knitted brow seem to fix his adversary's gaze. For in contrast to Donatello and Verrocchio whose Davids are depicted after the event in victor's pose, Michelangelo portrays his David in that state of concentration between rest and motion immediately prior to loosing the sling shot for the fatal blow. Michelangelo's David expresses through his posture and bodily movement the inner state of the biblical hero engaged upon this superhuman act, banishing fear and carrying out his task secure in his faith in God – this being in essence the ideal which shines forth from his body and spirit, for the original meaning of the sculpture was unquestionably a religious one.

From the Middle Ages David's victorious struggle against Goliath had been seen as an Old Testament epitome of Christ's victory over Satan. In a more general sense also, David as youthful hero had become a guiding light and model for knightly virtue and, by extension, civil courage. So it was that, at the beginning of the 16th c., with the Republic of Florence cast as beleaguered protectress of autonomy

Michaelangelo's "David"

against the absolute rule of princes, David's struggle for justice and freedom could again be systematically exploited. Following the expulsion of the Medici in 1494 and the political interlude of Savonarola, the new constitution of 1502 restored republican government to Florence, with Piero Soderini appointed Gonfaloniere della Giustizia for life. Mainly relying for support on the middle and lower social classes, he however antagonised the patriciate and in 1512 the Soderini-led republic was toppled. It was during Soderini's term of office that the decision was taken to move Michelangelo's marble statue of David, originally intended for the façade of the Cathedral, and erect it in front of the Palazzo Vecchio where it has stood since 1504, a symbol, here also visible from afar, of the triumph of the small over the powerful.

By an irony of history the statue's left arm was broken during the unrest at the time of the renewed expulsion of the Medici in 1527. The young Giorgio Vasari and a friend gathered up the pieces; these were replaced in 1543 without the figure suffering too greatly.

In the meantime the republican-minded citizens of Florence, who in their struggle for freedom identified so closely with heroes such as David, had long since been made subjects paying tribute to a Medici prince. Michelangelo's David continued to stand in front of the Palazzo Vecchio because the Medici Duke of Tuscany had his own reasons for revering it, just as his subjects had theirs – ruler and ruled united in admiration for the larger than life-size figure of the youth who so perfectly epitomised courage, pride and beauty.

Nor are those who view the statue today less moved to admiration as they contemplate the beauty of this extraordinary masterpiece.

visitor destroyed one of the figure's toes in September 1991 with a hammer the sculpture now has to be viewed behind glass.

To the right of the David is a bronze portrait of Michelangelo by Daniele da Volterra, probably the most authentic of the known portraits of the artist.

The walls of the Tribuna del David, like the walls of the Galleria, used to be hung with great 16th c. tapestries but their state of conservation caused them to be removed during the comprehensive rearrangement of the museum in the mid-1980s, when they were replaced by Florentine works of the 16th c. by such artists as Alessandro Allori, Stefano Pieri and Santi di Tito.

The three "**Florentine Rooms**" (Sale Fiorentine) hold 15th c. works of art. The first room contains the "Adimari Chest", with a grand wedding procession on the front. Clothes were kept in this type of long chest in the 15th c. The highlight of the second room is a Madonna by Sandro Boticelli, from soon after 1470, and there is another work attributed to Boticelli in the third room, the "Madonna del Mare", from around 1470, which with its gentler appearance and softer outlines, shows marked differences from the Madonna in the previous room.

The "**Byzantine Rooms**" (Sale Bizantine) house the oldest works in the Academy collection, dating from the late 13th and the 14th c. The first room has one of the museum's most important works, Pacino di Bonaguida's "Tree of Life" (c. 1310). It shows Christ's Crucifixion on a tree with twelve branches, and below it Genesis from Man's Creation to his expulsion from Eden, and above the Heavenly Host, saints, Christ and the Virgin Mary. The second and third Byzantine rooms contain works by artists including Taddeo Gaddi, one of the major artists of the 14th c.

The "**Tuscany Room**" (Salone delle Toscane) has 19th c. works by members of the Accademia delle Belle Arti, together with the plaster casts by Lorenzo Bartolini (1777–1850) and Luigi Pampaloni (1791–1847) for their subsequent sculpture in marble.

First floor

The first floor rooms which were opened up in 1985 show Florentine works of art which supplement those from the late 14th to mid-15th c. on display in the Byzantine and Florentine Rooms.

★Giardino di Boboli   H/J7

Location
Piazza Pitti

Buses
B, C

Open Nov.–Feb.
9am–4.30pm,
Mar.–May
9am–5.30pm,
Jun.–Aug.
9am–7.30pm,
Sep.–Oct.
9am–4.30pm

Behind the Palazzo Pitti (which also has one of the entrances, see entry) and between the Forte di Belvedere and Porta Romana (see entries) are the **Boboli Gardens**, 45 ha (111 acres) of hillside park, which owe their name to the Boboli or Bobolini family, former owners of some of this land acquired after Cosimo I acquired the Palazzo Pitti in 1549. Work on the park was begun between 1550 and 1560 by Niccolò Pericoli (known as "Tribolo" i.e. the "tormented"), continued by Bernardo Buontalenti (1585–88) and completed by Alfonso Parigi the Younger (1628–58).

Full of inviting walks, the gardens are among the finest classical parks of this kind and have various features worth seeing, as well as providing a beautiful view of Florence and the Arno.

North-east of the Palazzo Pitti is the **Fontana del Bacco** (1560), a tortoise fountain with the court dwarf of Cosimo I as Bacchus astride its back.

Near the fountain is **Buontalenti's grotto** (1583–88) with the figures of Ceres and Apollo in the niches to the right and left of the entrance. Inside the grotto the stalactites, once surrounded by water, turn out to be shepherds with sheep. The corners of the grotto are where Cosimo I installed Michelangelo's "Slaves", now in the Galleria dell'Accademia (see entry) and replaced here in the early 20th c. by plaster casts.

The **amphitheatre** opposite the south-east façade of the Palazzo Pitti was built in 1618 by Giulio and Alfonso Parigi, and reconstructed in 1700. It was used by the Grand Duke to stage magnificent festivities. The obelisk is from Egypt and the granite basin from Rome.

The **Kaffeehaus** (coffee house) is on the eastern edge of the gardens and its terrace looks out over Florence. It was given its German name by the Italians because in 1776 it was built by Zanobi del Rosso for Grand Duke Peter Leopold of Hapsburgh-Lorraine, later Emperor Leopold II.
  It is a few minutes' walk from the nearby exit to the Forte di Belvedere (see entry).

Not far from the Kaffeehaus is the **Neptune Fountain**. By Stoldo Lorenzi (1565), it has Neptune standing on a rock surrounded by Tritons and Sirens.

A few yards higher up, on the south-east edge of the park, is the "Abbondanza", the enormous **statue of Plenty**, begun by Giambologna and completed by Pietro Tacca 1636/1637.

Just a few paces south-west we come to the entrance to the **Giardino del Cavaliere**, and the Museo delle Porcellane. The "Cavalier's Garden", with its monkey fountain, is on a terrace above the ramparts. This is where Italy's first potatoes were grown, and silkworms used to be bred.

The **Porcelain Museum** has been housed in the 18th c. Palazzina del Cavaliere since 1973. It has displays of Italian, French and German porcelain and a collection from Vienna formerly in the possession of the

Fountain of Isolotto with the Statue of Oceanus by Giambologna

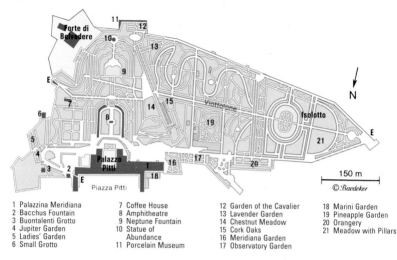

1 Palazzina Meridiana
2 Bacchus Fountain
3 Buontalenti Grotto
4 Jupiter Garden
5 Ladies' Garden
6 Small Grotto

7 Coffee House
8 Amphitheatre
9 Neptune Fountain
10 Statue of
   Abundance
11 Porcelain Museum

12 Garden of the Cavalier
13 Lavender Garden
14 Chestnut Meadow
15 Cork Oaks
16 Meridiana Garden
17 Observatory Garden

18 Marini Garden
19 Pineapple Garden
20 Orangery
21 Meadow with Pillars

Grand Dukes of Tuscany (viewing currently by appointment only, tel. 0 55212557).

Viottolone This is the impressive alley of cypresses, chestnut oaks and parasol pines that extends downhill to the Piazzale del Isolotto.

Piazzale del Isolotto In the centre of the oval piazza (1618) is a fountain with Giambologna's statue of Oceanus as its central figure (the original is in the Museo Nazionale del Bargello, see Palazzo del Bargello), and at its feet the Nile, the Ganges and the Euphrates.

The **Palazzina della Meridiana** adjoins the Palazzo Pitti and contains the Gallerie del Costume (open 1st, 3rd, 5th Sun., and 2nd, 4th Mon. in the month), a collection of costumes from the 18th c. to the First World War, and the Collezione Contini Bonacossi (Entrance via the Galleria d'Arte Moderna in the Palazzo Pitti; visits only by prior arrangement; tel. 0 55218341). The neo-classical palace, which faces the gardens, was begun in 1776 and substantially extended in the early 19th c. The Italian Royal Family stayed here on many occasions until the end of the monarchy. Nowadays it is once more furnished as it was in the 19th c. although it has not been possible to achieve a complete reconstruction.

Impruneta

Excursion
13 km (8 mi.) S

A visitor who is driving through the hilly Chianti district south of Florence should make a stop in Impruneta. This little town, with its population of about 15,000, is famous for its ceramic and pottery studios as well as its chemical and engineering works.

Santa Maria
dell'Impruneta

The 11th c. basilica of Santa Maria dell'Impruneta is in the centre of town. Walls and towers were built around the building when it was renovated in the 14th and 15th c. It was badly damaged in the Second World War.
   Features worth seeing in the interior are two richly ornamented tabernacles by Michelozzo (1453–56), resembling the church of

Santissima Annunziata (see entry) in Florence, the Cappella della Croce and the Cappella della Madonna, both containing work by Luca della Robbia.

★Loggia dei Lanzi   J6

Also known as the Loggia della Signoria, the Loggia dei Lanzi owes its name to the "Lanzichenecchi", or "Landsknechte", the German lancers stationed here as his guard by Cosimo I. Known too as the Loggia dell'Orcagna (after Orcagna, a major artist and its possible architect), this arcade on Florence's main square was built between 1376 and 1382 under the direction of Benci di Cione and Simone di Francesco Talenti, and it precisely counterpoints the Palazzio Vecchio (see entry).

Location
Piazza della
Signoria

Bus
23

The arcade, one of the finest examples of Florentine Gothic architecture, was used by the Republic for official ceremonies. This is where ambassadors and princes were received, Priors and Gonfaloniere installed. With the dissolution of the Republic the Loggia lost this political function and assumed a purely decorative role. After it was restored in the last century it resumed its original official use, and is now once again decked out with tapestries and garlands on festive occasions.

On the façade above the round arches are panels with allegorical figures of the cardinal and theological virtues, made by various artists to designs by Agnolo Gaddi (1384–89). On the roof is a terrace from which there is access to the Uffizi Gallery (see Palazzo degli Uffizi).

The **interior** of the arcade holds some important works of sculpture. To the right and left of the entrance are two lions, one from classical Greece and the other a 16th c. copy (Vacca).

Proceeding clockwise, next comes the bronze statue of Perseus by Benvenuto Cellini (1545–54), an impressive masterpiece because of its delicacy of workmanship and bold composition. In the centre of the opposite wall is the "Rape of Polyxena" in marble by Pio Ferdi (1866), followed by classical statues of women along the back wall (very much restored). In the centre of the other side is another marble group, Giambologna's "Hercules fighting with Nessus the Centaur" (1599). Another treasure at the front is "The Rape of the Sabine", another forceful marble group by Giambologna (1583). It is said not to have been given this title until later, so the artist was clearly seeking to demonstrate his skill and his art through this theme of young masculine strength, feminine beauty and old age.

★Loggia di Mercato Nuovo   J6

The Loggia di Mercato Nuovo (Loggia of the New Market), built by Giovanni Battista del Tasso 1547–51 and formerly frequented chiefly by silk-merchants and goldsmiths, is nowadays a **market-place** for Florentine handicrafts on every day but Sunday. The hall, which is open on all sides, is supported by 20 columns. A marble plaque in the centre of the Loggia marks the spot where bankrupt traders were exposed to the jeers and jibes of the public.

Location
Via di Porta Rossa

Buses
6, 11, 36, 37

On the south side of the Loggia is the "Fontana del Porcellino", the "piglet" fountain, as Pietro Tacca's bronze wild boar (1612) is nicknamed by the locals. It is a copy of a Roman marble in the Uffizi. Tourists throw coins into the fountain and make a wish to return to Florence.

Fontana del
Porcellino

Loggia del Pesce   L6

Location
Piazza dei Ciompi

Bus
B

Like the Loggia di Mercato Nuovo (see entry) the Loggia del Pesce (**Fish Hall**) was designed as a freestanding building. The architect was Vasari (1567) and it was originally part of the old market on the present Piazza della Repubblica. It has only stood here on the Piazza dei Ciompi, the site of the flea market, since the end of the 19th c.

★Monti del Chianti

Excursion
S of Florence

A drive through the Monti del Chianti takes you through some of the most attractive scenery Italy has to offer. The Chianti hills, with their vineyards, olive groves and woods of chestnut and oak, lie between Florence in the north and Siena in the south, between the valleys of the Arno and the Ombrone. Visitors who merely want to enjoy the landscape and not visit all the sights can take in the area in a day. Route 222, the Via Chiantigiana, twists and turns through this famous wine region (see Practical Information, Wine) and plenty of vineyards welcome wine-lovers for a tasting.

A trip through the Chianti district can be combined with a visit to Certosa del Galluzzo (see entry). Leave Florence on the road to Siena, the Via Senese, then turn right after 5 km (3 mi.) towards the monastery. Next stop just further south is Impruneta (see entry). A road east from the town centre leads to the 222 at the hamlet of Strada in Chianti. Driving south after 10 km (6 mi.) we reach Greve, the heart of Chianti Classico (the local wines can be tasted in the Enoteca del Chianti Classico), which has an impressive Piazza lined with arched colonnades.

The landscape beyond Greve is also extremely picturesque. About 20 km (12 mi.) further on there is another captivating view of the Monti del Chianti from the medieval fortress in Castellina. The best route back from Castellina in Chianti is to take the road west to Poggibonsi and then join the Siena-Florence motorway, which speedily returns the visitor to the starting point.

★Museo Archeologico Centrale dell'Etruria   K5

Location
Via della Colonna 36
Buses 6, 31, 32

Open Mon.–Sat.
8.30am–2pm;
Sun. 8.30am–1pm

This is the most important **archaeological museum** in northern Italy. Founded in 1870 its principal exhibits are finds from the areas of Italy settled by the Etruscans, as well as Egyptian, Greek and Roman antiquities. Collections begun by the Medici family are kept here. It is housed in the Palazzo della Crocetta which was built in 1620 for the Grand Duchess Maria Magdalena of Austria.

The museum is divided into the Topographical Museum of Etruria, the Egyptian Museum and the Museum of Etruscan, Greek and Roman antiquities (Antiquarium Etrusco-Greco-Romano).

In **room 1**, immediately by the entrance, is a bronze chimera (4th c. BC) with a lion's body, two heads, one of a lion and one of a goat, and with a serpent's tail. In the right front claw of this mythological creature is an inscription which identifies the statue as a sacrificial animal.

Museo
Topografico
dell'Etruria

The Topographical Museum has a collection of finds from Etruria which provide a good illustration of the highly civilized and cultured life of the Etruscans (brightly coloured sarcophagus of the Larthia

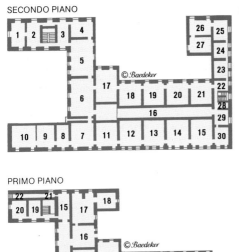

Museo Archeologico

SECOND FLOOR (SECONDO
PIANO)
  Museum of Etruscan,
  Greek and Roman
  Archaeology
  (continuation)
1, 2 Prehistoric department
3–6 Italian and
  Mediterranean
  comparisons
7–15 Vases of various origins,
  Etruscan terracottas and
  sculptures
  16 Temporarily closed
17–30 Etruscan urns,
  sarcophagi, objects
  found in tombs, wall-
  paintings

FIRST FLOOR (PRIMO PIANO)
1–8 Museo Egiziano
  (Egyptian Museum):
  statues, reliefs, papyri,
  amulets, sarcophagi,
  mummies, a chariot
  made of Syrian wood
9–22 Museum of Etruscan,
  Greek and Roman
  Archaeology: Etruscan
  scuptures, sarcophagi,
  bronzes, coins, jewellery

Seianti, between 217 and 147 BC, from Martinella near Chiusi). In
the garden can be seen reconstructions of graves and funerary
monuments.

The Egyptian Museum, which ranks second in importance to the one
in Turin, has statues, busts, ceramics, reliefs, sarcophagi, mummies,
pictures and utensils from various Egyptian dynasties, including a
very well-preserved wooden chariot (from the time of Rameses I, 14th
c. BC).

Egyptian Museum

The Etrusco-Greco-Romano department has displays of Etruscan urns
and sarcophagi, including the Ramta Uzenai marble sarcophagus from
Tarquinia; Etruscan, Greek and Roman bronzes, including the famous
"Idolino" – the Greek statue of an ephebe, a young man undergoing
military training (5th c. BC), the "Horse's Head" – a Greek bronze from the
Roman period, the "Chimaera" – an Etruscan bronze with the body of a
lion, the head of a ram and a serpent's tail, the "Orator" (dedicated to
Aulus Metellus, 3rd c. BC), and a statue of Minerva, a copy of a Greek
work and found in Arezzo in 1554.

Antiquarium
Etrusco-Greco-
Romano

Also of interest: the coin rooms with collections of coins minted in
Etruria, medieval and modern Roman coins, and Italian coins; the col-
lection of precious stones with gems, cameos and gold and silver
articles, and the collection of vases with the famous "Françoise Vase",
by Klitias from the studio of the Greek Ergotimos (6th c. BC).
  Also worth seeing are the Etruscan Gallery of Plaster Casts, the
Gallery of Etruscan Painting, the collection of hieroglyphics begun by
Lorenzo de'Medici (the Magnificent) and the pre-historic department.

Museo Bardini K7

Location
Piazza de'Mozzi 1

Buses
12, 13

Open Mon., Tue.,
Thu.–Sat.
9am–2pm; Sun.,
pub. hols.
8am–1pm

The **Bardini Museum** contains works of art, furniture, ceramics, tapestries, arms, etc. from the Classical, Renaissance and Baroque periods. The collection was bequeathed to the city of Florence in 1923 by the art dealer Stefano Bardini. It is now on show to the public in the 19th c. palace where he lived. Among the interesting works are a Caritas, an allegory of Love by Tino di Camaino and three pictures by Donatello; also a small plaster "Deposition" by Michelangelo.

On the upper floor is the Galleria Corsi, an art collection bequeathed to Florence by Fortunata Carobbi in 1937. It consists of paintings in different styles and from various epochs.

Museo della Fondazione Horne K6

Location
Via dei Benci 6

Bus
23

Open Mon.–Sat.
9am–1pm

The wealthy English art critic Herbert Percy Horne (1864–1916) gave the State a valuable collection of paintings, sculptures, drawings, furniture and ancient ornaments and utensils which are now on display in the Palazzetto Horne **(Horne Museum)**.

This building, also transferred to the State, was built in the late 15th c. for the Alberti family, probably by Simone del Pollaiolo (Cronaca), and later belonged to the Corsi family. The collection was seriously damaged in the 1966 floods, especially the ground floor exhibits.

The first floor holds 14th–16th c. paintings, including works by Simone Martini, Benozzo Gozzoli, Pietro Lorenzetti, Filippino Lippi and Bernardo Daddi. Among exhibits on the second floor are furniture made in Florence, drawings, roundels and terracottas (all 15th/16th c.).

★Museo Marino Marini H6

Location
Piazza S.
Pancrazio/
Via della Spada

Buses
6, 9, 11

Open Mon.,
Wed.–Sat.
10am–5pm,
Sun. 10am–1pm

The first museum in Florence to show modern art, this museum was installed in 1988 in the redundant church of San Pancrazio for the work of the Tuscan artist and sculptor Marino Marini (1901–80).

The much modified church's façade is basically 14th c. but also has many features identified with Alberti, the architect who carried out a great deal of alterations for the Rucellai family between 1457 and 1467 and was also responsible for the Rucellai Chapel. Having spent many years as a tobacco factory and then most recently an army depot, the church started undergoing conversion in the early 1980s supervised by renowned architects Lorenzo Papi and Bruno Sacchi, who have made the building, with its enmeshing of stairs and galleries and combined effect of woodwork, cast concrete and iron struts, a highly successful setting for the works of art on display.

The museum holds 176 of Marini's graphics, drawings, paintings and sculptures, many of them bequeathed to the city of Florence before his death. Beginning with the picture of the "Maidens" in 1916 they span all his themes and creative periods and obviously include many variations of his famous figures on horseback. Whereas the early works show the horse mostly at ease with mankind, after the 1940s it is bucking and rearing in an effort to dislodge its rider. Marini's other favourite themes included "Pomona", an ample fertility goddess, and images of dancers and clowns.

★Museo Nazionale del Bargello   K6

The massive bulk of the sturdy tower and crenellated walls of the Bargello, the mighty palace that the citizens of Florence built after 1250 as testimony to their victory over the nobility, is one of the city's landmarks. Located in Piazza San Firenze, between Via del Proconsolo, Via delle Vigna Vecchia, Via dell'Acqua and Via Ghibellina, nowadays it houses the **National Museum** (Museo Nazionale del Bargello).

From 1261 it was the seat of the Podestà, the governing body of the city. After 1502 this was the site of the Rota (ecclesiastical court) and prison, and in 1574 the palace became the seat of the Bargello (chief constable). In 1859 Italy's first national museum (outside the Vatican) was installed in the palace, which contains many important works by 14th–16th c. Tuscan artists, particularly Donatello, della Robbia and Michelangelo.

The **courtyard** is worth visiting for its architecture alone (photo p. 90). It is surrounded on three sides by an arcade (round arches, octagonal columns, groin valuting). On the fourth side an open staircase leads to the upper floors. Pillars and walls are decorated with the coats of arms of the Podestà, the members of the Rota and the quarters and boroughs of the city. In the centre of the courtyard is an octagonal fountain, and nearby the site of the scaffold when the Bargello was also a prison.

Today the courtyard and arcade are used to display sculpture, and hold works by Niccolò di Piero Lamberti, Vincenzo Danti, Cosimo Cenni, Vincenzo Gemito, Bartolomeo Ammannati, Domenico Poggini and Giambologna.

Michelangelo Room The tasteful courtyard leads into the rooms containing works by Michelangelo: a marble "Brutus" (c. 1540); "Madonna and Child with the young John the Baptist", a tondo carved for Bartolomeo Pitti about 1504; "David" (c. 1531), also known as "Little Apollo"; "Drunken Bacchus", Michelangelo's first large sculpture (1497–99).

Other works are by 16th c. artists. Worthy of particular mention are Jacopo Sansovino's Bacchus (c. 1520), the bronze bust of Michelangelo by Daniele da Volterra, the bust of Cosimo I by Benvenuto Cellini (1557) and other of Cellini's works, including his marble statue of Narcissus (1540).

The **Loggia** on the first floor has Giambologna's bronze statue of Mercury (1564) and his important allegory of "Architecture", as well as sculpture by Baccio Bandinelli and Francesco Moschino.

Donatello Room Here the statues by Donatello include his "St George" (1416, marble statue formerly in a niche in the church of Orsanmichele), marble "David" (1408–09), bronze "David" (made in 1430 for Cosimo the Elder), "St John as a Child" (Casa Martelli) and the "Marzocco Lion" (1420). Other artists represented in this room are Desiderio da Settignano, Vecchietta, Luca della Robbia and Bertoldo di Giovanni. Filippo Brunelleschi's and Lorenzo Ghiberti's models for the competition for the north portal of the Battistero (see entry) complete the display.

Other rooms Also to be seen on the first floor are frescoes in the Chapel of the Podestà, ivory carvings (Ivory Room), a collection of majolica (Majolica Room) and the work of enamellers and goldsmiths (Room of

Location
Via del Proconsolo 4

Buses
14, 23

Open 8.30am–1.50pm, closed 1st, 3rd, 5th Sun., 2nd, 4th Mon. in the month

Ground floor

First Floor

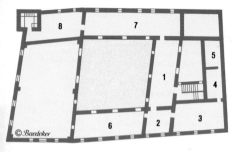

SECOND FLOOR (SECONDO PIANO)

1 Sala di G. della Robbia
  Glazed terracottas, by Della
  Robbia, plus works by Rustici,
  Bandinelli, Giambologna
2 Sala di A. della Robbia
3 Sala del Verrocchio
  Busts and reliefs, by Verrocchio
  and others
4, 5 Medici colléction of coins
  and medals
6 Sala del Camino
  Small bronze figures
7 Sala delle Armi
  Collection of weapons
8 Sala della Torre
  Tapestries, textiles

FIRST FLOOR (PRIMO PIANO)

A Tower
B Loggia
  "Mercury" and "Allegory of
  Architecture", by Giambologna.
  Works by 15th and 16th c.
  Florentine artists
1 Salone del Consiglio
  Generale or Salone di
  Donatello
  "San Giorgio", "San
  Giovannino", "David", "Il
  Marzocco", by Donatello, "Il
  Sacrificio di Isacco", by
  Brunelleschi. Works by L. della
  Robbia, Ghiberti, Michelozzo
2 Sala Islamica
  Tapestries, etc.
  (15th and 16th c.)
3 Salone del Podestà
  Enamels and goldsmiths' work
4 Cappella del Podestà
  Frescoes, probably by Giotto
5 Sagrestia
  Frescoes (14th c.)
6 Sala degli Avori
  Wood carvings (14th and 16th
  c.), ivory carvings
7 Sala Bruzzichelli
  Tuscan art (furniture, glass, etc.
  16th and 17th c.)
8 Sala delle Maioliche
  Majolica (15th and 16th c.)

Museo Nazionale

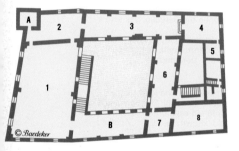

del Bargello

GROUND FLOOR (PIANTERRENO)

A Entrance and vestibule
B Courtyard with octagonal
  fountain
1 Michelangelo Room
  "David" (c. 1531), "Brutus"
  (1540), "Drunken Bacchus"
  (c. 1498), by Michelangelo
  "Bacchus" by Sansovino
  Bust of Cosimo I, by Cellini
  Costanza Bonarelli, by Bernini
2 Changing exhibitions
3 Sala del Trecento
  14th c. Florentine
  sculpture, inc. works by
  T. di Camaino, A. Arnoldi,
  S. Talenti, Arnolfo di
  Cambio

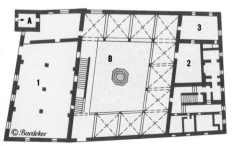

Inner courtyard of the Palazzo del Bargello

the Goldsmiths), while the Bruzzichelli Room has 16/17th c. Tuscan furniture and glassware.

Giovanni and Andrea della Robbia Rooms Works in glazed terracotta by Giovanni della Robbia and a portrait bust of Costanze Bonarelli by Bernini. Also works in glazed terracotta by Andrea della Robbia.

Second Floor

Verrocchio Room As its name implies, this room chiefly contains works by Verrocchio, including his "Noblewoman", "David" (bronze), "Madonna and Child (high relief) and "Resurrection of Christ" (high relief).

Other artists represented in this room are Antonio Rossellino, Mino da Fiesole, Antonia del Pollaiolo, Francesco Laurana and Matteo Civitati.

Two rooms contain the famous Medici **coin collection** that was started by Lorenzo de'Medici and constantly added to by his successors.

Bronze "David" by Donatello

Other exhibits that can be seen on the second floor include tapestries and textiles from Florence, 13th–17th c. weapons, and a collection of small bronzes.

★★ Museo dell'Opera del Duomo K5

Location
Piazza del
Duomo 9

Buses
1, 6, 7, 11, 13,
17, 33

Open Apr.–Oct.,
Mon.–Sat.
9am–7.30pm;
Nov.–Mar.,
Mon.–Sat.
9am–7pm

A host of artists created notable works of art – sculpture, gold and silver items, embroidery, etc. – to furnish the Cathedral, the Campanile and the Baptistry (see Duomo Santa Maria del Fiore and Battistero). Security and weathering meant these could not be allowed to stay in place inside and outside the building, so at an early stage they were removed for safekeeping. Since 1891 they have been kept in the **Cathedral Museum**, the building that in the 15th c. had been the site of the studios and workshops for the artists and craftsmen working on the cathedral.

Over the portal of the Museo dell'Opera del Duomo (Museo di Santa Maria del Fiore) – literally the museum of the cathedral building works – is a bust of Grand Duke Cosimo I by Giovanni Bandini dell'Opera (1572).

Ground floor

One of the items in the **anteroom** is a bust of Brunelleschi who was responsible for the dome of the cathedral. The following two little rooms contain the original wooden model of the lantern of the cathedral signed by Brunelleschi and tools which were used in the building of the dome.

Old cathedral façade By the entrance to this room can be seen a mark showing the water-level of the Arno on 4th November 1966. The room contains statues that were incorporated in the old façade of the cathedral and which were removed before it was demolished in 1587. There is also a drawing (on the right of the entrance) dating from the second half of the 16th c. showing the old façade of the Duomo Santa Maria del Fiore (see entry). The most interesting works include, along the wall left of the entrance, the statue of St Luke (by Nanni di Banco), the statue of John the Evangelist (by Donatello) and the statue of St Matthew (by Bernardo Ciuffagni); along the left-hand wall the statue of Pope Boniface VIII (by Arnolfo di Cambio). On the wall opposite the entrance the statues of "S. Reparata", "Madonna and Child" and the "Madonna of the Nativity" (all by Arnolfo di Cambio). On the right-hand wall are "The Virgin interred in the Sepulchre" (plaster cast, by Arnolfo di Cambio) and St Augustine and St Gregory (by Niccolò di Piero Lamberti).

The **small room** holds missals and precious reliquaries together with other gold and silver works from the Cathedral Treasury, together with a model of the cathedral façade.

The **goldsmith's octagon** adjoining the small room contains relics from 1300 to 1800.

The **Mezzanine** holds one of the most famous sculptures in Western art, Michelangelo's Pietà, the marble group fashioned by the artist in his old age but never completed. The limp, broken figure of the lifeless Christ, the face of Mary with only a hint of her suffering, the grief-stricken visage of Joseph of Arimathea, possibly a self-portrait, the unfulfilled nature of the whole group (the figure of Mary Magdalene on the left was added later) – all this combines in an incomparable expression of the concept of death and man's helplessness in the face of mortality. Michelangelo smashed this piece because he was not satisfied with the quality of the marble. His pupil Calcagni reassembled the fragments and, except for the figure of Christ, added the finishing touches.

First Floor

The **Cantoria Room** contains the two marble "singing galleries" which used to support the console of the cathedral organ. They stood under the dome until 1686 when they were dismantled on the occasion of the wedding of Grand Duke Cosimo III and Violante Beatrice of Bavaria. The cantoria on the left-hand wall is by Luca della Robbia (1431–38). Against the end-wall of the room are the figures of John the Baptist

(1423–27) and of Habakkuk, known as the "Zuccone" (1434–36), both by Donatello, who was also responsible for the cantoria on the right wall, and the group of Abraham and Isaac (1421) against the adjoining wall.

This room contains the **bas-reliefs** which formerly decorated the panels on the lower storey of Giotto's Campanile (see Duomo Santa Maria del Fiore, Campanile); these were replaced by copies between 1965 and 1967. The panels with the allegorical figures are by Andrea Pisano (first two bottom panels on the long-right-hand wall, bottom row on right-hand wall opposite, bottom row on the long left-hand wall, bottom row on the left-hand wall opposite), Luca della Robbia (bottom row on the long right-hand wall), by artists of the school of Pisano (top row on the right-hand wall opposite, top row on the long left-hand wall, top row on the left-hand wall opposite) and Alberto Arnoldi (top row, long right-hand wall).

"Pietà", a marble group by Michelangelo

The greatest treasures of the **Altar Room** are the silk and gold needlework panels with scenes from the life of St John the Baptist, from designs by Antonio Pollaiolo (long left-hand wall), and the silver altar of the Battistero (left-hand wall opposite), one of the finest examples of the art of the Florentine silversmiths. It was begun in the Gothic style in 1366 and completed during the Renaissance (1480). The altar is decorated with prophets and sibyls, scenes from the life of John the Baptist and other scenes from the scriptures.

The other works in the room are by 14th and 15th c. artists (including Giovanni della Robbia, Tino da Camaino, Giovanni di Balduccio, Giovanni Bandini and Andrea Pisano). This room currently also holds some panels from Ghiberti's "Porta del Paradiso", which were replaced in the Battistero (see entry) by a replica in 1990. Here they can be seen close to in quiet surroundings.

Museo Stibbert   J2

In 1860 the Scottish officer Fredrick Stibbert began collecting art treasures in the Villa Montughi just outside Florence, then in 1906 he presented them to the city.

The collection of antique European and Asian weaponry – suits of armour, helms and swords, sabres, daggers and powder-flasks – is especially interesting; the highpoint in the "Sala della Cavalcata", the Cavalcade Room, is a 16th c. train of 14 knights on horseback and 14 foot-soldiers, complete with weapons and armour.

The other exhibits – furniture, paintings, fabrics and other works of art – show the feeling for art and the taste of the collector.

Location
Via Federico
Stibbert 26

Bus 4

Open Fri.–Wed.
9am–1pm. Guided
tours on the hour
except Sun. when
visitors are free to
wander

Museo di Storia della Scienza   J6

Location
Piazza dei Giudici 1

Buses
3, 13, 23, 31, 32

Open Mon.–Sat.
9.30am–1pm
Mon., Wed., Fri.
also 2–5pm

From 1574 to 1841 this austere medieval fortress-like building was the headquarters of the Rota court (hence the name of the square, *giudici* = judges). Since 1930 the palace has held the **Museum of the History of Experimental Sciences**.

The collection includes instruments and scientific objects, some belonging to the Medici and some from other Florentine institutes: optical and mathematical apparatus, including a mechanical writing device, electrical apparatus, instruments for astronomy and cosmography and physical and anatomical models. One room is devoted to Galileo and his discoveries. Among the items on display here are a telescope, compasses and a lens which helped in the discovery of the satellites of Jupiter.

Museo Storico Topografico "Firenze com'era"   K5

Location
Via dell'Orluolo 4

Buses
14, 23

The historical museum "Firenze com'era" ("**Florence as it used to be**") was opened in 1903 in the old convent of the Oblates (opposite Santa Maria Nuova) with its fine 15th c. cloister. Its paintings, drawings, prints and photographs look back over the development of the city of Florence since the end of the 15th c. It also tells of the everyday life of the Florentines, their various festivals and their great processions.

The museum is closed on Thursday and open for the rest of the week from 9am to 2pm and on Sunday and public holidays from 8am to 1pm.

Museo Zoologico "La Specola"   H7

Location
Via Romana 17

Buses
11, 36, 37x

The **Zoological Museum** is in the Palazzo Torrigiani, also known as "La Specola", the observatory, because Grand Duke Pietro Leopoldo built an astronomical and meteorological observatory here in 1775. The museum's collection of anatomical specimens in wax is particularly interesting. Many of them were moulded, in an improbably true-to-life fashion, in the studio of Clemente Susini (1754–1814).

The museum is open Monday, Tuesday, Thursday, Friday and Saturday between 9am and noon and on Sunday from 9am to 1pm; closed holidays.

★Ognissanti   H5

Location
Piazza Ognissanti

Buses
9, B, C

Open 8am–noon,
4–7pm

The church of "Ognissanti" (**All Saints Church**), one of the first Baroque churches in Florence, dates back to a 13th c. building but was completely renovated in the 16th and 17th c. Restoration work had to be carried out in 1872 and after the flood of 1966.

The main features of the exterior are the glazed terracotta relief "Coronation of the Virgin with Saints", ascribed to both Giovanni della Robbia and Benedetto Buglioni, and the Romanesque Campanile. Inside, at the second altar on the right, are Domenico Ghirlandaio's "Madonna della Misericordia" (Madonna of the Protecting Cloak, 1470), and a fresco with a Pietà by Domenico and Davide Ghirlandaio (1472). The sacristy contains a painting on wood of "Christ Crucified" in the style of Giotto and a fresco of the Crucifixion by Taddeo Gaddi.

Entered through the transept or from the square (left of the façade), the **cloister** consists of Ionic columns and has 17th c. frescoes with scenes from the life of St Francis.

The cloister leads into the **refectory** (open Mon., Tue., Sat. 9am–noon) with its fresco of the Last Supper by Ghirlandaio that takes up the whole of the rear wall. Also here is Ghirlandaio's "St Jerome in his Chamber" (1480) and Sandro Boticelli's famous "Saint Augustine at Study".

Opificio e Museo delle Pietre Dure   K5

There is a long and unique tradition to **"Florentine mosaic"**, as it is called, which consists of semi-precious stones inlaid in stone. Skilled craftsmen were especially in demand for the princes' chapel of San Lorenzo (see entry) in 1588. They started in shops in the Palazzo degli Uffizi (see entry) and then after 1796 moved to the Convent of San Niccolò where, chiefly for restoration purposes, this special Florentine craft is still carried on today.

Adjoining the studio is a museum full of interesting examples of the art of these consummate craftsmen, as well as their tools and some particularly valuable stones.

Location
Via degli Alfani 78

Buses
1, 6, 7, 10, 11, 17, 20, 25, 31, 32, 33

Open Mon.,–Sat. 9am–2pm

★★Orsanmichele   J6

The present **church**, a very well-preserved 14th c. building, developed from an oratory (Orsanmichele is the abbreviated form of San Michele in Orto) and a corn hall, for trading in grain, which held a miraculous picture that came in time to attract more worshippers than buyers, with the consequence that in the late 14th c. the building's religious significance came to predominate.

The delicate articulation of the external walls, the ornamentation, arches, niches, figures, mouldings, the marble infill in the window openings and the uncluttered tracery of the pillared arcades make the church's architecture of the highest order. The beauty of the architecture is complemented by important works of sculpture.

Location
Via dei Calzaiuoli

Bus
23

Open 9am–noon, 4–6pm

Commissioned by the guilds at the end of the 14th c., the fourteen intricately **carved niches** on the façade contain statues of the patron saints of the various guilds. Most of the figures – some now replaced by copies – date therefore from the early 15th c. Among them are some of the very finest examples of Renaissance sculpture and indeed of western sculpture generally.

Starting in the Via dei Calzaiuoli, the niche farthest on the left boasts a work of the Early Renaissance, a bronze statue of St John the Baptist (1414) by Lorenzo Ghiberti, carved for the cloth merchants and wholesalers guild. Cascading down in folds the drapery gives the figure an almost dance-like grace, suggesting a still extant feeling for the Gothic style. The contrasting stance and expressive, energetic face are on the other hand pure Renaissance. There follows a bronze group "Christ and Doubting Thomas" (1465–83) in the High Renaissance style, cast by Andrea del Verrocchio for the Tribunale di Mercanzia; until about 1450 this niche held a statue (now in the Santa Croce Museum) of St Louis of Toulouse, sculpted by Donatello for the Parte di Guelfa.

Then come statues of St Luke the Evangelist (1597–1603), carved by Giambologna for the guild of magistrates and notaries, and St Peter the Apostle (c. 1420), commissioned by the butchers and executed by

Bronze statue of John the Baptist by Ghiberti

a sculptor in Donatello's circle.

Occupying the next two niches are Nanni di Banco's St Philip (1410–12, for the tanners' guild), a decorative robed figure still essentially two-dimensional, and by the same artist but this time for the stonemasons and carpenters guild, a group of four crowned saints (1414–17) portraying four Early Christian sculptors martyred under Diocletian (plinth relief). Evidently influenced by classicism, Nanni's figures with their pronounced contrasts, toga-like dress and Roman beards, are reminiscent of ancient-classical statues and portrait heads. While still in essence a niche figure, Donatello's St George (statue of a knight, *c.* 1416, original in the Bargello) occupying the armourers' niche broke fresh ground, preparing the way for free-standing sculptures.

The bronze of St Matthew the Evangelist by Lorenzo Ghiberti (1424, for the bankers' guild) shows a new confidence in the treatment of the figure when compared with his St John. Instead of being front-on in the traditional manner, the figure is rotated slightly to the side; at the same time the left hand, freed from gathering in the robe or clutching an attribute, rises in front of the breast in the gesture of a classical orator.

Occupying a further two niches are statues of St Stephen (1427–28, by Ghiberti for the wool merchants) and the slender erect figure of St Eligius by Nanni di Banco (*c.* 1420) for the smiths' guild. Next to it, commisioned by the guild of linen drapers and second-hand dealers, is Donatello's St Mark the Evangelist (1411–15), the saint's wild, sparse hair, protruding brow, deep-set eyes and heavily furrowed beard expressive of an intellectual intensity and inner excitement.

The other three niches held St James (post 1422) by Niccolò di Pietro Lamberti for the furriers, the "Madonna della Rosa" (1399), attributed to Giovanni di Piero Tedesco, for the doctors' and pharmacists' guild, and St John the Evangelist (1515) by Baccio da Montelupo for the silk-weavers and goldsmiths.

The **interior** of the two-naved church is impressive on account of its frescoes, paintings and stained-glass windows. At the back of the left-hand nave is the altar of St Anne with Francesco da Sangallo's marble sculpture "Madonna and Child with St Anne" (1526). The right-hand nave ends with Orcagna's famous Gothic marble tabernacle (1349–59), its rich ornamentation setting off the miraculous picture of the Madonna (by Bernardo Daddi, 1347). Reliefs on the plinth show scenes from the life of the Virgin (front) and "Death and Assumption of the Virgin" with a self-portrait of Orcagna (back;

1359). The tabernacle is decorated with angels and prophets, sibyls, apostles and allegorical figures of the virtues. Pietro Migliore's marble grille with a bronze trellis (1366) is also an interesting feature.

Orsanmichele is connected to the Palazzo dell'Arte Lana (see entry) by a bridge, and opposite is the little church of San Carlo dei Lombardi (see entry).

Orti Oricellari   H5

Adjoining the Palazzo Venturi-Ginori is part of the famous Orti Oricellari, the **gardens** that became the site of the Accademia Platonica (neo-Platonic academy) when Bernardo Rucellai transferred it here in 1498. The Academy was visited by Pope Leo X in 1516 and Emperor Charles V in 1530.

In the centre of the gardens stands a gigantic statue of Polyphemus (8.4 m (27.6 ft) high) by Antonio Novelli, a pupil of Giambologna.

Location
Via degli Orti
Oricellari

Buses
26, 27, 35

Orto Botanico   K4/5

The "Giardino dei Semplici" **botonical gardens** were founded in 1545 by Cosimo I for the study of exotic plants. It is the headquarters of the Italian Botanical Society, the "Società Botanica Italiana", and together with the school and the museum forms part of the "Institute of Botany".

The garden is open Mondays, Wednesdays and Fridays from 9am until noon, and the museum (entrance Via La Pira 4) Mondays to Fridays for the same hours.

Location
Via Micheli 3

Buses
1, 6, 7, 10, 11, 17,
20, 25, 31, 32, 33

★Ospedale degli Innocenti   K5

In 1419 the silk merchants' and silk tailors' guild commissioned the architect Filippo Brunelleschi, designer of the Cathedral dome, to build a **foundling hospital**. The Ospedale degli Innocenti (abandoned children were called Innocenti, "innocents", after the slaughtered children of Bethlehem) marks the beginning of Renaissance architecture in Florence. Until as recently as 1875, mothers wanting to leave newborn babies in the care of the orphanage while remaining incognito could place them in a revolving wooden drum (ruota) at one end of the columned hall.

The outstanding feature of the Ospedale is the **loggia** with its harmonious, column-borne arches. The superlative architecture is complemented by frescoes beneath the arcades and in the lunettes above the doors, and by ten coloured medallions in glazed terracotta of swaddled infants by Andrea della Robbia (circa 1463).

The vestibule leads to the church of **Santa Maria degli Innocenti** and thence, via a door, to a cloister designed by Brunelleschi. The lunette has a glazed terracotta "Annunciation" by Andrea della Robbia.

On the first floor, in addition to the picture gallery – the Galleria dello Ospedale degli Innocenti – there is a collection of **frescoes** removed from their original positions. Among them are works by Florentine artists,

Location
Piazza della SS
Annunziata

Buses
1, 6, 31, 32

including Poccetti, Bicci di Lorenzo, Lorenzo Monaco, Allori, Rosselli, Ghirlandaio, Fra Bartolomeo, Perugino and della Robbia.

The **Galleria dello Ospedale degli Innocenti** (open Mon.–Sat. 8.30am–2pm, Sun. and public holidays 8am–1pm) houses paintings, sculptures, miniatures and furniture from the 14th to the 18th c. Among the finest are the works by Giovanni del Biondo, Rossellino, Benedetto da Maiano and, in particular, Domenico Ghirlandaio and Andrea del Sarto, as well as the terracotta Madonna by Luca della Robbia.

Palazzo Altoviti-Valori   K6

Location
Borgo Albizi 18

Buses
13, 14, 23

The Palazzo Altoviti in the Borgo degli Albizi, a street with many fine town houses, first belonged to the Albizi family and then to the Valori and Guicciardini families. In the 16th c. Baccio Valori decorated it with busts of famous Florentines (Ficino, Vespucci, Alberti, Guicciardini, Dante, Petrarch, Boccaccio, et al) which is why the locals nicknamed it the "Rogues' Gallery".

Palazzo Antinori   J5

Location
Piazza Antinori 3

Buses
6, 11, 36, 37

In Piazza Antinori, opposite the church of San Gaetano (see entry), stands the town house of the Antinori family. The austere and elegant palace was built between 1461 and 1466 in the style of Giuliano da Maiano.

For many generations the Antinoris have devoted themselves to the production of good wine. The palace has an "enoteca" where visitors can taste the wine and try Tuscan delicacies, and admire the beautiful courtyard and its fountain.

Palazzo dell'Arte della Lana   J6

Location
Via dell'Arte della Lana

Buses
13, 14, 23

Florence prospered in the Middle Ages by producing and processing wool and selling the finished products. This is evident in this palace of the guild of weavers and wool merchants which had 200 shops and employed 30,000 workmen. The irregular palace complex, linked to the church of Orsanmichele (see entry) by a bridge (built in 1569 by Buontalenti), was begun in 1308. After it was restored in 1905 it became the headquarters of the Dante Society. Today the palace houses a shop, and some cross vaulting can be seen in its showrooms.

The inner rooms, the Saloni di Orsanmichele, have some fine paintings (Taddeo Gaddi's "Entombment"). On the corner of Via dell'Arte della Lana and Via Orsanmichele is the 14th c. Gothic tabernacle of Santa Maria della Tromba.

Palazzo Bartolini Salimbeni   J6

Location
Piazza S. Trinita 1

Buses
6, 11, 36, 37

This palace was built between 1517 and 1520 by Baccio d'Agnolo and thoroughly restored in 1962. The people of Florence reproached the architect for having used too many Roman elements (the Classical forms of Bramante and Raphael) more suited to a church than to a town house. The architect responded by inscribing above the portal "carpere promptius quam imitari" – it is easier to carp than to imitate.

The Palazzo Corsini on the banks of the Arno

Another inscription above the windows gives the clue to the secret of the success of the former occupants: "per non dormire" – by not sleeping!

Palazzo Corsini   H6

The Palazzo Corsini stands beside the Arno (10 Lungarno Corsini, with its entrance in Via del Parione), and its impressive façade is best viewed from the opposite bank (it is incomplete, lacking a left wing to match the right wing).

Location
Via del Parione 11

Buses
9, C

The palace, still owned by the Corsini family, was built by Pier Francesco Silvani and Antonio Ferri (1648–56) in the 16th c. style but with some Baroque elements, such as the spiral staircase inside the palace, which is one of the most important examples of Baroque architecture in Florence.

Galleria Corsini The palace holds the most important private collection in Florence (on the first floor, viewing by appointment, tel. 218994). It was founded in 1765 by Lorenzo Corsini, a nephew of Pope Clement XII. The pictures are not arranged in chronological order but mainly according to the old criterion of decoration and symmetry, the idea being that a painting should fit in with the decor of a room and not need viewing for its own sake.

On display are fine examples of the Italian and foreign schools of the 17th c. and of Florentine art of the 15th and 16th c., including Raphael. There are several statues and busts of Pope Clement XII (1730–40) who was a member of the Corsini family.

★Palazzo Davanzati · Museo della Casa Fiorentina Antica

J6

Location
Via Porta Rossa 13

Buses
6, 11, 36, 37
Open Tue.–Sun.
8.30am–2pm.
Closed alternate
Sun. and Mon.
(Currently only
the ground floor
is open)

The austere and majestic five-storey façade of the Palazzo Davanzati is divided up on the ground floor by three massive doors, topped by a loggia and decorated in the centre by a splendid coat of arms of the Davanzati family (in the summer the curtains are fastened to the iron bars in front of the windows).

The Davizzi built a townhouse here in 1300; one of the family was Gonfaloniere of the Republic in 1294. In the 16th c. the palace was acquired by the Bartolini family and later (1578) by the Davanzati. In 1906 the building was bought by the art dealer Elia Volpi and restored to its former glory. Since 1956 it has held the **Museum of the Old Florentine House**.

The museum covers three floors and contains furniture, drawings, sculpture, tapestries, ceramics, textiles and everyday objects from the Middle Ages, the Renaissance and the Baroque period. The "Parrot Room" on the first floor is especially interesting. It gets its name from its decoration. The walls are painted to look like tapestries with parrots. The room has a painted wooden ceiling. The exhibits have been assembled from the Museo Nazionale del Bargello (see Palazzo del Bargello), other collections in Florence and from gifts. They provide a glimpse of the highly-cultivated life of the citizens of Florence who furnished their houses with valuable art treasures and other items.

Palazzo Frescobaldi

H/J6

Location
Piazza
Frescobaldi 1

Buses
11, 36, 37

In the Piazza Frescobaldi, on the left bank of the Arno at the end of the Ponte Santa Trinità (see entry), stands the palace of the Frescobaldi family. Built in the 13th c., it was used by Charles de Valois, the brother of the French king, as his residence when his peace mission on behalf of Pope Boniface VIII brought him to Florence in 1301 (one of the consequences of his mediation was Dante's being sent into exile).

The palace was remodelled in the 17th c. The Frescobaldis are today one of Italy's most prosperous landowners, and include some outstanding vineyards among their property.

★Palazzo Gondi

K6

Location
Piazza San
Firenze 1

Bus
23

The Palazzo Gondi, one of the finest examples of 15th c. Florentine palaces, was built between 1490 and 1501 by Giuliano da Sangallo but not completed until 1874 by Poggi. The main feature of its façade is the way the stone has been meticulously worked on the individual storeys, becoming flatter towards the top.

The courtyard, one of the most charming of the Renaissance, is especially worth seeing. Here again one is struck by the careful use of the material and the artistic craftsmanship (on the capitals, the staircase and the fountain).

Palazzo Guadagni

H6/7

Location
Piazza di Santo
Spirito 10

Bus
B

This Palazzo in Piazza di Santo Spirito has a classical austerity and beauty. Simone del Pollaiolo, known as Cronaca, built it (probably 1503–06) for Riniero Dei. The three storeys, in different styles, are topped by an open loggia. In 1684 it was acquired by the Marchese Guadagni and later by the Dufour-Berte family.

★ Palazzo Medici-Riccardi   J5

The majestic bulk of the Palazzo Medici, opposite the church of San Lorenzo (see entry), bespeaks the power of a ruling dynasty. At the same time its limitation to bare essentials testifies to the wise lack of ostentation of the Medici family at that time. They presided over a democratic-republican community and would never have chosen to behave like city kings.

The palace was built between 1444 and 1464 by Michelozzo for Cosimo the Elder. All the Medici princes lived and ruled here until Cosimo I (1540) moved into the Palazzo Vecchio (see entry). In 1655 it was acquired by the Riccardi family who enlarged it by extending the side of the palace; in 1818 it was bought by the Grand Dukes of Tuscany. Today it houses the Medici Museum (ground floor), the Prefecture (first floor) and the Biblioteca Riccardiana. Its valuable art treasures and furnishings have been severely depleted through being plundered, destroyed or sold off.

An interesting feature of the **façade** is that each of the three storeys is very different from the others. The windows on the ground floor are supported on brackets that look as though they are "kneeling", and surmounted by wide arches, every other one with a triangular gable. The windows on the first floor have beautiful decoration, while the second floor is overhung by a heavy cornice. On the corner opposite San Lorenzo (see entry) is the Medici coat of arms (seven balls topped by a lily).

The archway leads into the square **courtyard**, with twelve marble medallions above the colonnade and the statue of Orpheus by Baccio Bandinelli, then comes the smaller garden courtyard.

Location
Via Cavour 1

Buses
1, 6, 7, 11, 17, 33

Open Mon., Tue., Thu.–Sat. 9am–12.45pm, 3–5.15pm; Sun., pub. hols. 9am–12.45pm

Chapel of the Magi A stairway leads up from the main courtyard to the palace chapel on the first floor (currently closed for renovation). It was designed by Michelozzo and the wall frescoes, the "Procession of the Magi to Bethlehem", are by Benozzo Gozzoli, and his main work. They incorporate two historical events, the magnificent assembly of bishops which took place in Florence in 1439 and which led to the union of the Roman and Greek churches, and the visit to Florence in 1459 of Pope Pius II, the great humanist Aeneas Silvius Piccolomini. There are portraits of some of the people who took part in these events including Joseph, the Patriarch of Constantinople (as the oldest of the Magi), John

The massive Palazzo Medici-Riccardi illustrates the power of the Medicis

"Orpheus" by Bandinelli keeps watch in the inner courtyard of the Palazzo Medici-Riccardi

VII, Emperor in the East, and Lorenzo de'Medici (as a young boy). The frescoes are very well preserved and with their bright colours present a vivid and lively picture of Florence in the 15th c. and the culture and prosperity of the Renaissance. The altarpiece is a copy of Filippo Lippi's famous "Nativity".

Palazzo Nonfinito/Museo di Antropologia ed Etnologia   K6

Location
Via del
Proconsolo 12

Buses
14, 23

The Palazzo Nonfinito is, as its name implies, unfinished, a fact belied by its exterior. Alessandro Strozzi commissioned the architect Bernardo Buontalenti to build a new town house for his family near the Palazzo Pazzi (see entry). Neither Buontalenti nor his successors, however, were able to complete the large building with the beautiful inner courtyard.

Since 1869 the Palazzo has housed the Museo Nazionale di Antropologia ed Etnologia (**Museum of Mankind**) with anthropological and ethnological collections from all over the world.

The Museum is open Thursday, Saturday and every third Sunday in the month from 9am to 1pm, and is closed from July to September.

Palazzo Pandolfini   K4

Location
Via San Gallo 74

Buses
1, 7, 25, 33

The famous painter Raphael designed a palace for Giannozzo Pandolfini, the Bishop of Troia, and Giovanni Francesco and Aristotile da Sangallo put his plans into effect about 1520.

The charm of the palace lies in its simple elegance and the perfect expression of elements of the Roman Renaissance. It was originally intended to extend the palace to the right so that the portal would have been in the middle. However under Pope Clement VII, a Medici – his name can be seen next to that of Leo X on the right-hand side – it was obviously decided to leave the building half-finished as you see it today.

Palazzo di Parte Guelfa   J6

The Gothic window above the covered steps and the battlements of the palace date back to the 14th c. This building, in one of the Italian towns engulfed in the feud between the Guelphs, loyal to the Pope, and the Ghibellines, followers of the Emperor, was in the 13th c. confiscated from the defeated Ghibbelines by the Captain of the Guelph party for administration purposes. The 15th c. extension to the building was led by the architects Brunelleschi and Francesco della Lune.

The interior of this medieval palace – today the headquarters of various organisations – contains beautiful rooms of harmonious proportions; the decoration of the walls and ceiling was carried out by, among others, Giambologna, Luca della Robbia and Donatello.

Location
Piazza di Parte
Guelfa

Buses
6, 11, 36, 37

Palazzo dei Pazzi   K6

The palace was built for Jacopo de'Pazzi (executed in 1478 after the conspiracy against Lorenzo and Giuliano de'Medici). The work was originally under the direction of Brunelleschi (1430) but was later taken over by Giuliano da Maiano (1462–72) whose contribution is marked by its meticulous finish and love for architectural detail.

The Pazzi family, who moved to Florence from Fiesole (see entry) in the Middle Ages, personified commercial acumen and hunger for power. Once Lorenzo de'Medici had survived their murder bid their attempt to break the power of the Medicis was doomed to failure. The family was banned and their palace came into the possession of the Cibo family and then later the Strozzis and Quarantesis.

Location
Via del
Proconsolo
10/Borgo degli
Albizi

Buses
14, 23

★★Palazzo Pitti   H/J6/7

The Palazzo Pitti ranks as Florence's most important palazzo together with the Palazzo Vecchio (they are joined by a passage) and the Palazzo Medici-Riccardi (see entries). Its size is impressive – it covers a surface area of 32,000 sq.m (344,320 sq.ft), and its façade is 205 m (672 ft) across, and 36 m (118 ft) high at the centre – and so is its architecture, an effect that is heightened by the way the square fronting it slopes slightly uphill towards it.

The art gallery (Galleria Palatina or Pitti) in the Palazzo Pitti is one of the most important in the world, almost on a par, so far as works of art are concerned, with the collections of the Uffizi (see Palazzo e Galleria degli Uffizi). The palace also houses the Museo degli Argenti (Silver Museum), the Galleria d'Arte Moderna (Gallery of Modern Art), the Contini Bonacassi collection, the Museo delle Carrozze (Carriage Museum) and the Appartamenti ex Reali (Royal Apartments). In the adjoining Palazzina della Meridiana are the Galleria del Costume and the Collezione Contini Bonacossi (see Practical Information, Museums).

A respected and wealthy Florentine merchant family, the Pittis were equal to the Medici in terms of pride and ambition. Consequently in 1447 Luca Pitti laid plans for a magnificent palace on the left bank of the Arno

Location
Piazza Pitti

Buses
B, C

Open Tue.–Sat.
8.30am–6.50pm,
Sun., pub. hols.
8.30am–1.50pm

a little above the town. The architect Luca Fancelli was in charge of the preliminary work (1457–66), possibly based on designs by Brunelleschi. Between 1558 and 1570 the wife of Cosimo I, Eleonora of Toledo, who had acquired the palace in 1549, had it completely renovated and considerably enlarged by Bartolomeo Ammanati, who was followed by other architects, interior designers and artists.

The new owners, the Medici, and Cosimo III in particular, purchased valuable pictures to decorate the apartments. These form the basis of the Galleria Palatina. Classical and contemporary statues were also added.

The Palazzo Pitti became the residence of the Italian kings (1864–71) when Florence was the capital of a partially united Italy. In 1919 King Victor Emanuel III finally gave it to the city, which had the museums enlarged.

Architecture at its most creative can be seen in the façade of the palace with its massive ashlar stonework, high-vaulted windows and stepped storeys, and in the Rondò di Bacco, the Mannerist courtyard by Ammanati (1558–70), looking like a grotto enlivened by "rustication". Adjoining it is the terrace of the Boboli Gardens (see Giardino di Boboli) with its fountains and statuary.

Galleria Palatina/Galleria Pitti

The entrance to the Galleria Palatina or Galleria Pitti (first floor) is via the ticket sales point to the right of the courtyard. The gallery pic-

Palazzo Pitti

30 m

Fontana del Carciofo

Giardino di Boboli

Cortile dell' Ammannati

PRIMO PIANO

© Baedeker

1–25 GALLERIA PALATINA / PITTI   A–V APPARTAMENTI REALI

tures are not in chronological order but are arranged as part of the decor as an adjunct to the state-rooms and their costly furnishings. The collection was begun about 1620 by Cosimo II and finally made accessible to the public by the Italian kings. The rooms are named after the themes of the pictures they contain or the artists represented.

Especially interesting are the works by Raphael (1483–1520), Andrea del Sarto (1486–1530), Titian (1490–1576), Tintoretto (1518–94) and Rubens (1577–1640).

The Sale Castagnoli (room 18) is reached from the staircase via the vestibule, the Sala Degli Staffieri and the Galleria delle Statue where the following tour begins. The following sequence of rooms correspond to the numbering on the plan and in the rooms themselves.

In the centre of the room stands the "Italian Venus" which Napoleon commissioned from Antonio Canova in 1810. There are four pictures tracing the development of Titian ("Concert", "Portrait of a Lady", and portraits of Pope Julius II and Pietro Aretino). "Venus, Amor and Vulcan" is an early work of Tintoretto. Other major works in the Venus room include "Return of the Hunters" by Sustermans, "Return from the Hayfields" and "Ulysses in the Phaecian Isle" by Rubens, and "Seascape at Sunset" by Salvatore Rosa.

Sala di Venere

Among the 16th and 17th c. works in this room particularly worth mentioning are Titian's "Maria Magdalena", the first of a series of pictures on this theme painted for the Duke of Urbino between 1530 and 1535, and his "Portrait of a Nobleman". Andrea del Sarto's "Descent from the Cross" was painted in 1523/1524 for the high altar of Mugello church. The Medicis acquired it in 1782, replacing it in the church with a replica. "The Dying Cleopatra" (1638/1639) is a late work by Guido Reni.

Sala di Apollo

The painted ceiling on the theme of War in the Room of Mars is by Pietro da Cortona, with the Medici coat of arms in the centre. Mirroring the ceiling's theme is Rubens' very large "The Consequences of War", showing Venus vainly entreating Mars not to go to war. When he painted it in 1637 Rubens was still absorbing the impact of the Thirty Years' War. Other works include Tintoretto's portrait of Alvise Cornaro, Rubens' "Four Philosophers" (with his self-portrait top left), Murillo's "Madonna with the Rosary", Titian's portrait of Cardinal Ippolito de'Medici, and Van Dyck's portrait of Cardinal Guido Bentivoglio.

Sala di Marte

The ceiling of the Jupiter Room is also painted by Pietro da Cortona, and refers to the fact that the room was also a throne room. The major works of art in this room include "The Three Ages of Man", attributed to Giorgione, Guercino's "Madonna with the Little Swallow", Andrea del Sarto's "John the Baptist" and Fra Bartolomeo's "Descent from the Cross". "La Velata" (*c.* 1516), the veiled woman, or "La Fornarina", is one of Raphael's finest female portraits.

Sala di Giove

The works by Raphael in the Saturn Room include portraits of Tommaso Inghirami, and Agnolo Doni, as well as "Vision of Ezekiel" and "Madonna with Baldachin". There are also paintings by his contemporaries Perugino, Fra Bartolomeo, Andrea del Sarto and Ridolfo del Ghirlandaio.

Sala di Saturno

Unlike the previous rooms, which have 17th c. decor, the Iliad Room decor is from between 1819 and 1825. The ceiling, depicting Olympus, and the scenes from Homer's Iliad in the lunettes, were painted by Luigi Sabatelli. Opposite one another hang two versions by Andrea del Sarto of the Assumption of the Virgin. Velasquez' "Philip IV of Spain",

Sale dell'Iliade

Sala dell'Illiade in the Palazzo Pitti

Raphael's "La Gravida" and Sustermans' portrait of Count Waldemar Christian are particularly worth seeing.

Sala della Stufa	The little Room of the Stove was first decorated in 1627 by Florentine artist Matteo Rosselli, with the remaining walls covered by Pietro Cortona in 1637 and 1640/1641, on the theme of the four Ages – golden, silver, copper and iron.
Sala di Ulisse	The ceiling of the Ulysses Room shows the homecoming of Ulysses, an allusion to the return to Florence of Ferdinand III from Lorraine. The most important work in this room is Raphael's "Madonna dell'Impannata" (*c.* 1512).
Sala di Prometeo	The Room of Prometheus contains almost all of the Galleria Palatina's "tondi", which like the other works in this room are from the 15th and 16th c., and are by such artists as Filippo Lippi, Sandro Botticelli, Ridolfo del Ghirlandaio and Guido Reni.
Corridoio delle Colonne	The works in the Corridor of the Columns are mainly 17th c. Flemish and Dutch landscapes.
Sala della Giustizia	The Justice Room chiefly brings together works from the 16th c. Venetian School, with chief among them Titian's portrait of Tommaso Mosti (or his brother Vincenzo Mosti).
Galleria del Poccetti	The frescoes in the small gallery – it was an open loggia until 1813 – were first attributed to the Florentine artist Poccetti but later were found to be by Filippo Tarchiani.
Sala Castagnoli	The room is called after the artist Giuseppe Castagnoli, who was

responsible for the painting of the ceiling (from 1815). There are two enormous marble statues from the Villa Medici in Rome on two sides of the room. The table of the muses in the centre of the room was made between 1800 and 1855 in the Opificio delle Pietre Dure (see entry).

The Quartiere del Volterrano, the series of rooms beginning with the Sala delle Allegorie, were the winter quarters of the Grand Duchess in the time of the Medicis. The first room is the only one where the decor dates from the Medicis, the rest were refurnished after 1815. These have been in public ownership since 1911 but not all the rooms are accessible.

Quartiere del Volterrano

Appartamenti Monumentali

The collection of works of art in the Palazzo Pitti's Galleria Palatina is complemented by the Appartamenti Monumentali, the former Royal Apartments lived in by Victor Emmanuel II, Umberto I, Queen Margherita and Victor Emmanuel III. The magnificent rooms (the visitor should note the frescoes and stucco-work here, too) contain costly furniture, paintings, statues, tapestries, etc. Most of the furnishings are 19th c., but some rooms also have furniture that is Florentine Baroque.

Galleria d'Arte Moderna

The Gallery of Modern Art is on the second floor of the Pitti Palace. It was founded about 1860 and has been continuously expanded through

Open 2nd, 4th Mon., 1st, 3rd, 5th Sun. in the month 8.30am–1.50pm

Appartamenti Monumentali: the "White Room" or Ballroom

Palazzo Pitti

Façade of the Palazzo Pitti

gifts or transfers of works of art from other national or municipal galleries. It gives an impressive overview of 19th and 20th c. painting in Tuscany and other parts of Italy. There are also excellent examples of 19th and 20th c. sculpture. A special section is devoted to the works of the "Macchiaioli" (see History of Art) and this Tuscan school is represented here by Giovanni Fattori, Silvestro Lega, and Telemaco Signorini, amongst others. The final section is a collection of works by contemporary Italian painters, including Severini, Soffici, De Chirico and Morandi.

There is access from the Galleria d'Arte Moderna to the Collezione Contini Bonacossi (see Practical Information, Museums).

Museo degli Argenti

Open as Galleria d'Arte Moderna

On the ground floor and mezzanine of the Palazzo Pitti, in the rooms where the Medicis spent the summer months (entrance left of the palace courtyard), is the Silver Museum, which in addition to the work of silversmiths and goldsmiths also has displays of precious stones, jewellery, carved ivory and amber, painted glass and porcelain. The admission ticket also covers a visit to the Museo delle Porcellane (see Giardino di Boboli) and to the Galleria del Costume (see Practical Information, Museums).

The museum's collection, founded after the First World War, is based on the silver owned by the Medici family. Other exhibits come from the Uffizi (see Palazzo degli Uffizi), the Bargello (see Museo Nazionale del Bargello in the entry for Palazzo del Bargello), and the treasures of the princely archbishops of Salzburg and the kings of Italy.

On display are 17th and 18th c. jewel caskets and reliquaries, 16th and 17th c. vases and crystalware, 16th and 17th c. tapestries, carved ivory and amber, the Medicis' jewellery collection; goblets, golden tableware, silver ewers and platters.

Museo delle Carrozze

Like the silver collection, the Carriage Museum is also on the ground floor of the Pitti palace. On show are state coaches, barouches and carriages of every kind which were used by archdukes and kings in the 18th and 19th c., including the carriages of the Duke of Modena, Francesco II and King Ferdinando of Naples.

Not open at present

★Palazzo Rucellai   H6

The architect Bernardo Rossellino built this palazzo between 1446 and 1451 to designs by Leon Battista Alberti. It is one of Florence's finest Renaissance mansions, and was commissioned by Giovanni Rucellai, a wealthy merchant who acquired his wealth and status in the 15th c.

Alberti and Bernardo Rossellino, as architect and artist, were able to give free rein to their talents on this building, as their rich client readily provided them with the means to do so. Their clarity of conception and breadth of execution can be seen in the precision of the façade with its tapering pilasters, variety of window shapes, carefully hewn blocks of ashlar and storeys of gradually diminishing height. It was a milestone in the architectural history of the Renaissance. Above the first-floor windows can be seen a stone frieze of billowing sails, the trade-mark of the Rucellai family, owners of the palazzo till the present day.

Location
Via della Vigna
Nuova 18

Buses
6, 9

Since 1985 the ground floor of the palazzo has contained the Museum of the History of Photography (Museo di Storia della Fotografia "Fratelli Alinari", open Tuesday to Sunday, 10am to 7.30pm), one of the best of its kind in Italy. Work by Italian and foreign photographers of the 19th and 20th c. as well as a collection of photographic equipment is on display.

Museo di Storia
della Fotografia

The Loggia dei Rucellai, the striking arcaded building opposite the palazzo, was built, also to Alberti's designs, between 1460 and 1466. The loggia has been glazed and is nowadays used for exhibition purposes.

Loggia dei
Rucellai

★Palazzo Spini-Ferroni   J6

The largest of Florence's medieval palaces, this was built in 1289 for the Spini family (then later owned by the Ferronis), probably to plans by Arnolfo di Cambio. Restored in 1874, its massive walls, great height and emphatic crenellation make this extensive complex on the banks of the Arno most impressive. Little is left of a medieval tower and a ground floor loggia, or of the stone seating that ran round the palace and provided a place for both locals and waiting customers to rest awhile.

Location
Piazza Santa
Trinità

Buses
6, 11, 36, 37

Salvatore Ferragamo, who died in 1960, made shoes for Hollywood stars, including Greta Garbo and Marilyn Munroe. In 1995 a museum was established in the Palazzo Spini-Ferroni where 10,000 creations by the master are on display. Visitors by appointment only.

Museo Salvatore
Farragamo

★Palazzo Strozzi   J6

In the 15th c. the Strozzi family, who considered themselves just as noble as the Medici, determined to outdo the ruler of Florence Lorenzo de'Medici. Rather than build something that would vie with the Palazzo Medici-Riccardi (see entry) on a footing of grandeur, the wealthy mer-

Location
Piazza Strozzi

Buses
6, 11, 36, 37

chant Filippo Strozzi planned to build a house for his family that would be outstanding not for its size and splendour but for its meticulous workmanship. The Palazzo Strozzi was built between 1489 and 1538 and is accounted the finest of Florence's Renaissance palaces. In the year it was completed, it was seized by Cosimo I and not returned to the Strozzi family until 1568. Today it houses cultural institutes.

In this building the architects, Benedetto da Maiano and (after his death) Cronaca, or Simone del Pollaiolo, brought together the great achievements of Renaissance architecture, with articulation of classical beauty in the overall and detailed design and consummate craftsmanship in every aspect of the building. The impact of the façade depends on the balanced composition of the storeys, the portal, the windows and the cornice, as well as on the art of the stonemason evident in every one of the ashlar blocks, with horizontally-aligned bosses that project progressively less towards the top of the building.

The wrought-iron work (rings in the walls for tethering horses, torch-holders and lanterns on the corners) is from around 1500 and was by Niccolò Grosso, a famous blacksmith who would only accept commissions if he was paid in advance. The elegant inner courtyard by Cronaca is worth seeing. The Galleria Strozzina in the bottom two floors of the building stages occasional art exhibitions of old and new works. There is also a little museum on the ground floor telling the history of the building and including a wooden model of the palazzo by da Maiano.

Palazzo dello Strozzino   J6

Location
Piazza Strozzi 2

Buses
6, 11, 36, 37

The younger line of the Strozzi family commissioned Michelozzo to build a palazzo in 1458, before the Palazzo Strozzi opposite (see entry) was built. It was completed by Giuliano da Maiano between 1462 and 1465.

In 1927 the courtyard was incorporated into the Odeon Theatre by its architect Marcello Piacentini.

★★Palazzo degli Uffizi   J6

Location
Piazza della
Signoria/Piazzale
degli Uffizi
Entrance:
Loggiato degli
Uffizi 6

Bus
23

Open Tue.–Sat.
8.30am–10pm;
Sun., pub. hols.
8.30am–1.50pm

Around 1540 Cosimo I de'Medici, Duke of Florence and, after 1569, Grand Duke (Granduca) of Tuscany, moved out of the family palace (see Palazzo Medici-Riccardi) into the Palazzo Vecchio (see entry), which thus became the Palazzo Ducale (Ducal Palace). This left no room for the law-courts and governing body of Florence and plans were drawn up for offices of their own, the Uffizi, to be built adjoining the Palazzo Ducale. The foundation stone was laid in 1560. In 1565 a corridor was hastily built (in less than six months) from the Palazzo Vecchio through the Palazzo degli Uffizi and over the Ponte Vecchio to the Palazzo Pitti (see entries). The works which were carried out under Vasari, Buontalenti and Parigi came to a temporary halt in 1580.

The Palazzo degli Uffizi took in the old customs building, the Zecca, where the famous "florins" were minted, and the Romanesque church of San Piero Scheraggio. This coincided with the construction of artists' studios and workshops. Rooms were also allocated for the study of natural sciences and alchemy. In 1585/1586 space was even found for a theatre where the first operas in the history of music were performed. Today the palace houses the Uffizi Galleries and the National Archives.

Archives On May 27th 1993 five people were the victims of a bomb attack on the Uffizi and more than 200 paintings and sculptures were damaged. After years of restoration new rooms and a new entrance area was opened in 1998. A further extension of the exhibition is planned.

Side wing of the Palazzo degli Uffizi; in the background the Palazzo ▶
Vecchio

Palazzo degli Uffizi

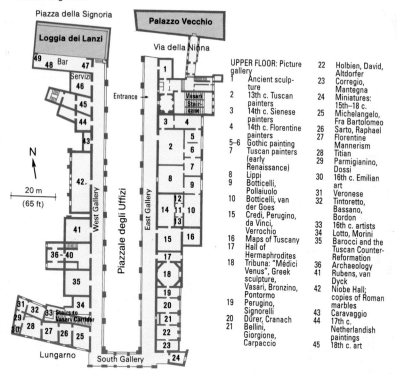

Piazza della Signoria

Loggia dei Lanzi

Palazzo Vecchio

Via della Ninna

Entrance →

N

20 m
(65 ft)

West Gallery

East Gallery

Piazzale degli Uffizi

Lungarno

South Gallery

UPPER FLOOR: Picture gallery
1 Ancient sculpture
2 13th c. Tuscan painters
3 14th c. Sienese painters
4 14th c. Florentine painters
5–6 Gothic painting
7 Tuscan painters (early Renaissance)
8 Lippi
9 Botticelli, Pollaiuolo
10 Botticelli, van der Goes
15 Credi, Perugino, da Vinci, Verrochio
16 Maps of Tuscany
17 Hall of Hermaphrodites
18 Tribuna: "Médici Venus", Greek sculpture, Vasari, Bronzino, Pontormo
19 Perugino, Signorelli
20 Dürer, Cranach
21 Bellini, Giorgione, Carpaccio
22 Holbien, David, Altdorfer
23 Corregio, Mantegna
24 Miniatures: 15th–18 c.
25 Michelangelo, Fra Bartolomeo
26 Sarto, Raphael
27 Florentine Mannerism
28 Titian
29 Parmigianino, Dossi
30 16th c. Emilian art
31 Veronese
32 Tintoretto, Bassano, Bordon
33 16th c. artists
34 Lotto, Morini
35 Barocci and the Tuscan Counter-Reformation
36 Archaeology
41 Rubens, van Dyck
42 Niobe Hall; copies of Roman marbles
43 Caravaggio
44 17th c. Netherlandish paintings
45 18th c. art

Layout The Palazzo degli Uffizi is U-shaped around the Piazzale degli Uffizi, extending from the Palazzo Vecchio down to the Arno and then back to the Loggia dei Lanzi (see entry). On the ground floor the Palazzo has colonnades, columns alternating with pillars where stallholders still display their wares and which from time immemorial has been animated by the bustle of the people of Florence and visitors to the city. On the upper floors are the offices and works of art.

The uniformly articulated façades conceal a disparate interior that developed from the mingling of 14th and 16th/17th c. buildings. This was also the first European building to use cement and iron reinforcements.

To avoid long waits at the ticket office of the Uffizi visitors can telephone 0 55294883 without extra charge, collect their tickets at a special counter and go through a separate entrance; groups can also have a guided tour of the museum. In addition **tickets** are available from tobacconists.

★★Galleria degli Uffizi

The Uffizi contain one of the most important collections of paintings in the world, which, besides Florentine and Italian art, also includes a large number of foreign works and valuable Classical sculpture. The collections began as the private gallery of the Medici princes, and were bequeathed to the city of Florence by the Electress Anna Maria Ludovica von der Pfalz, the last heiress of the house of Medici, who died in 1743.

The Uffizi are, however, valued not simply for their paintings, but also for the beautiful setting they provide, and the corridors are bedecked with oriental grotesques, Classical sculpture and precious tapestries.

The greatest treasure is undoubtedly the unique collection of Florentine Renaissance painting, deemed a vital part of this city's contribution to European art. These works from the Florence of between about 1300 and 1500 set the trend for the whole of Western art, so the following pages therefore briefly introduce and interpret a representative selection of them. This account follows the hanging of the pictures in chronological order according to when they were painted, beginning with Room 2 on the 2nd floor of the Uffizi and making it relatively easy to follow the museum's own tour guideline. However, beyond Room 13, an octagonal gallery in the Tribune, the works are no longer in chronological order, but according to schools, regions and countries (e.g. German, Dutch, North Italy, etc.) from about 1500 to 1700.

Room 2 of the gallery brings together three large Madonnas from around 1300, illustrating the debut of **Tuscan art** and one of its first high points.

Room 2

Cimabue's "Madonna Enthroned", or "Madonna in Maestà" (c. 1275) is still entirely in the Byzantine tradition of painting the Virgin, who looks like a statue, aloof from reality. She is surrounded by symmetrically arranged angels, gracefully supporting the throne. In a crypt-like area below there are four prophets. The Madonna's gesture, pointing towards the Infant Jesus with her right hand, is as traditional as his gesture of benediction. There is no sign of any tender exchange between mother and son. Cimabue's Infant Christ is dressed like a Roman general and his Virgin's mantle takes the form of the many thin folds of Byzantine drapery.

By contrast, Duccio's "Madonna Enthroned" (1285) already shows more movement, with gentle colouring and a flowing line. Yet she too still

"Madonna Enthroned" by Giotto   *"Madonna and Child" by Masaccio*

113

appears ethereal and aloof. The first appearance of a human, realistic dimension is in the "Madonna Enthroned" by Giotto (c. 1310, p. 113). The throne is so near as to be almost within reach, the figures have weight and solidity, making eye-contact with one another and the beholder, standing firmly on the ground and thus realistically in three-dimensional space. Giotto was the first artist to represent the Virgin not as an insubstantial queen of heaven, but as a woman with a physical presence. Even the minor figures appear animated and have different facial expressions. Giotto enlivens the whole picture with new colourfulness, no longer using simply the plain earthy colours of Byzantine art, but also employing colours of greater and more highly differentiated luminosity. But the backgrounds remain the traditional gold ground, intended to emphasise the solemnity of the scene. Giotto's most important and historical achievement, however, was in his composition. He was the first artist to conceive of a well defined pictorial space that realistically takes into account the eye of the beholder. The white drapery of the angels and the white robe of the Virgin together form the angles of a well-contrived pyramidal composition, further empha- sised by the triangular pediment of the throne. With this pyramidal com- position, Giotto created a model that was to hold good for centuries.

Giotto's more personal, individualistic and, above all, realistic way of seeing and painting was to lead to a true Renaissance in art compared with the Byzantine concepts that had gone before. Henceforth painting was to be an art in its own right, particularly as opposed to sculpture which it was finally to overshadow.

Room 3

Sienese Art In the meantime, however, there continued to be more con- servative painters such as the Sienese artist Simone Martini, whose "Annunciation", dating from about 1333, is still very much Gothic in style. Its gilded setting, with its turrets, gables and decoration, is redolent with motifs from Gothic architecture. The "Annunciation" is a work of great refinement and elegance, from the angel's fluttering garment to the shyly recoiling Virgin. The movements are of a lyrical tenderness and sensitivity; the sculptural nature of the figures is subordinated to two- dimensional draftsmanship, i.e. the lines are emphasised and thus accen- tuate the slenderness of the finely articulated figures. Just as Northern Gothic architecture created buildings that were tall, slender and embell- ished with complex decoration, the Gothic ideal of beauty expressed itself in art in slim, delicate and almost ethereal female images.

Other works of the 14th c. Sienese school in Room 3 are the "Madonna in Glory" (1340) and panels showing scenes from the Life of Blessed Humility (1341) by Pietro Lorenzetti, a follower of Giotto. His brother Ambrogio Lorenzetti is represented by his scenes from the life of St Nicholas, in which narrative force is combined with a feeling for form and colour and attempts at representation using perspective.

Room 4

Florentine Art The most prominent of Giotto's Florentine followers rep- resented here are Bernardo Daddi (d. 1348) and Taddeo Gaddi (d. 1366), whose altarpieces are characterised by delicate colours and soft, grace- ful lines in realistic representations of people and places.

Room 5/6

High Gothic Gothic continued to dominate art in the period that fol- lowed, and the early 15th c. works of Lorenzo Monaco "The Adoration of the Magi" (1420) and "The Coronation of the Virgin" (1413) are still using the standard forms and colours of the international style of Gothic.

However, the chief representative of the "International Style" in Italy was Gentile da Fabriano, and his "Adoration of the Magi" (1423) strik- ingly conveys the artist's Gothic ideal of beauty. This picture dates from the period of transition from Gothic to Renaissance. In its lavish atten- tion to detail it testifies to the high aspirations of Palla Strozzi, the wealthy commissioner of the work. There is, however, still no sign of a radical break with tradition. Gentile shows no interest in the individual- ism characteristic of Renaissance art, but instead revels in the fairy-tale splendour reminiscent of Burgundian manuscripts.

Early Renaissance The work of his contemporary Masaccio is totally different. The "Madonna and Child with St Anne" (c. 1420), painted with Masolino, is one of the early works of this painter who revolutionised art by introducing a sense of perspective, three dimensions on a two-dimensional surface. He ranks with Brunelleschi and Donatello as one of the founders of the Renaissance, in which the image based on accurate observation of nature was to lead to a new experience of reality. Masaccio's altarpiece, with its energetic draftsmanship and relief-like modelling of the very real natural beauty of the faces and figures, is testimony to his greatness as an innovator.

Nearby hangs the "Coronation of the Virgin" (c. 1430–35) by Fra Angelico, the Dominican monk who was a contemporary of Masaccio, but whose deeply religious concept of art steeped in the mystic tradition takes him in the opposite direction, although it would be wrong to characterise him as conservative or old-fashioned. Whilst his paintings are dominated by gold backgrounds, and his figures appear rather ethereal, their form determined by drapery, Fra Angelico employs a richly colourful palette, and uses circular and semi-circular arrangement of figures to achieve an impressive composition in a unifying pictorial perspective.

Yet Fra Angelico undoubtedly seems a traditionalist compared with such a passionate exponent of perspective as Paolo Uccello. His "Battle of San Romano" was painted in about 1456 to commemorate the Florentines' victory over the combined troops of Siena and Milan in 1432. It was originally hung high up on a wall in the Palazzo Medici, which is why it appears a view from below. This is no gory battle-scene, however, more like a joust, where the protagonists appear almost like marionettes. The extreme foreshortening, broken lances, tumbled horses and riders, and puppet-like warriors, their forms reduced to pure volume, reflect Uccello's deep interest in problems of perspective. On the whole, though, he paints in a way that is rather anti-naturalistic, abstract and even modernistic when the red and blue horses are considered.

Confident application of perspective construction is evident in Domenico Veneziano's "Virgin and Child enthroned with four saints" (c. 1445). Instead of traditional individual panels for the saints, as in a polyptych, he paints one large altarpiece, in whose harmonious architectural space the saints stand in a semi-circle, two to the left and two to the right of the Virgin's throne, set in the arcade. A Venetian by birth, Domenico is a master of painting with light, his art representing an innovation with its abundance of fine nuances and delicate shades of colour that contrasts with the solid areas of strong colour of his Florentine contemporaries. The use of oil as an additional fixative with the tempera makes it possible to achieve the most delicate blues. Domenico's greatest contribution was the realistic representation of light and shade through painting. A beam of light falls diagonally from the top right of the picture, illuminating part of the room. This painting is the first in which sunlight is represented naturally, instead of using the traditional gold background.

Portraiture provided another focus for early Renaissance art. This evolved from the study of classical medallions, and profile portraits were particularly well received. The portraits of the Duke and Duchess of Urbino by Piero della Francesca from around 1465 are a good example. The heads of Federico da Montefeltro and his wife, Battista Sforza, are presented in full profile. The Duke is facing left, since as a young man he had lost his right eye in a tournament. This concession apart, Piero did not flatter any of his sitters by withholding even the slightest irregularity that was characteristic of their features. He has conscientiously reproduced the Duke's aquiline nose, each individual wrinkle, the thin lips, the stern look, and the stockiness of this ruler, whom he held in high esteem. Nor has the wasted, waxen face of his spouse escaped the artist.

Besides this stringently realistic characterisation of the Duke and Duchess, the background is also of interest as a rare example of early Renaissance landscape. It shows how much the ruling couple were worth, documenting their claim to power over their land, the Dukedom of Urbino, with its hillside towns and ports. When depicting the landscape, with its fine gradations from light to dark, Piero della Francesca, who was from Arezzo, was clearly inspired by the brown tones of his native Umbrian hills.

Room 8

Another example of Florentine portrait painting is **Filippo Lippi's** "Virgin and Child with two angels" (c. 1460). Largely detached from its religious subject matter, this late work by Lippi is the portrait of an elegantly dressed, girl-like beauty, her half-profile revealing the high, smooth, fashionably shaven forehead of the time, with a veil artistically woven into her golden hair. She is seated on an ornate chair at an open window, and two angels, smiling with delight, are lifting the baby Jesus up to her. The scene radiates cheerfulness and grace, although the Infant Christ looks rather grave. The rocky landscape seen through the window, taken in conjunction with the child's sorrowful expression, presumably is a reference to Golgotha and the Crucifixion. Of greater importance to the artist, however, is the bond of affection between mother and child, the tender physical touching and the eye-contact. Art's religious content became increasingly secularised towards the end of the 15th c., and subservient to the representation of interpersonal relationships. Women and motherhood, children's upbringing, and family happiness were important themes for discussion and representation by contemporary artists.

Lippi's other works, such as the Tarquinia Madonna (1437), the "Virgin enthroned with saints" (c. 1445), the "Coronation of the Virgin" and the "Adoration in the forest with St Romuald and the child John", combine the monumental three-dimensional figures of Masaccio with buildings and landscapes flooded with light, and an elegantly flowing line.

Room 9

The pictures, like the statuettes by the **Pollaiolo brothers**, are distinguished by powerful forms, bodies full of movement that result from a searching anatomical analysis. This is particularly evident in "Hercules and Antaeus" and "Hercules and the Hydra". On the other hand, the form of St Jacob taking up the whole of the altarpiece from the Cappella del Cardinale di Portogallo in San Miniato al Monte shows the trend towards monumental altarpieces rather than smaller polyptychs.

The early work of Sandro Botticelli also merits special attention. His Virgins are still strongly reminiscent of the style of his teacher, Filippo Lippi. "Valour" (1470) is regarded one of the early works, as is the portrait of an unknown man with the medallion of Cosimo the Elder, a charming contrast between full and half profile.

Rooms 10–14

Botticelli painted the altarpiece "Adoration of the Magi" around 1475 when he was about 30, during the "golden age" of Florence and the rule of Lorenzo the Magnificent, who was four years younger. Art historians question whether Botticelli's picture of the three kings was commissioned by the Medici themselves, or by their friend Giovanni del Lama for the Dominican church of Santa Maria Novella in Florence. In any event the Florentine ruling classes had Botticelli paint their portraits among the onlookers. He arranged the group in the classical pyramid, with the holy family at its peak, and below them the kings, in this case members of the Medici family ranked centrally in their socio-political order (the father, Cosimo the Elder, ruler of Florence, with his sons Giovanni and Piero de Medici). At the sides of the triangle are the younger Medici, Cosimo's nephew, the thoughtful, black-haired and sombrely dressed Lorenzo the Magnificent and his prouder, more animated, flamboyantly dressed brother Giuliano, who was murdered in the Pazzi conspiracy in 1478. They are framed by groups of humanists, aristocratic and wealthy friends and artists, against a Classical-style background of landscape and architecture. The actual theme of the Holy Story recedes into the background and serves only as a pretext for a magnificent representation of the Medici and their supporters.

Patrician Florence was not, however, solely interested in superficial, sensual pleasures. There was also an intense study of Classical literature and philosophy. Botticelli's "Birth of Venus" and "Primavera" should be interpreted against this historical background. Both works were commissioned by Lorenzo di Pierfrancesco de Medici, a cousin of Lorenzo the Magnificent. In the "Birth of Venus" (1482/1483) Botticelli combines Classical and Christian thought in accordance with Renaissance ideas, as a rebirth of the spirit from Classical mythology and Christian theology. Thus he paints a female nude modelled on a Classical statue of Venus, the Love Goddess, and indirectly summons up again the image of Christian baptism, associated with, for example, Christ being baptised in the Jordan. In the view of Marsilio Ficino, a contemporary philosopher and a notable teacher at the Florence's Platonic Academy, founded by Cosimo de Medici, Venus should be seen as an allegory of heavenly love, embodied in a beautiful woman. The contemplation of earthly beauty and perfection creates a longing to go back to the origin of the beauty and hence ultimately to God, its Creator.

The extent to which the Florentine intellectuals differ, with such ideas, from traditional philosophy elsewhere is made clear by comparing their work with Flemish painting as exemplified by Rogier van der Weyden's "Entombment" (*c.* 1450) in the same room, and by the Portinari Altarpiece, which was commissioned by Tommaso Portinari, who ran the Medici bank in Bruges, and completed by **Hugo van der Goes** shortly before the "Birth of Venus". Although the altar impresses with its naturalism and realism, it shows that on the whole art north of the Alps was still extremely religious in character. A nude in these circumstances would be unthinkable, and figures are enveloped in concealing drapery.

Botticelli's "Primavera" (1485–87), by contrast, has scantily clad maidens dancing gracefully in a meadow strewn with spring flowers, a reference to the three Graces of antiquity. Venus appears in the centre of the picture, her son Cupid above her head, and Mercury is on the extreme left, while the right-hand side shows the metamorphosis of the nymph Chloris – following her rape by the wind god Zephyr – into Flora, the goddess scattering flowers. At first sight it seems to represent a celebration of

"Primavera" by Botticelli

spring, as suggested by the picture's title, arbitrarily chosen much later by Vasari, but the picture's meaning is much more complex. Its prime source is Classical literature. Ovid describes the metamorphosis of the earth nymph Chloris in his "Fasti". The three Graces are known as the daughters of Atlas or Hesperides from Classical writings. The spring mood is undoubtedly drawn from the work "De rerum natura" by Lucretius.

A further level of meaning is derived from contemporary philosophical views of ideal love and beauty. Spring heralds the awakening of human emotions and desires, and Mercury drives the dark clouds of melancholy away with his staff so that these may unfold undisturbed. The group of Zephyr, Chloris and Flora visually represents the conflict between lust, chastity and beauty.

The elegantly clad figure of Venus in the centre of the picture, with her inviting gesture, is highly reminiscent of a Virgin, and thus embodies the synthesis of earthly and heavenly love. She is a typical "Venus humanitas", a symbol of spiritual, moral, divine love, an example of perfect humanity.

Room 15

When Botticelli died in 1510 a new generation of artists was already at work, and there was the famous triumvirate in the early 16th c. of **Leonardo da Vinci**, Michelangelo and Raphael. Leonardo was a pupil of **Andrea del Verrocchio**, and worked with him on "The Baptism of Christ in the Jordan" (c. 1470–72). Verrocchio had begun as a goldsmith and worked for most of his life as a sculptor. The figures of Christ and John the Baptist show his powerful, even rather hard modelling, in keeping with his being a sculptor. The kneeling angel facing us, hands folded on chest, although very graceful, appears rather ordinary, with his bony head and short, curly hair. Leonardo's kneeling angel, painted in profile, is lovelier, with his blond hair falling in soft waves over his neck, his tender look, and the rich drapery of his flowing garment.

Leonardo da Vinci lived at a time of scientific discovery in terms of the world and mankind which made Holy Writ increasingly less plausible as the only model for explaining the complicated interactions of the universe. Leonardo sensitively captures the atmosphere of crisis of his time in the "Adoration of the Magi" (1481). In the centre of this unfinished picture the Madonna appears with the child as a stabilising influence. She is encircled by a heaving mass of people, young and old, who greet the birth of the Son of God partly with wonder and amazement, partly with doubt and fear. In Leonardo's version the Nativity, which hitherto has been portrayed as some kind of folk tale, gains a new dimension of world redemption. In a chaotic world which is falling apart – hence the ruins, warriors and wild horsemen in the background – those who have come to adore are putting all their hope in a little child, who is to give them power and strength. The figures press forward out of the darkness, and are almost dazzled by the light of the Saviour. Whether their longing for salvation can be fulfilled, however, remains to be seen. The Virgin and Child are strangely isolated within the structure of the picture, and the adoring throng are conceived as very much at a distance, giving a rather murky effect. As Leonardo sees it, the Infant Child's promise of salvation is to be regarded with some scepticism.

Room 16

Room 16 is the last in the first part of the tour of the Uffizi, which is devoted to **Florentine and Tuscan art** from c. 1300 to 1500, mostly in chronological order. The art of the Italian Renaissance which followed is taken up in Room 25 onwards, with works by Raphael and Michelangelo. The following rooms are arranged according to schools of painting.

Room 17

Of particular interest in this room are the marble **Hermaphroditus**, a Roman copy of the Greek original from the 2nd/3rd c. BC, and the "Cupid and Psyche" group.

Room 18

Tribuna In the centre is the "Medici Venus", the most famous Classical marble sculpture in Florence and thought to be a late Greek version of the "Aphrodite of Cnidus" by Praxiteles. Other important statues are the

"Apollino" (after Praxiteles), "Arrotino" ("Scythian sharpening a knife"; Pergamon School, 2nd or 3rd c. BC), the "Wrestlers" (Pergamon School) and "Dancing Faun" (3rd c. BC, copy).

The walls are mainly hung with Mannerist portraits of the Medici family from about 1530 to 1570, the most outstanding being those by Pontormo, Bronzino and Vasari.

Pietro Perugino was from Umbria and was a pupil of Andrea del Verrocchio in Florence. His "Madonna with saints" and various portraits display a balanced composition, three-dimensional realism and sub-dued colour. As Raphael's teacher he paved the way for the classical art of the High Renaissance. **Luca Signorelli's** "Holy Family" (c. 1495) and "Madonna and Child", on the other hand, show much more turbulence and movement through extreme foreshortening of parts of the body and flaring colour. His painting influenced the young Michelangelo.

Room 19

This room holds German Renaissance art by **Lucas Cranach** including his portrait of Martin Luther and his wife Katharina, a self-portrait, an impressive "Melanchthon" and a rather erotic "Adam and Eve", and by **Albrecht Dürer** – "Virgin and Child" (1526), "Portrait of the Father" (1490) and "Adoration of the Magi" (1504), painted shortly before his second Italian journey.

Room 20

Venetian painting, characterised by soft, tonal colour and balanced light, together with harmonious landscapes and restful figures, is represented by **Giovanni Bellini's** "Religious Allegory" (c. 1485) and "Scenes from the life of Moses" (Judgment of Solomon, Trial by Fire) and by **Giorgione's** "Portrait of a Maltese horseman".

Room 21

German and Flemish painters Works by Albrecht Altdorfer, "Scenes from the life of St Florian" (c. 1525) and a portrait of Richard Southwell by Hans Holbein the Elder (1536), as well as works by Gerard David, Joos van Cleve and Lucas van der Leyden.

Room 22

Mainly religious works by Antonio Allegri, better known as **Correggio** after his birthplace, a representative of High Renaissance art in Northern Italy (Emilia), whose diagonal pictorial compositions with light effects and unusual depths of perspective had a lasting influence on later Baroque painting.

Room 23

The other works of interest in this room are the "Triptych" (1466) by the North Italian painter **Andrea Mantegna**, which depicts the Ascension, the Adoration of the Magi and the Circumcision, also a "Madonna of the Rocks" (1489). His true-to-life representation of people and his religious humanism strongly influenced the work of Albrecht Dürer.

Miniatures from the 15th to 18th c.

Room 24

Michelangelo's "Holy Family" (1504/1505), known as the Doni Tondo, was painted on the occasion of the marriage of Agnolo Doni and Maddalena Strozzi. It is devoid of any religious sentiment. The family appears as though carved out of a block, unmistakably demonstrating Michelangelo's strong interest in sculpture. Interpretation of the pic-ture's themes and composition is a matter for dispute. Viewed from below, and with strongly contrasting colours, the family forms a com-plex interrelated group, amidst naked youths on the rim of a large basin in the background. A young boy is looking over the balustrade. A recent interpretation of this setting is that it is an act of baptism, and the boy is John the Baptist. But it may also simply be a forerunner for the profusion of naked figures in the frescoes of the Sistine Chapel that Michelangelo was to paint some years later, as could be the unnaturally bright, iridescent colours, also to be found in the Sistine Chapel.

Room 25

Michelangelo's "Holy Family"

Of significance in this room also is the "Vision of St Bernhard" by **Fra Botolomeo**.

Room 26

This room contains three important works by **Raphael**: a self-portrait (*c.* 1506) showing him aged twenty-three, his charming "Virgin Mary with the Goldfinch", an effective triangular composition, and "Pope Leo X with the Cardinals Giulio de'Medici and Luigi de'Rossi".

The Pope presents himself to the onlooker as a modern man in the spirit of the Renaissance. He wishes to be seen as a humanist, a lover of literature, and a collector of precious things. Raphael depicts him between 1517 and 1519 as an individual, not simply a holder of office, and at the same time creates a balance between ideal form and true appearance, by representing the Pope, a lover of the arts and music, as a self-assured, strong-willed, intellectual character, despite his unprepossessing appearance, but without superimposing an attitude of power. In accordance with the Pope's wishes, Raphael also painted two Cardinals in the background, the Pope's close relatives, confidants and protégés, a fact which caused him to be reproached for nepotism. Raphael solves the difficult problem of a group portrait of subjects of unequal rank by showing the Pope seated, glancing up from his perusal of a valuable codex of miniatures, with his two confidants, Cardinal Luigi Rosso and Giulio de Medici – later Pope Clement VII – framing him on either side. Another interesting feature is the contrast between the idealised figures on the one hand, and, on the other, the true-to-life details of the handwriting, the finely engraved bell and the chair knob, with its reflection of part of the papal chamber.

Another painting worth singling out is **Andrea del Sarto's** "Madonna with the Harpies", a monumental altarpiece that is typical of Florentine

High Renaissance art by a painter who combines Raphael's soft, tonal technique with Michelangelo's monumentality and Leonardo da Vinci's atmospheric sfumato.

The year of Raphael's death (1520) is taken as the onset of **Mannerism**, the late phase of the Renaissance, that lasted until about 1600, and was characterised by anti-classical and unnatural forms and colours.

Room 27

One of the early Mannerists was Rosso Fiorentino, whose predilection for two-dimensional composition, and cool, pale colours can be seen in his "Moses defending the daughters of Jethro" (1523), based on the Old Testament story of Moses driving the shepherds from the well so that the flocks of the seven daughters of Jethro can drink. The picture is composed along strictly geometrical lines, with two pyramids roughly equal in size, meeting at Moses' left knee. The bottom one is light-brown, with its base the edge of the picture, whilst the top one is brightly coloured and upside down. The three naked figures that form the bottom triangle are anatomically correct, and yet appear unnatural, almost like articulated dolls.

The abstract quality of the representation is reminiscent of Uccello's technique (cf. "Battle of San Romano"), yet also shows how, after Raphael, painting moved away from the classical ideals, and the unreal and surreal have taken the place of what was believed to be a harmonious world.

Jacopo da Pontormo's "Supper at Emmaus" (c. 1525) was painted for the Carthusian convent near Florence. His works are influenced by his teachers Leonardo da Vinci and Andrea del Sarto fused with inspiration from the late work of Raphael and the monumental art of Michelangelo. Another influence was Dürer, especially his Passion cycle. "Supper at Emmaus" is distinctive for the spiritual yet mysterious representation of Christ and the young men at the same time as the treatment of the Carthusian monks in a naturalistic way with the effective use of light. Pontormo's pupil Agnolo Bronzino painted religious and mythological subjects, but was chiefly admired for his formal portraits of elegant, rather cool sitters (Room 18, Tribuna).

Works by the Venetian painter **Titian** in this room include his "Venus of Urbino" (1538), "Ludovico Beccadelli" (1552), "Venus and Cupid" (1560), "Eleonora Gonzaga della Rovere", "Francesco Maria, Duke of Urbino" and "La Flora", one of his finest portraits of women. The "Venus of Urbino" was painted for the Duke of Urbino, and is fascinating in the way it uses colour, with the shades of red pulling the different parts of the picture together diagonally and in spatial perspective.

Room 28

Girolamo Francesco Maria Mazzola, known as **Parmigianino** after Parma, his birthplace, was first influenced by Correggio, then by the Roman High Renaissance, and finally he got caught up in the Mannerist Movement. The "Madonna with the Long Neck", painted between 1534 and 1540, is a good example of the distortion characteristic of Mannerism with its highly elongated figures and strange light.

Room 29

Also here can be found works by **Doss Dossi**, one of the chief masters of the Ferrara School, first half of the 16th c., with romantic, atmospheric religious and mythological scenes.

Paul Veronese is represented in this room by his works "Holy Family with St Barbara" and the "Annunciation".

Room 31

The following paintings are displayed in this room: "Leda and the Swan", "Venetian Admiral", "Adam and Eve" and various portraits by **Tintoretto**; "The Concert" and "Two Hounds" by **Jacopo Bassano** and "Man in a Pelt" by **Paul Bordon**.

Room 32

Mostly small-scale works by **Mannerist** artists of the 16th century including Alessandro Allori, Agnolo Bronzino, Zucci and Giorgio Vasari.

Room 33

Palazzo degli Uffizi

Room 34

The following works in this room are of importance: portraits of the poets Giovanni Antonio Pantera and Cavaliere Pieto Secco Suardo (1563), of **Giovanni Battista Moroni** as well as a "Holy Family with St Jerome and St Anne" (1534) by **Lorenzo Lotto**.

Room 35 (sometimes closed)

This room is devoted to Baroque and Tuscan Counter-Reformation art.

Room 41

Van Dyck's portraits of the Emperor Charles V and Giovanni di Montfort, plus some of **Rubens'** finest works – "Henry IV at Ivry" and "Henry IV entering Paris", "Isabella Brandt" (his first wife) and "Entry of Ferdinand of Austria into Antwerp".

Room 42

Niobe Room Pride of place in this room, decorated in the Classical style between 1779 and 1780, is

"Youthful Bacchus" by Caravaggio

taken by "Niobe and her Children", a Roman copy, discovered in Rome in 1583, of 5th and 4th c. BC Greek originals, and the finest classical sculpture in Florence after the Medici "Venus". In the centre is the "Medici Vase" from the 2nd c. BC; there are also other Classical statues, and paintings mostly by 18th c. artists (Canaletto).

Room 43

Flemish painters 17th c. landscapes and genre paintings including works by Segher, Jakob van Ruisdael, Jan Steen, Gabriel Metsù, and Frans van Mieris.

Room 44

Caravaggio's "Medusa", "Youthful Bacchus" (1589), and "Sacrifice of Isaac" (1590).

The Uffizi's **Rembrandts** are "Self Portrait as an Old Man (1664), "Portrait of an Old Man" (the so-called "Rabbi"; 1658 or 1666) and "Self Portrait as a Young Man" (1633/1634).

Room 45

Room 45 is used for changing exhibitions of 18th c. work.

Corridoio Vasariano

The entrance to the Vasari corridor in the Uffizi is between Room 25 and Room 34. The Corridoio Vasariano, which crosses the Arno along the Ponte Vecchio (see entry), is named after Giorgio Vasari who built it for Cosimo I in 1565. It enabled the Medicis to walk unseen from the Palazzo Vecchio to the Palazzo Pitti (see entries).

The Corridoio Vasari contains a rich collection of portraits by Italian and foreign artists. These are primarily self portraits, but there are also portraits and copies of self portraits. The collection is constantly being updated, so portraits by modern artists such as James Ensor and Carlo Levis can be found alongside the work of Leonardo, Raphael,

122

Michelangelo, Rembrandt and Velásquez. Viewing of the Corridoio Vasariano is by appointment only: tel. 0 5523885.

★★Palazzo Vecchio   J/K6

The austere beauty of the city and the pride and tenacity of the people of Florence are embodied in the Palazzo Vecchio (or della Signoria) in a unique way. The city's principal palace came into existence when Florence was beginning its rise to power and greatness, was a witness to the decades of its artistic and cultural heyday, and stayed on as the symbol of its glorious past. The defiant fortress-like structure of the main building serves to express the power exercised by the Florentine community from the 14th to the 16th c.; its bold and lofty tower (94 m (308 ft)), with its clock dating from 1353, symbolises the fierce pride of the people of Florence, while the furnishings within the palace reflect their love of art.

Arnolfo di Cambio is said to have begun the building (1299–1314). Thereafter several patrons and architects (Michelozzo) were responsible for modifying the work and for the additions and alterations. Initially the palace was the official residence of the Priors (Palazzo dei Priori) and the Gonfaloniere, which therefore made it the seat of the governing body of the Republic, the "Signoria". Its other names, Palazzo del Popolo and Palazzo del Comune, are accounted for by the republican-democratic nature of Florence, even when it was ruled by the Medici, although they governed from their palace, the Palazzo Medici (see entry). It was Cosimo I, Duke then Grand Duke of Tuscany, who moved into the city's principal palace in 1540, after which it was known as the Palazzo Ducale (Ducal Palace). Soon, however, he moved into the Palazzo Pitti, so the name of Palazzo Vecchio (old palace) became current. Between 1865 and 1872, during the Italian struggle for unity, it was for a while the seat of the Government, the Chamber of Deputies and the Foreign Ministry. Thereafter it became the equivalent of the City Hall, and the state rooms were thrown open to the public as a museum.

Exterior To the left of the main entrance is a copy of Donatello's Marzocco, the heraldic lion of Florence with the city's coat of arms between its paws, and next to it a copy of Donatello's bronze statue of "Judith and Holofernes". The original is to be found in the Sala del Gigli (see below). On the right is a copy of Michelangelo's "David" and a marble statue of Hercules and Cacus by Bandinelli (1533). Directly beneath the battlemented gallery are frescoes showing the coats of arms of the communes of Florence.

The ground floor has three courtyards, the armoury and the great stairs that lead to the upper floors. The first courtyard and the armoury are especially interesting.

The small inner courtyard, the **"Primo Cortile"**, was redesigned by Michelozzo in 1470 (magnificent columns!). In the centre is a graceful fountain with a putto and dolphin (1476), a copy of the original by Verrocchio which is now inside the palace on the second floor. Around the top of the walls are 18 large townscapes, painted on the occasion of the wedding of Francesco de'Medici and Johanna of Austria (1565). Beneath the arcade can be seen Perino da Vinci's marble group "Samson and the Philistine".

The armoury (**Camera dell'Arme**) is worth visiting as it is the only room to have survived from the 14th c. palace.

Scalone del Vasari In the second courtyard is the ticket office and the great staircase is by Vasari (1560–63).

Location
Piazza della Signoria

Bus
23

Open Mon.–Wed., Fri., Sat.
9am–7pm; Sun. and pub. hols.
8am–1pm

Ground Floor

Palazzo Vecchio

Salone dei Cinquecento This vast room 53.7 m (176 ft) long, 22.4 m (71.5 ft) high and 18.7 m (61.3 ft) wide, is the work of Simone del Pollaiolo, known as Cronaca (1495). The walls were once decorated by two famous paintings, Michelangelo's "Soldiers Bathing" and Leonardo's "Battle of Anghiari", but both have been lost. The ceiling is divided into 39 panels richly decorated with allegories and scenes from the history of Florence and of the Medici family.

On the left is what is known as the "Audience Room", which was reserved for receptions and official ceremonies, with niches containing statues of the Medici: Cosimo I, Pope Leo X, Giovanni delle Bande Nere, Alessandro, Pope Clement VII, Franceso I (by Bandinelli, de'Rossi and Caccini).

Against the opposite wall is Michelangelo's famous "Genius of Victory" ("Genio della Vittoria", 1532–34), which was probably executed for the tomb of Pope Julius II in Rome. The statue shows the artist's supremely confident mastery in his shaping of the marble and his creative genius in the beauty and movement of the body. In the alcoves next to this are Roman statues: Ganymede, Mercury, Apollo and Bacchus.

Paintings, frescoes, statues ("Hercules" by Vincenzo de'Rossi) and tapestries complete the room's furnishings.

Quartiere di Leone X Leo X's quarters lead off from the Salone dei Cinquecento (on the opposite side of the entrance, right). Today this is where the mayor and city council have their offices.

Studiolo di Francesco I de'Medici To the right of the entrance a door leads to Francesco's study, designed by Vasari and richly decorated with paintings, frescoes and statues. Eminent painters (Poppi, Tito, Naldini) and sculptors (Giambologna: "Aeolus" or small Apollo) were employed on this "jewel casket" of Florentine late-Renaissance art.

A secret staircase leads to the **Tesoretto**, Cosimo I's little study, with ceiling paintings by pupils of Vasari.

On the other side of the Salone dei Cinquecento are the Ricetto (anteroom), the Sala degli Otto di Pratica and the Sala del Dugento with a magnificently carved wooden ceiling by Michelozzo.

Second floor

Sala dei Gigli The Lily Room has a large fresco by Ghirlandaio (1481–85). Today this room also contains the famous bronze group "Judith and Holofernes" by Donatello (1455–60). It was decided in 1988, after extensive restoration, that it should no longer stand outside, and has been replaced by a replica on its former site at the main entrance.

The **Salle della Carte Geografiche**, the linen-room, is lined with beautiful wooden presses decorated with contemporary maps (1563–75). Also on show here is a magnificent globe, the largest of its kind.

Cancelleria In the Chancellery of the Secretary of the Republic stands a bust of Niccolò Machiavelli and the original of Verrocchio's "Putto and Dolphin" (copy in the courtyard).

Sala dell'Udienza The Audience Room has a richly carved ceiling (by Giuliano da Maiano) and frescoes (including figures by Domenico Ghirlandaio).

Cappella della Signoria This contains a large fresco by Ridolfo Ghirlandaio.

The **quarters of Eleonora of Toledo**, the consort of Cosimo I, who died young in 1562, consist of the Camera di Gualdrada (the fresco on the bedroom ceiling shows the young Florentine woman who refused to kiss Emperor Otto IV because that was her husband's prerogative); Camera di Penelope (story of Odysseus); Camera di Ester or Dining

SECONDO PIANO

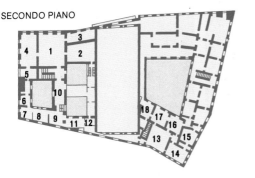

PRIMO PIANO

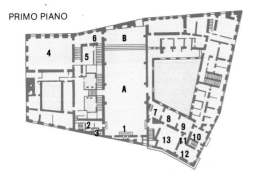

PIANTERRENO

© Baedeker

Palazzo Vecchio
Palazzo
della Signoria

SECOND FLOOR (SECONDO PIANO)
1 Sala degli Gigli
2 Salle della Carte Geografiche
3 Cancelleria, former office of N. Machiavelli
4 Sala dell'Udienza
5 Cappella della Signoria
6 Sala di Gualdrada
7 Sala di Penelope
8 Sala di Ester o Sala da Pranzo
9 Sala delle Sabine
10 Salotto
11 Sala verde
12 Cappella di Eleonora
13 Sala degli Elementi
14 Loggiato
15 Camera di Ercole
16 Camera di Giove
17 Camera di Cibele
18 Camera di Cerere

FIRST FLOOR (PRIMO PIANO)
A Salone dei Cinquecento
B Udienza
1 "Il Genio della Vittoria", by Michelangelo
2 Studiolo di Francesco I de' Medici
3 Tesoretto, Cosimo I's writing desk, by Vasari
4 Sala dei Dugento
5 Sala degli Otto di Pratica
6 Ricetto
7 Sala del Duca Cosimo I
8 Sala di Lorenzo il Magnifico
9 Sala di Cosimo il Vecchio
10 Sala di Giovanni delle Bande Nere
11 Cappella di Leone X
12 Sala di Clemente VII
13 Sala di Leone X

GROUND FLOOR (PIANTERRENO)
A Primo Cortile (courtyard)
B Camera dell' Arme
C Scalone del Vasari

Palazzo Vecchio: inner courtyard ...

... one of the sumptuously decorated rooms

Room (head of Apollo and fine lavabo); Salotto with interesting historical illustrations; Camera delle Sabine (ceiling painting: the Sabine women resolve the conflict between their menfolk and the Romans); Camera Verde, the "Green Room", with an adjoining study, and Cappella di Eleonora (the paintings are by Bronzino).

The "**Quarters of the Elements**", with paintings by Vasari and his pupil Gherardi (1556–66), consist of the Sala degli Elementi (allegories of Earth, Air, Fire and Water in the Mannerist style); Loggiato di Saturno (lovely view of Florence from the terrace); Camera di Ercole (scenes from the story of Hercules); Rooms of Juno, Jupiter, Cybele and Ceres, and a small writing room.

From the "**Ballatoio**" it is possible to climb up to the tower room which affords a magnificent panoramic view of the city. The route to the top passes the Alberghettino, a prison cell, ironically christened the "little hotel", where Cosimo the Elder was incarcerated before he was sent into exile (1433) and Savonarola was imprisoned for a few days in April 1498.

The tour of the palace ends with a visit to the **Quartiere del Mezzanino**. The mezzanine, which Michelozzo created by lowering the ceilings, contains works from the Collezione Loeser (paintings and sculptures by 14th and 16th c. Tuscan artists).

Piazza di Bellosguardo

Location
SW of the city
centre

As the name suggests, there is a splendid view of Florence from the Piazza di Bellosguardo, south-west of the centre, with the Villa di Bellosguardo and its beautiful garden. To the right of the Piazza stands the Villa Belvedere al Saracino (built by Baccio d'Agnolo in 1502 for Francesco Borgherini) and to the left is the Villa dell'Ombrellino. A bust of Galileo commemorates the fact that he lived here from 1617 to 1631.

Piazza del Duomo   J/K5

The Piazza del Duomo, the square around the cathedral (see Duomo Santa Maria del Fiore), is one of the most important sites in European art, with the cathedral, Giotto's Campanile and the Baptistry (see Battistero). The cathedral square, adjoined on the west by the Piazza San Giovanni with the Archbishop's Palace (see Palazzo Arcivescovile), is overlooked by several imposing buildings, including the Loggia del Bigallo (see entry), the Palazzo della Misericordia, the Palazzo dei Canonici, the Palazzo Guadagni (see entry), the Museo dell'Opera del Duomo (see entry) and the Palazzo Niccolini.

Location
city centre E of the station

Buses
1, 6, 7, 11, 13, 17, 33

The oldest and most distinguished association of Florentine citizens for social and charitable purposes, founded in 1326, when the plague ranged in Florence, to aid the sick poor and to attend to their burial. Michelangelo was a member of the order which used to wear red hoods (these are now black) and which has its headquarters near the Duomo Santa Maria del Fiore (see entry). The duties of the Order used to include accompanying the condemned prisoners to the place of execution. Nowadays the confraternity runs a modern ambulance service and a first-aid centre. It has over 2000 members, all volunteers, and is funded by donations.

Arcicon-fraternita della Misericordia

Piazza Goldoni   H6

A statue commemorating the famous Venetian dramatist Carlo Goldoni (1707–93) by Ulisse Cambi (erected 1873) is a feature of this square by the Arno named in his honour and on which seven streets converge.

Also in the square is the Ricasolis' town house, a building ascribed at one time to Michelozzo (1396–1472). But since it was only begun in 1480 and finished early in the 16th c., it is evident he could not have been the architect.

Location
city centre S of the station

Buses
9, C

Piazza della Repubblica   J6

Almost every visitor to Florence is bound to visit this square in the heart of the city if only to patronise one of the many cafés that line the Piazza della Repubblica with their tables and chairs.

This was the site of the Roman forum. It served as the Mercato Vecchio, the Old Market, until 1888 when the market booths were demolished and the Loggia del Pesce (see entry) that stood here was moved elsewhere. The market was replaced by the Arconte (1895), a monumental triumphal arch, and a series of administrative buildings. The statue of "Abbondanza", a copy of Donatello's version of "Plenty" which from its pillar looks out over the square, was the first profane statue to go on display in a public square since the end of antiquity.

Location
city centre

Buses
6, 11, 36, 37

Piazza San Giovanni   J5

The Piazza San Giovanni only acquired its present dimensions when, for technical reasons to do with traffic engineering, the Episcopal Palace was moved back some 50 m (165 ft).

St Zenobius' Column, erected here in 1384, recalls a tradition that in 429, as the relics of the saint of San Lorenzo were being transferred to

Location
next to the Cathedral

Buses
1, 6, 7, 11, 13, 17, 33

the church of Santa Reparata, predecessor of the Cathedral, a withered elm burst into leaf again.

Loggia del Bigallo

The Loggia del Bigallo, a typical Late Gothic structure, was commissioned by the Confraternity of the Brothers of Mercy (Compagni della Misericordia) to provide a place for "displaying" lost or abandoned children offered for adoption. The marble loggia and the little palace to which it belongs were built in 1353–58, probably by Ambrogia di Renzo. In 1445 Ventura di Moro and Rossello di Jacopo Franchi decorated the strips below the double arches with frescoes – scenes from the life of St Peter the Martyr, now replaced by copies. The originals are preserved in the council room inside the palace (and elsewhere), where works by 14th and 15th c. Florentine artists can also be seen (viewing by prearrangement only).

Palazzo Arcivescovile

The Episcopal Palace was built initially between 1573 and 1584 by Giovanni Antonio Dosio for Cardinal Alessandro Medici, later Pope Leo XI, but only finally completed by Ciurini in 1735. This long period of construction is reflected in a mixture of medieval and later styles. In 1895 the palace was moved back *en bloc* some 50 m (165 ft) to accommodate the city's increasing traffic.

Piazza Santa Croce K6

Location
E of the city
centre

Buses
13, 14, 19, 23, 31,
32

In front of the church of Santa Croce (see entry) is a square which would have been unusually large for the Middle Ages, and was clearly intended for festivals and popular assembly or as a site for the Franciscan monks to preach their sermons. Focal points are the 17th c. fountain on the west side of the square, the large monument to Dante and two palazzi.

A type of football was played here as early as the 16th c.; a commemorative plaque on the façade of the Palazzo dell'Antella marks the boundary line. The tradition has been carried on till the present day, and every June the piazza is the setting for the "Calcio Storico Fiorentino", a game of football in 16th c. costume.

Museo Santa Croce

The Santa Croce Museum (open Tue.–Sun. 10am–7pm) shows the Spanish artist Salvatore Dali in an unusual light – namely as a sculptor. In addition etchings and lithographs are also on exhibition.

Piazza di Santa Maria Novella H5

Location
city centre

Buses
4, 7, 10, 13, 14, 23,
25, 28, 31, 32, 33, 62

This bustling five-cornered square before the church of Santa Maria Novella (see entry) is closed to traffic, and looks most attractive, with its grass and flowers. The two marble obelisks surmounted by bronze lilies and supported by four tortoises are by Giambologna (1608), and mark the turning point for the annual horse race, the "Palio dei Cocchi".

Loggia di San Paolo

Opposite the church of Santa Maria Novella (see entry), on the south side of the square, is the Loggia di San Paolo which was commissioned in 1466 by the head of the Ospedale di San Paolo. It is modelled closely on Brunelleschi's Loggia degli Innocenti (the Porch of the foundling Hospital). The columns were replaced in 1789. It too is decorated with terracotta medallions by the Florentine artists Andrea and Giovanni della Robbia.

★Piazza della Santissima Annunziata   K5

Adjudged the most beautiful square in Florence, the tone of the spacious Piazza della Santissima Annunziata is set by four buildings of artistic importance – the church of Santissima Annunziata (see entry) at the top, the portico by Brunelleschi of the foundling hospital, the Spedale degli Innocenti (see entry) on the right, the colonnades of the Confraternità dei Servi di Maria, the work of Antonio da Sangallo and Baccio d'Agnolo, on the left, and Ammanati's Palazzo Riccardi-Manelli (see entry).

Location
city centre E of
the station

Buses
6, 31, 32

The statues in the square are the equestrian figure of Grand Duke Ferdinand I, Giambologna's last work, and completed by his pupil Tacca in 1608, and two bronze fountains of sea-creatures, dating from 1629 and the work, with his assistants, of Pietro Tacca, the versatile Carraran sculptor, metalworker and architect.

The imposing Palazzo Riccardi-Manelli (formerly Palazzo Grifoni) in Santissima Annunziata is the seat of the provincial and regional governments of Florence and Tuscany. The three-storey building, with its fine dignified façade, dominates the square opposite the church of Santissima Annunziata.

**Palazzo
Riccardi-Manelli**

Ugolino Grifoni, a wealthy official under Grand Duke Cosimo I, commissioned the architect Bartolomeo Ammanati to erect a palace over the top of old houses, a task which he skilfully accomplished between 1557 and 1563. The combination of red brick and predominantly light-grey stone is especially effective.

★Piazza della Signoria   J6

The Piazza della Signoria has been the political centre of the city since the 14th c. when houses belonging to Ghibelline families had to make way for the new square. It is notable for its important buildings and statues – the Palazzo Vecchio, Palazzo degli Uffizi, Loggia dei Lanzi (see entries) and the copies of statues by Michelangelo and Donatello (see Palazzo Vecchio).

Location
city centre

Bus
23

In the 1980s the Piazza della Signoria did not look its best. When archaeologists carried out trial excavations they discovered unexpected treasures under its paving, with finds from the Roman and Etruscan periods, the Middle Ages, even the Bronze Age. However the Florentines were not prepared to have the finest of their squares transformed into a permanent building site or subterranean excavation, so the authorities finally bowed to public pressure and filled in the excavations in 1989.

The square contains two kinds of **memorial**. A granite disc in the pavement, not far from the Fountain of Neptune, marks the spot where Savonarola and his companions Buonvicini and Malruffi were executed and burnt at the behest of Pope Alexander VI. Near the fountain is the equestrian statue by Giambologna (1594) of Cosimo I who was elevated to Grand Duke of Tuscany by Pope Pius V in 1569.

The most impressive monument in the square, however, is the Fonte di Piazza (del Nettuno), the Fountain of Neptune (photo p. 6). The Piazza della Signoria was to be given a magnificent work of art to commemorate the marriage of Francesco de'Medici, son of Cosimo I, to Princess Johanna of Austria (1565), since this union was to take the Medicis into the ranks of the great ruling houses of Europe – Francesco was even to receive the title of Grand Duke. So a fountain which had already been begun to the left of the entrance to the Palazzo Vecchio had to be fin-

Fonte del Nettuno

ished in a hurry, and between 1563 and 1575 Bartolommeo Ammanati and his assistants worked to make this the largest fountain in Florence, with the god Neptune, four horses and three tritons. They may have been in too much of a hurry, since the Florentines were to jeer "Ammanato, che bel marmo hai rovinato" – what lovely marble you've ruined, Ammanato!

★Piazzale Michelangelo L7

Florence's finest viewpoint, 104 m (341 ft) above sea level, is named after Michelangelo, an artist who did not always get the best of treatment from the people of Florence. It was designed by Giuseppe Poggi and laid out between 1865 and 1870. The statues in the centre of the square are bronze copies of Michelangelo's famous "David" and the four "Times of the Day" for the Medici tombs in the New Sacristy of San Lorenzo (see entry).

Location
SE of the city
centre

Bus
13

Florence's most important sights can easily be picked out and identified from the Piazzale Michelangelo. The Palazzo Vecchio (see entry), the city's tallest building, can be recognised by its tower topped by a belfry. Close by is the battlemented, smaller tower of the Bargello (see Palazzo del Bargello). Nearby is the more slender spire of the Badia Fiorentina (see entry). By the river can be seen the Franciscan church of Santa Croce (see entry), overlooking the Arno. In the opposite direction, well in the background near the station, the church tower and spire of Santa Maria Novella (see entry) are visible. But the massive building that dominates the cityscape is the Cathedral, the Duomo Santa Maria del Fiore (see entry), with its imposing dome and richly decorated belfry. To the left of the Cathedral the smaller white roof is the Baptistry (see Battistero) and the red dome is the New Sacristy of San Lorenzo (see entry).

Ponte alla Carraia H6

The oldest **bridge** over the Arno after the Ponte Vecchio, the Ponte alla Carraia collapsed several times and had to be rebuilt, for example in 1304 when the bridge was crowded with spectators trying to watch a spectacle on the Arno, or as a result of flooding. It was built in its present form, with five arches, by Ammanati in 1559.

Buses
9, C

The Ponte alla Carraia was also blown up by German troops during the Second World War but it was possible to rebuild the bridge in its original form.

Ponte alle Grazie K6/7

The first **bridge** upstream of the Ponte Vecchio (see entry) is the Ponte alle Grazie which was built in 1237 on the orders of Mandella, Podestà of Florence. The bridge withstood the 1333 flood but was so badly damaged in the Second World War that it had to be rebuilt in its modern form. The name of the bridge comes from a nearby chapel dedicated to the Virgin.

Bus
23

Ponte Santa Trinità H/J6

The Ponte Santa Trinità is the most elegant **bridge** in Florence. It was first built in 1252 but soon collapsed. Rebuilt more solidly in stone, it

Buses
6, 11, 36, 37

◀ *The busy Piazzo della Signoria with the massive Palazzo Vecchio*

was again destroyed when the Arno burst its banks in 1333 and 1557. It was built in its present form by Ammanati between 1567 and 1570 (reportedly in consultation on artistic matters with Michelangelo). When it was blown up by German troops in 1944 the people of Florence gathered up the fragments which made it possible to rebuild it in its original form between 1955 and 1957. On the corners of the bridge stand allegorical figures of the four seasons; they were placed here in 1608.

★★Ponte Vecchio   J6

Buses
B, C

It is possible that the Ponte Vecchio, the "**Old Bridge**" at the narrowest point on the river, dates back to Etruscan times. It is known for certain this is where there was a wooden bridge for the Roman consular road, the Via Cassia, to cross the Arno. On account of its age the Ponte Vecchio has undergone more repair following collapse or flooding than any other bridge in the city.

Shops and dwellings have been built on it since the 13th c. It was convenient for the butchers who could throw their waste straight into the river, to the delight of the fish and those Florentines who had to keep the city clean. The number of shops increased to such an extent, however, that Grand Duke Ferdinando I decreed "for the benefit of strangers" that only goldsmiths might have shops on the bridge, a ruling that has been observed right up to the present day.

In the middle of the bridge is a bust of Florence's most famous goldsmith, Benvenuto Cellini (1900).

The Corridoio Vasariano (see Palazzo degli Uffizi), constructed in the 16th c. to link the Palazzo Vecchio and the Palazzo Pitti (see entries), leads through the first storey of houses on the bridge.

The picturesque Ponte Vecchio, now lined only with jeweller shops

Porta alla Croce   M6

The Porta alla Croce, the **Cross Gate**, on the Piazza Beccaria and built in 1284, is all that is left of the city wall fortifications. Inside is a badly damaged fresco by Michele di Rodolfo, "Madonna and Child with St John the Baptist and St Ambrose".

Location
Piazza Beccaria

Buses
8, 12, 31, 32, 33, 80

Porta Romana   G7

The Via Cassia, the road to Rome, passes through the Porta Romana, the **Roman Gate**, the mightiest and best-preserved of Florence's city gates.
   Above the arch inside the gatehouse, which was built in 1326, is a fresco of the 14th c. Florentine school, "Madonna and Child and Four Saints" (Franciabigio).

Location
Via Romana

Buses
12, 38, 42

Porta San Frediano/Porta Pisana   G6

From the Arno a section of the old city wall leads to the Porta San Frediano. This **gate** is also known as Porta Pisana because it was from here that the road to Pisa left the city. This massive structure was built between 1332 and 1334, probably to designs by Andrea Pisano. The formidable doors are 13.2 m (44 ft) high and 25 cm (10 in.) thick.

Location
Borgo S. Frediano

Bus
6

Porta San Giorgio   J7

The Porta San Giorgio (**city gate**), just below the Forte di Belvedere (see entry), was completed in 1260, and is part of the second circle of walls on the left bank of the Arno, the course of which can still be traced from the positions of the city gates of San Niccolò (see entry), San Miniato, San Giorgio and Porta Romana and San Frediano (see entries). The interior fresco of the Madonna is by Bicci di Lorenzo; on the outside is a relief of St George.

Location
Costa S. Giorgio

Bus
C

Porta San Niccolò   L7

The Porta San Niccolò (**city gate**) was equally suited for defence by land and, in conjunction with the Zecca tower on the opposite bank of the Arno, for sealing off the river. The tower of the bastion, built in 1324, forms the beginning of the city wall in the east on the left bank of the Arno.

Location
Piazza Poggi

Bus
C

Rotonda del Brunelleschi   K5

The Rotonda di Santa Maria degli Agnoli (or Angeli), also known as Rotonda del Brunelleschi, forms the nucleus of an octagonal church which Brunelleschi (hence the name) began after 1433 for the cloth-merchants' guild but never completed.
   The Rotonda is thought to be the first Renaissance building to be based on a central plan. In 1936 neighbouring buildings were demolished with the result that the Rotonda is now free-standing. It presently contains the Centro Linguistico di Ateneo, which means that as a rule it is not possible to visit the interior.

Location
Via degli Alfani

Buses
1, 6, 7, 10, 11, 17, 20, 25, 31, 32, 33

Porta San Frediano   Porta San Niccolò

San Carlo dei Lombardi · San Carlo Boromeo   J6

Location
Via Calzaiuoli

Bus
23

Opposite Orsanmichele (see entry) stands the little Gothic single-naved **church** of San Carlo which was built between 1349 and 1404 first by Neri di Fioravante and Benci di Cione and then by Simone Talenti. It did not get its present name until the 17th c. when it was entrusted to the care of Lombards – St Carl Borromeo was Bishop of Milan. Until then it had been dedicated to St Michael and St Anne.

San Felice   H7

Location
Piazza San Felice

Buses
11, 36, 37

The history of the **church**, which stands opposite the Palazzo Pitti (see entry), extends far back into the Middle Ages (1066). The façade, a classic example of simple yet effective Renaissance architecture, was built about 1450.

The church contains works by the Giotto school ("Christ Crucified"), by the schools of Filippino Lippi (triptych), Ridolfo Ghirlandaio ("Madonna and Child"), and of Neri di Bicci (triptych) and a terracotta group from the school of Giovanni della Robbia.

★ San Firenze   K6

Location
Piazza San Firenze

Bus
23

The Baroque complex of San Firenze (**former church**) consisting of two church façades with a palace between them is in the Piazza San Firenze not far from the city's main square, the Piazza della Signoria (see entry). Its appearance reflects its chequered history. The church of San

Filippo Neri was built by Gherardo Silvani (1633–48) on the site of an old oratory dedicated to San Fiorenzo (hence the name "Firenze") that had been passed to the brotherhood of priests of St Philip Neri. The church façade (1715) is by Ferdinando Ruggieri. The church of Sant'Appolinare was built nearby between 1772 and 1775, with a façade also in accordance with Ruggieri's 1715 designs. At the same time a palazzo was built between the two churches, originally incorporating the cloister areas. Nowadays San Firenze is the seat of the Tribunale, the judicial authority.

San Frediano in Cestello   H6

This Carmelite **church** and convent, formerly known as Santa Maria degli Angeli, then became a parish church dedicated to St Frediano. The church was transformed in the 17th c. when it became Baroque in character, as is evidenced by its distinctive little cupola and graceful campanile.

Inside can be seen the famous "Smiling Madonna", a 13th/14th c. Tuscan painted wooden statue.

Location
Piazza di Cestello

Bus
6

San Gaetano   J5

The finest 17th c. façade in Florence belongs to the Baroque **church** of San Gaetano. The original 11th c. church (San Michele Berteldi) was completely rebuilt in the early 17th c. Inside, pale figures against black stone imbue the place with a special atmosphere. In the second chapel on the left is "The Martyrdom of St Laurence" by Pietro da Cortona.

In the Cappella Antinori in the adjoining monastery is a "Christ Crucified" by Filippo Lippi.

Location
Piazza Antinori

Buses
6, 11, 36, 37

San Giovanni(no) dei Cavalieri   K4

The **church** of San Giovanni(no) dei Cavalieri (the Maltese Knights of St John) changed its name as often as its architects. First it was the Oratory of Mary Magdalene, with a home for "fallen" women (1326), then "San Pier Celestino", "San Niccolò" (1533) and finally San Giovanni Decallato (St John the Baptist Beheaded) or San Giovanni dei Cavalieri, the patron saint of nuns from Jerusalem who had a convent (with a fine cloister) near the church. Inside is a "Nativity" (1435) by di Lorenzo and a "Coronation of the Virgin" by di Bicci.

Location
Via San Gallo 66

Buses
8, 80

★San Giovanni degli Scolopi   J5

John the Evangelist ranks second in importance after John the Baptist as patron saint of Florence, and it was in his honour that in 1579 the architect Ammanati began to build this **church** and the adjacent college for the Jesuits opposite the Palazzo Medici (see entry). It was not completed, however, until 1661, when the architect was Alfonso Parigi the Younger. With the banishment of the Jesuits from Florence in 1773 the church was handed over to the "Padri Scolopi".

The façade and the interior, richly adorned with marble and frescoes, show this to be a church on which no expense was spared.

Location
Via Martelli/Via de'Gori

Buses
1, 6, 7, 11, 17, 23

San Jacopo sopr'Arno   J6

Location
Borgo San
Jacopo 34

Buses
11, 36, 37

From the Ponte Trinità (see entry) there is a splendid view of the little Romanesque **church** of San Jacopo "on the Arno" (12th c. but much altered subsequently) with its beautiful Campanile (1660, by Gherardo Silvani). The church has a porch dating from about 1000, the only one of this period in Florence.

The interior, nowadays used for exhibitions, has frescoes and altarpieces by 18th c. Florentine artists.

Near the church, on the corner of Borgo San Jacopo and Via dello Sprone, is a lovely **fountain** by Buontalenti.

★★ San Lorenzo   J5

Location
Piazza San
Lorenzo

Buses
1, 6, 7, 11, 17, 33

Open 7.30am–
noon, 3.30–
6.30pm

San Lorenzo counts as one of the major sites of art in the Western world. The **church** of St Laurence, the Old Sacristy, the New Sacristy, the Princes' Chapel and the Laurenziana Library are works of the highest architectural importance in their own right and contain priceless art treasures. It was here, in their parish church, that the Medici, unrivalled as patrons, spurred on the artists of their city – Brunelleschi, Donatello and Michelangelo – to even greater achievements.

It is said that the church of San Lorenzo was founded by St Ambrose in 393 outside the city walls of that time. It was rebuilt in the 11th c. in the Romanesque style. It was that important exponent of Florentine Renaissance architecture, Brunelleschi, who was commissioned by the Medici (from 1419 onwards) to give it its present

The bare brick façade of San Lorenzo remains unfaced

form. The work was completed after his death but in accordance with his plans by Antonio Manetti (1447–60). Michelangelo supplied designs (drawings and models in the Casa Buonarotti, see entry) for the façade but they were never implemented, so the bare bricks are still visible.

Among the stalls selling souvenirs, clothing, etc., to the right of the façade in the Piazza San Lorenzo, can be found the **monument** to Giovanni delle Bande Nere (1360–1429), father of Cosimo I and founder of the ducal Medici dynasty (by Baccio Bandinelli, 1540).

Brunelleschi's light, harmonious **interior** of the church displays the clear-cut articulation of Renaissance architecture: a beautiful marble pavement, columns with Corinthian capitals supporting the broad arches, an intricate coffered ceiling with delicate rosettes. The harmonious proportions of the church's side chapels, aisles and nave denote architecture of the highest order.

At the end of the **nave** are two bronze pulpits by Donatello, the artist's final masterpiece (c. 1460), completed by his pupils Bartolomeo Bellano and Bertoldo di Giovanni, vividly depicting scenes from the life of Christ and the saints.

Above the door to the cloister is a **marble balcony** thought to have been   Left aisle

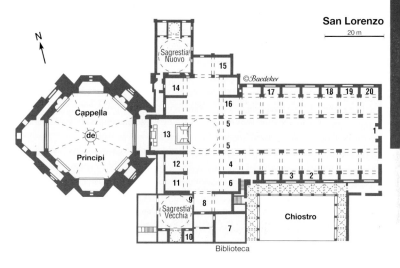

San Lorenzo
20 m

1   Façade wall, by Michelangelo
2   "Crocifisso tra la Madonna e San Giovanni" (15th and 17th c.)
3   "Martirio di Sant'Arcadio e Compagni" by Sogliani
4   "Martirio di San Lorenzo" by Bronzino (1565–9)
5   Bronze pulpits, by Donatello and his pupils
6   Capella Martelli
7   Vestibule of the Biblioteca
8   Cappella di Ss Cosma e Damian
9   Tomb of Pietro and Giovanni de'Medici, by A. del Verrocchio (1472)
10 Marble basin, by the school of Donatello
11 Altar, by the school of Ghirlandaio
12 Wooden statue, "Madonna col Bambino" (late 14th c.)
13 Cappella Maggiore
14 Monument to Pietro Benvenuti
15 Tomb of Maria Anna Carolina
16 Marble tabernacle, by D. da Settignano
17 "Adorazione dei Magi" by G. Maccietti
18 "San Lorenzo", by N. Lapi
19 "Sposalizio di Maria", by R. Fiorentine (1523)
20 "Martirio di San Sebastiano" by Empoli

designed by Donatello. Opposite Donatello's bronze pulpit is a fresco by Agnolo Bronzini, "Martyrdom of St Laurence" (1569).

In the **Cappella Martelli** (left) are a diptych by Filippo Lippi, "Annunciation" (1440; on the altar), one of his major works, and a monument to Donatello (1896) by Dario Guidotti and Raffaello Romanelli.

From the left aisle a door leads to the **cloister**, built in the style of Brunelleschi (1475).
A door on the first floor leads to the Biblioteca Medicea Laurenziana (see below).

The left arm of the transept leads into the **Sagrestia Vecchia** (old sacristy). Intended by its founder, Giovanni Bicci de'Medici, to be a burial chapel but linked with the public function of a sacristy, it was Brunelleschi's first complete architectural work (1420–28), and in its construction, articulation and proportions was to have a profound influence on European architecture.

Here, too, the impact of the building is heightened by **works of art**. Four medallions under the dome show scenes from the life of St John the Evangelist and four stucco reliefs in the arches depict the seated Evangelists. Recently cleaned and restored the reliefs now shine forth again in the luminous colours of the Early Renaissance. These are all by Donatello as are the bronze doors in the apse representing martyrs and apostles in animated discourse. On the left-hand wall is the magnificent tomb of Piero and Giovanni de'Medici (sons of Cosimo the Elder) by Andrea Verrocchio (1472). Beneath the marble table in the centre is the sarcophagus of Giovanni Bicci de'Medici and his wife Piccarda Bueri (the parents of Cosimo the Elder).

On the **high altar** is a "Crucifixion" by Baccio da Montelupe.

Right aisle

Opposite Donatello's bronze pulpit (in the side chapel) is a tabernacle by Desiderio da Settignano (1461). In the last chapel but one (going towards the exit) can be seen a painting by Rosso Fiorentino, "The Marriage of the Virgin" (1523).

The **Biblioteca Laurenziana** (Laurentian Library; open Mon.–Sat. 9am–1pm), built on to the church of San Lorenzo and its cloister (access to the Library is via the first floor of the cloister, see above), owes its artistic importance, its architecture and its contents to the Medici family. The library was founded by Cosimo the Elder as a collection of documents and books and enlarged by Lorenzo the Magnificent. It was transferred to Rome but part of it was returned to Florence under Pope Clement VII (also a Medici), who gave orders for a building which gave the public access to the collection. Work started in 1524 to Michelangelo's designs.

Despite the difficult external conditions – it had to be built on the weak foundations of a 13th c. monastery – the library was consecrated in 1571. It shows that Michelangelo, who, after he left Florence in 1534, continued to take part in the building work by means of letters and models, was at the height of his powers as an architect. The importance of the Biblioteca Laurenziana as a work of art is due to the three-dimensional articulation of the façade, the vestibule and the reading room, the staircases, and the confident use of all the decorative elements of Renaissance architecture.
The collection of manuscripts includes important papers from Ancient Egypt and valuable manuscripts by Napoleon.

Tomb of Giuliano de Medici by Michelangelo with figures representing Night and Day

Cappelle Medicee

Although the Medici chapels form part of San Lorenzo they are now administered as a museum in their own right, separately from the church. They consist of the Medici family vault (Cappella dei Medici) and the New Sacristy (the oldest Medici chapel, see San Lorenzo, Old Sacristy). The entrance to the Medici chapel leads first into a crypt with tombs of members of the Medici family, then into the memorial chapel of the Medici princes, the Cappella dei Principi.

Cappella dei Principi In 1602 Grand Duke Ferdinando I had the idea of building a particularly splendid family vault for the Medici dynasty. The plans were so sumptuous that the rumour went round that the intention was to transfer the tomb of Jesus Christ from Jerusalem to Florence, for such an extravagant building could not be intended for mortal men.

The final design came from Giovanni de'Medici (illegitimate son of Cosimo I) and was put into effect by the architect Buontalenti (1604 onwards). After his death the work was continued by Mario Nigetti (until 1640). Despite a great deal of effort the chapel was not completed until the death in 1737 of the last Medici to rule Florence; the huge dome, 59 m (194 ft) high but very heavy-looking, was not completed until the 19th c. The furnishings attest to the importance of the Medici family: ceiling paintings showing scenes from the Old and New Testaments, precious mosaics on the walls, 16 coats of arms of Tuscan cities inlaid with semi-precious stones and, high above, the huge coat of arms of the Medici.

Six Medici Grand Dukes are buried in the Chapel. They are (clockwise) Cosimo I (d. 1574), Francesco I (d. 1587), Cosimo III (d. 1723), Ferdinando I (d. 1609), Cosimo II (d. 1621) and Ferdinando II (d. 1670). Their wall tombs and sarcophagi, executed with artistry and costly materials, were

Location
Piazza Madonna
degli Aldobrandini

Open Tue.–Sat.
8.30am–1.50pm;
closed 2nd and
4th Sun. and 1st,
3rd, 5th Mon. in
the month

the work of highly skilled craftsmen, but the gloomy pomp of the chapel has a chilling air about it, an indication that the heyday of Renaissance art came and went with the 16th c. Behind the altar is the entrance to the reliquary and treasure chapels.

The Cappella dei Principi leads into the **Sagrestia Nuova**, the New Sacristy, built, with interruptions, by Michelangelo between 1520 and 1534, and designed to offset Brunelleschi's Old Sacristy (see above). The term "sacristy" is misleading since this is in fact a funerary chapel for the Medici.

The chapel was Michelangelo's first work as an architect and where he simultaneously applied his talents as painter and sculptor. This can be seen in the articulation of the internal walls, the three-dimensional treatment given to the architectural elements, the niches and pediments, arches and gables, both projecting and inset. The interior with its predominant "colours" of dark grey and brilliant white was evenly lit by the windows in the dome.

Besides acting as architect, Michelangelo was also commissioned to sculpt the tombs for members of the Medici family. He completed only two of the tombs, however, those of Giuliano, Duke of Nemours, and Lorenzo, Duke of Urbino (Lorenzo the Magnificent, his brother Giuliano, murdered in 1478, and Duke Alessandro, murdered in 1537, are all also entombed in the chapel but without monuments). Neither Giuliano, with his military commander's baton, nor Lorenzo with the grotesque helmet on his head (maybe a sign of his feeble-mindedness) are depicted as actual likenesses. Michelangelo, when reproached with this fact, responded that in a thousand years it would not matter to anyone what the two deceased really looked like. He deliberately wanted to transcend pure portraiture and create timeless figures, hence the simple names for them of "la vigilanza" (Vigilance) and "il pensiero" (Thought).

Giuliano de Medici, seated and robed as a Roman general, his baton in his hand, looks with a watchful eye over the Virgin and St Cosmas and St Damian, a group of saints much venerated by the Medicis, placed on the tomb of Lorenzo the Magnificent. Below Giuliano, on the slanting sarcophagus lid, lie the figure of Night, with crescent moon and stars in her hair, and poppy, owl and mask, and the figure of Day, unfinished, with an inscrutable rough-cut stone gaze into the void. Both are modelled on Classical lines. Night is reminiscent of a Leda from a Roman sarcophagus and Day is similar to the Belvedere torso. Michelangelo was thus quite consciously coming to terms with Classical sculpture while giving it a new Christian philosophical dimension.

The seated figure in the niche in the opposite wall represents Lorenzo de Medici. His head rests on his left hand, a pose indicative of pensiveness. Below the figure, on the sarcophagus lid, are the allegorical representations of Dusk, or Evening (left), and Dawn, or Morning (right). The male figure of Dusk embodies mental fatigue, the inert bulk of the sleeping body, contrasting with the female figure that symbolises awakening, the body and spirit slowly regaining in strength. This contrasting pair also illustrates the struggle within Lorenzo, who was mentally deranged when he died. Lorenzo, like his opposite counterpart, also looks to the Virgin in the hope of redemption.

The Virgin, in her turn, is looking at the altar on the wall facing her, thus referring to Christ's sacrificial death, and the consequent Resurrection and eternal life. In this way all the figures communicate with one another, their interlocking gaze covering the room, an original concept of Michelangelo's.

Unfortunately the chapel reveals little of Michelangelo's grand design for the work as a whole. Giuliano de Medici's tomb, for example, should have had the two river gods of the Arno and the Tiber at its base, glorifying Tuscany and Latium as the two provinces ruled by Giuliano. In the niches to the left and right of the Duke of

Nemours there should have been allegorical representations of Heaven and Earth in stone. The ceiling above should have held the display of trophies that can now be seen in the way through to the New Sacristy. And above it all, in the semicircle of the wall articulation, there should have been a fresco of the Resurrection, drawing the eye heavenwards via painted cassettes in the light area of the dome. With this chapel Michelangelo sought to bring architecture, sculpture and painting together to create a philosophical and artistic image that would reflect the path of life from the material world (river gods, sarcophagi), via humanity (day and night = life and death, Giuliano's statue) to the life eternal and the resurrection fresco.

★ San Marco   K4/5

The **church** of San Marco, built in 1299 by the Silvestrine order of monks, was transferred along with the monastery to the Dominicans of Fiesole (see entry) by Pope Eugene IV in 1436, the year of the Cathedral's consecration. Thanks to the generosity of Cosimo the Elder the church was largely reconstructed and the monastery was completely rebuilt. The work was entrusted to the architect Michelozzo (1431–52). Giambologna added the side altars, the Chapel of St Antonino and the Salviati Chapel in 1588. The church underwent alterations by Pier Francesco Silvani in 1678 and the façade was reworked in 1780.

Location
Piazza San Marco

Buses
1, 6, 7, 10, 11, 17,
20, 25, 31, 32, 33

The monastery is built around the church. The oldest part contains the Museo di San Marco, while the monks live in the rest.

The single-naved church holds valuable works of art. In the centre of the **interior** façade there is an interesting "Crucifixion" in the style of Giotto. On the left side of the church there is the funerary chapel of St Antony, considered Giambologna's main work of architecture (1580–89). He also contributed to the decor, with six life-size niche statues and six bronze reliefs of scenes from the life of St Antonino.

Returning to the exit, along the right side of the church, there are three **works of art** to note: the Baroque marble door by Cigoli leading to the sacristy, a Byzantine mosaic, "Virgin in Prayer" (705–707) from the Oratory of Pope John VII in Rome, and a "Madonna and Child" by Fra Bartolommeo della Porta (1509).

Museo di San Marco

The monastery of San Marco, built in Renaissance style by Michelozzo, with its superb collection of paintings and frescoes, gives a more focused impression of the spiritual life of the Dominicans and their interest in art than does the church.

Open Wed.,
Sat.–Mon.
8.30am–2pm;
Tue., Thu., Fri.
8.30am–4pm,
closed 2nd, 4th
Mon., 1st, 3rd, 5th
Sun. in month

In the late 15th and 16th c. fierce religious forces emanated from San Marco that were temporarily to transform Florence. Besides the Dominican monk Antoninus, later to become St Antonino, Archbishop of Florence, there was Savonarola, the revivalist preacher who was Prior of San Marco until his execution in 1494.

The monastery owes its fame, however, to the Dominican monk Fra Angelico (see Famous People), who painted the monastery rooms between 1436 and 1445, thus leaving us today with a "natural" museum. Fra Bartolommeo, an inspired early 16th c. artist, is also represented here by a number of his paintings.

Pilgrim's hospice Here there are panels by Fra Angelico from various   Ground floor

141

"The Annunciation" by Fra Angelico

museums in Florence, including "Madonna dei Linaioli" (1436, commissioned from Angelico by the linen weavers' guild), miniatures of the life of Jesus (1450), the famous "Deposition" (1435) and the "Last Judgment" (1430).

Cloister of St Antonino Immediately opposite the entrance can be seen the fresco "St Dominic at the Foot of the Cross"; diagonally opposite the entrance, in the lunette, is the fresco "Ecce Homo", both by Fra Angelico.

Works worth seeing in the **Great Refectory** include Fra Bartolommeo's fresco of the "Last Judgment".

Sala dei Lavabo Here there is another impressive work by Fra Bartolommeo, his large panel "Madonna with St Anne and other Saints" (1510).

The whole of one wall of the **chapterhouse**, where the monks confessed and atoned for their sins, is taken up by Fra Angelico's fresco of the "Crucifixion".

In the **Small Refectory** is a famous "Last Supper" by Ghirlandaio, similar to the one in the Ognissanti church (see entry).

First floor

Dormitorium There are over 40 cells on the first floor adorned with frescos by Fra Angelico and his pupils. His style is unmistakable in all the paintings and frescoes. He transforms the austere and stiff rigidity of the medieval saints into gentle tenderness. His saints radiate piety and innocence yet their features are not ethereal but entirely human. Man appears transfigured, the earthly bear traces of the celestial. There is scarcely a more intimate representation of the "Annunciation" than that of Fra Angelico (opposite the stairs).

At the end of the back corridor are the Prior's rooms, where Savonarola is commemorated together with St Antonino, Archbishop of Florence. The last two cells on the right of the front corridor overlooking the church recall the memory of Cosimo the Elder who often came here in retreat when he was ruler of the city.

The great hall of the **library**, the work of Michelozzo (1444), is notable for the austere beauty of its architecture and contains valuable manuscripts, missals and bibles.

The Library of San Marco with its austere architecture

San Martino   J/K6

Opposite the Dante House (see Casa di Dante), in a little square, is the unassuming **church** of San Martino where Dante was to marry Gemma Donati. Founded in 986 it passed to the Compagnia dei Buonomini, a charitable brotherhood which cared for the "shameful poor", once wealthy burghers who had lost everything they possessed. The present church is from the second half of the 15th c.

The church is worth a visit for its frescoes which depict the good deeds of the brotherhood – visiting the sick, sheltering pilgrims, etc., and thus provide a vivid picture of everyday life in Florence in the late 15th c.

Location
Via Dante
Alighieri

Bus
14

Open Mon.–Sat.
10am–noon,
3–6.30pm Sun.
10am–noon

San Michelino/San Michele Visdomini   K5

In the shadow of the cathedral (see Duomo Santa Maria del Fiore) stands the **church** of San Michelino, the Vicedomini family church (hence the name San Michele Visdomini), which had to make way for the cathedral and was rebuilt a few yards away in the 14th c. (renovated in the 17th c.). It contains altarpieces by Pontormo ("Holy Family and Saints"), Passignano, Empoli and Poppi.

Location
Via de'Servi

Buses
1, 6, 7, 11, 13,
17, 33

★★San Miniato al Monte   L8

A short walk up from the Piazzale Michelangelo (see entry) brings the visitor to the square in front of the **church** of San Miniato al Monte, with

Location
Monte alle Croci

143

another superb view over Florence. The church and monastery provide very good examples of the Romanesque Tuscan architecture of the late 11th and 12th c. (see History of Art, Romanesque Architecture), showing the closeness of the links to Classical Roman in its exterior and interior.

The name commemorates St Minias, who died a martyr in Florence around AD 250. The monastery church was built over his grave, probably around 1018 or 1013. It was not actually completed until the early 13th c. and originally belonged to Benedictine nuns, but between 1373 and 1552 was used by Olivetan monks, as it is today.

The gleaming white and green **façade** (c. 1100), with its triangular gable, is clad with marble panels which, with the great Romanesque-Roman arches, articulate the façade in geometric patterns of squares, rectangles, circles, etc. in various combinations. On the upper storey there is a late 13th c. mosaic of Christ between the Virgin and San Miniato. The gable is topped by a gilded eagle with a pack of wool in its claws, symbolising the wealthy cloth merchants' guild, long-term patrons of San Miniato.

After the old **Campanile** collapsed in 1499 a new one was begun in 1518 but never entirely completed. In the troubled times of the early 16th c. it served the Florentines, including Michelangelo, as defence against the troops of the Emperor.

The monastery church's impressive **interior** is of unusually harmonious proportions, with its decorative wall inlay, and takes the form of an early Christian basilica with alternating columns and pillars dividing nave and two aisles, lacking a transept but with a splendid timbered roof (repainted in the 19th c.). The raised choir, traditionally over the grave of St Minias, originally allowed the entering pilgrim a direct view into the crypt and sight of the bones of the saint, but this is now blocked by the Renaissance tabernacle.

Although San Miniato is basically a medieval Romanesque church building it is furnished with two outstanding examples of Renaissance art, Michelozzo's Cappella del Crocifisso at the end of the nave, and the Chapel of the Cardinal of Portugal, added on the left aisle and by Antonio Manetti with sculpture by Rossellino.

Michelozzo's barrel-vaulted **Cappella del Crocifizzo** (1448) in the nave was commissioned by Piero de Medici. On the back wall is an altarpiece by Agnolo Gaddi (c. 1396) showing scenes from the martyrdom of St Minias. It is interesting to see how the proud donor has set his stamp everywhere in this relatively small space. Piero's sign was a ring with an uncut diamond (symbolic of durability and toughness) and a bunch of feathers. These emblems are reproduced throughout the frieze and in the bronze screen. The back is embellished with an eagle, symbol of the guild, indicating that the guild was the builder and Piero de Medici was only reluctantly allowed to show that he was the donor. The coffered ceiling is in glazed terracotta, its light-blue and white colouring identifying it as the work of Renaissance artist Luca della Robbia.

The chapel of the **Cardinal of Portugal** (Cappella del Cardinale di Portogallo), on the left aisle, was commissioned by the Portuguese King Alfons V as a monument to his nephew, and built by Manetti between 1461 and 1466, very much on the lines of Brunelleschi's Old Sacristy for San Lorenzo. The decor brings together Christian and Classical concepts, with Antonio Rossellino's sarcophagus recalling a Roman Mithraic sacrifice, but decorated with putti and angels. The recumbent figure of the deceased is aligned with the empty judge's throne opposite as a warning of the Last Judgment. This monument, in its entirety,

◀ *The white and green façade of the Church of San Miniato al Monte*

The Bishop's Palace, near the Church of San Miniato

should be regarded a forerunner of Michelangelo's sarcophagi in the New Sacristy of San Lorenzo. The terracotta sculpture (Holy Ghost, four cardinal virtues) is by Luca della Robbia.

Steps on the right and left of the Capella del Crocifisso lead down into the hall **crypt** which has seven aisles with groin vaults and frescoes by Taddeo Gaddi depicting Saints and Prophets.

Presbytery The late 12th c. marble pulpit and choir screen, rich with decoration, are among the late Romanesque highlights of the church.

The mosaic in the **apse** of Christ Pantocrator flanked by the Virgin and St Miniato shows considerable Byzantine influence, and dates originally from 1297 but has since been considerably restored, and was totally renewed in the late 19th c.

The **sacristy**, reached from the right hand side below the apse, contains Spinello Aretino's masterpiece, his "Life of St Benedict" (post 1387). A doorway in the sacristy leads to the cloister with frescoes by Andrea del Castagno and Paolo Uccello.

Work on the cemetery, the **Cimitero delle Porte Sante**, was begun in 1857 in accordance with the plans of Nicola Matas, and it is the burial ground for many famous people from the late 19th c.

The massive **Palazzo dei Vescovi** (bishop's palace), to the right of the church, was begun by Bishop Andrea dei Mozzi in 1295 and completed by his successor Antonio d'Orso in 1320. It served the Bishops of Florence as their summer residence, high above the city, until it became

part of the monastery in 1534. Subsequently also used as a military hospital, a Jesuit college and, on occasions, for concerts, it is now back in the hands of the Olivetans.

The **popes** often spent long periods in Florence. Pope Stephen IX died here (buried in the church of Santa Reparata). His successor, Nicholas II, had previously been Bishop of Florence, an office which he retained.

The impressive interior of the Church of San Miniato al Monte

San Niccolò sopr'Arno   K7

An aedicula (built-up altar) in the style of Michelozzo and a lively fresco by Piero del Pollaiolo, "Madonna della Cintola" (1450), in the sacristy are the principal art treasures of the **church** of San Niccolò sopr'Arno which was built in the 12th c., reconstructed in the 14th c. and restored in the 16th c. After Florence was occupied by the troops of the Emperor and the Pope Michelangelo is supposed to have hidden in the belfry in 1530 to avoid possible arrest.

Location
Via San Niccolò

Bus
C

San Salvatore al Monte · San Francesco al Monte   L7

The **church** of San Salvatore al Monte (or San Francesco al Monte) tends to get overlooked because of the nearby church of San Miniato (see entry) but the church that Michelangelo called "la bella villanella" ("the beautiful country lass") is worth visiting for its outstanding clearcut architecture both inside and out. This is mainly the work of Cronaca (from 1499), who had considerable difficulties to overcome since the steepness of the site meant that building could only proceed if use was made of retaining walls.

Location
above the Piazzale Michelangelo, Viale Galileo

Bus
13

San Simone   K6

Restoration work after the 1966 floods revealed the extent of the trea-

Location
Piazza San
Simone, Via Isola
della Stinche

Bus
14

sures that the little **church** of San Simone had to offer. Founded in the 12th c. and completely remodelled in the 17th c. by Silvani it has extremely elegant architecture, frescoes and paintings that had almost been forgotten, including a "St Peter in Majesty" ascribed to the "Maestro della S. Cecilia", the master of St Cecilia.

Sant'Ambrogio   L6

Location
Piazza
Sant'Ambrogio

Bus
B

St Ambrose is one of the oldest churches in Florence. The building was remodelled at the end of the 13th c. and restored several times during the following centuries; the neo-Gothic façade was added in 1887. The single-naved **church** contains the tombs of famous Renaissance artists, including Cronaca (d. 1580), Mino da Fiesole (d. 1484) and Verrocchio (d. 1488). It is furnished with notable paintings and frescoes, among them the "Madonna del Latte" by Nardo di Cione, a triptych by Bicci di Lorenzo and Cosimo Rosselli's fresco of a procession.

A marble tabernacle by Mino da Fiesole (1481–83) in the Cappella del Miracolo (Chapel of the Miracle) depicts the event that gave the chapel its name. In 1230 a priest failed to dry the chalice properly; the next morning, it is said, the wine had turned to blood.

★★Santa Croce   K/L6

Location
Piazza Santa
Croce

Bus
23

Open 8am–
12.30pm,
3–6.30pm

"Santa Croce is a pantheon of the most worthy kind. The **church** has a serious and a gloomy solemnity, indeed it is a huge hall of the dead that no thinking person will enter without reverence" wrote Ferdinand Gregorovius, a German who travelled widely in Italy in the 19th c. This feeling is one the visitor can share on approaching the church and entering its broad interior.

The greatest church of the Franciscan order, Santa Croce was begun, probably by Arnolfo di Cambio, in 1294 on the site of an earlier building dating from 1228, and was consecrated in 1443 in the presence of Pope Eugene IV. The façade, articulated in multicoloured marble, and the campanile are 19th c.

The **interior** is basilican, of the type usual for a mendicant order, with a nave, two aisles, and transept at the end, and an open painted timber ceiling and octagonal columns supporting broad arches. It is the church layout best suited for the rousing sermons of the Franciscans who were much in demand in this traditional woolworkers' quarter of the city.

Its many tombs and cenotaphs (276 memorials in the floor) and important works of art make Santa Croce one of Italy's most impressive sacral buildings, and it is undoubtedly the largest Franciscan church, at 115.43 m (379 ft) long, 38.23 m (126 ft) wide at the nave and 73.74 m (242 ft) wide at the transept.

North aisle Opposite the first pillar can be seen the tomb of the famous scientist Galileo Galilei, by Giulio Foggini. On the right of the side door is the monument to Carlo Marsuppini, by Desiderio da Settignano, one of the finest of 15th c. monuments, and in the floor are memorials to Lorenzo Ghiberti, who made the bronze doors of the Baptistry, and his son Vittorio.

North transept It is worth looking at the monument on the left to the Florentine composer Luigi Cherubini (d. 1482). There is a row of five chapels along the east wall. The Cappella Bardi contains Donatello's "Christ Crucified", criticised as looking like a peasant by Brunelleschi, whose own, and, he hoped, finer "Crucifixion" was created for Santa

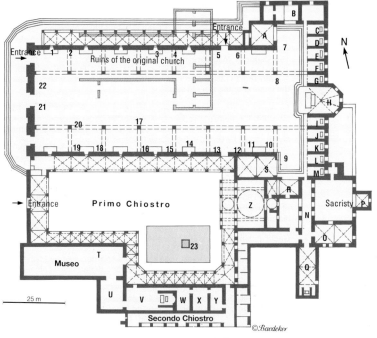

1 Frescos of Saints (15th c.)
2 Tomb of Galileo Galilei, by G. Foggini
3 Tomb of Lorenzo and Vittorio Ghiberti
4 "Pietà" by Bronzino
5 Monument to Vittorio Fossombroni, by Bartolini
6 Monument to Carlo Marsuppini, by D. da Settignano
7 Monument to Luigi Cherubini, by O. Fantacciotti
8 Monument to Leon Battista Alberti, by L. Bartolini
9 Tomb of Prince Corsini
10 Tomb of Ugo Foscolo
11 Tomb of Gioaccino Rossini, by G. Cassioli
12 Tomb of Leonardo Bruni
13 Donatello's recess with a relief "The Annunciation" (1435)
14 "Gesù nell'Orto" by Andrea del Minga
15 Tomb of Niccolò

Machiavelli, by Spinazzi (1435)
16 Tomb of Vittoria Alfieri, by Canova (1810)
17 Marble pulpit, by B. da Maiano (1472–6)
18 Cenotaph of Dante Alighieri, by S. Rica (1829)
19 Tomb of Michelangelo, by Vasari (1570)
20 "Madonna col Bambino", relief, by A. Rossellino (1478)
21 Monument to G. B. Niccolini, by P. Fedi (1883)
22 Monument to Gino Capponi, by A. Bortone (1884)
A Cappella Salviati
B Cappella Bardi with Crucifix by Donatello
C Cappella Bardi di Vernio
D Cappella Pulci e Beraldi
E Cappela Capponi
F Cappela Capponi
G Cappela Tosinghi/Spinelli
H Cappella Maggiore with high altar

I Cappella Bardi with frescoes by Giotto
J Cappella Peruzzi, with frescoes by Giotto
K Cappella Giugni
L Cappella Calderini
M Cappella Velluti
N Corridoio della Sagrestia
O Sales kiosk and exit to Scuola del Cuoio
P Cappella Rinuccini
Q Cappella del noviziato o dei Medici, by Michelozzo (1445)
R Cappella Baroncelli, with frescoes by T. Gaddi
S Cappella Castellani
T Room I of the Museum, former refectory
U Room II of the Museum, former small refectory
V Room III of the Museum, former Cappella Canigiani
W–Y Rooms 4–6 of the Museum, with important paintings
Z Cappella de'Pazzi, by Brunelleschi

Maria Novella (see entry). In the Cappella Bardi di Vernio the wall frescoes of scenes from the life of St Sylvester (1340) are by Maso di Banco, while the frescoes in the burial recesses are by Maso di Banco and Taddeo Gaddi. The Cappella Tosinghi-Spinelli has interesting stained-glass windows by the school of Giotto.

The **Cappella Maggiore** is covered with frescoes. Those in the vault show the "Risen Christ, the Evangelists and St Francis", and are by Agnolo Taddi (1380), who was also responsible for the wall frescoes of the Legend of the Holy Cross.

The east wall of the **south transept** also has five chapels. The Cappella Bardi is notable for Giotto's frescoes of the story of St Francis which are numbered among his most mature and major works (c. 1320). There are also remarkable frescoes by Giotto in the adjacent Cappella Peruzzi of scenes from the life of St John the Evangelist (right-hand wall) and of St John the Baptist (left-hand wall). These were particularly admired by the Renaissance painters and closely studied by Masaccio and Michelangelo. The last chapel on the left, the Cappella Velluti, has some damaged frescoes by a pupil of Cimabue ("Archangel Michael") and Giotto's "Coronation of the Virgin".
   In the south end of the transept is the Cappella Baroncelli. The frescoes of the Prophets at the entrance and of the Life of the Virgin on the walls are accounted the greatest work of Taddeo Gaddi, a pupil of Giotto. The adjoining Cappella Castellani has frescoes of the lives of the saints by Angelo Gaddi and his pupils, and a fine tabernacle by Mino da Fiesole.

The doorway (by Michelozzo) gives on to a corridor, also by Michelozzo, which leads to the **Sacristy**. This contains fine Renaissance cabinets and a "Crucifixion" by Taddeo Gaddi. Beyond the Sacristy is the 14th c. Cappella Rinuccini, covered with frescoes by Giovanni da Milano. At the end of the sacristy corridor is the Cappella del Noviziato (or dei Medici) which Michelozzo built for Cosimo the Elder in 1445. The altarpiece in glazed terracotta, "Madonna and Child" (1480), is by Andrea della Robbia.
   The Corridoio della Sagrestia gives on to the Scuola del Cuoio, the leather school, where hand-made leather bags and other leather goods can be purchased (see Practical Information, Shopping).

In the **south aisle** can be seen the monument of the composer Gioacchino Rossini (d. 1868), and the tomb of the Florentine politician Leonardo Bruni (d. 1444), Bernardo Rossellino's prototype of the Florentine Renaissance tomb. In a recess is the delicate relief of the Annunciation by Donatello (1435). About halfway along the aisle is the tomb of Niccolò Machiavelli (d. 1527), the great writer and politician, by Spinazzi (1787). Against the fifth pillar stands the octagonal marble pulpit by Benedetto da Maiano (1472–76) with scenes from the life of St Francis and allegorical figures. Nearer the door is Dante's monumental cenotaph (1829), Florence's tribute to the memory of the poet it had sent into exile and who died in Ravenna in 1321, followed by Vasari's monument to Michelangelo and, on the first pillar, Antonio Rossellino's relief "Madonna del latte" (1478).

Museo dell'Opera di Santa Croce

Open Mon., Tue.,
Thu.–Sun.
10am–12.30pm,
2.30–6.30pm
in winter 10am–
12.30pm, 3–5pm

On the right of the church is the entrance to the monastery buildings, where it is possible to visit two cloisters, the Pazzi Chapel and the Museo dell'Opera di Santa Croce, the museum of the building works of Santa Croce, housed in the former refectory and other monastery rooms.
   The first cloister, built in the late 14th/early 15th c., leads into the Cappella dei Pazzi.

The façade of Santa Croce: the most impressive of Italian sacred ▶
buildings

The **Pazzi Chapel** owes its fame to the architectural genius of Brunelleschi. He spent the period from 1430, or 1443, until his death in 1446 working on this classic early-Renaissance building for Andrea de'Pazzi. It was to serve as the burial chapel of the Pazzi family as well as the chapterhouse of Santa Croce's Franciscans.

The architrave of the porch is adorned with a frieze of small medallions bearing the heads of angels (Desiderio da Settignano) and the cupola has beautiful rosettes by Luca della Robbia who also carved the "Relief of St Andrew" (1445) above the wooden doors (by Giuliano da Sangallo; 1470–78).

The interior works as a harmonious whole, with clear articulation by pilasters, highlighted niches, curves and barrel vaulting, although the presence of the chancel means the chapel is not rectangular. The four terracotta medallions in the spandrels, showing the seated Evangelists, are by Luca della Robbia, as are the twelve tondi of the Apostles (white ceramic on a blue ground).

From the first cloister there is a way through to the two-storey **Chiostro Grande**, the Great Cloister, another beautiful work designed by Brunelleschi but built in about 1452 by Bernardo Rossellino.

The **museum** is in the refectory and adjoining rooms of the monastery. Numbered among its most important works of art are Taddeo Gaddi's huge "Last Supper" (120 sq.m (1291 sq. ft)), and his "Entombment" and frescoes of saints.

Other outstanding works include a "Crucifixion" by Cimabue, one of his later masterpieces, a bronze "St Louis" by Donatello (1423), Domenico Veneziano's fresco "St John the Baptist and St Francis", Maso di Banco's "Coronation of the Virgin", and Andrea della Robbia's terracotta group "Stigmata".

Santa Felicità   J6

Location
Piazza Santa
Felicità

Buses
B, C

The **church** of Santa Felicità was built over an early Christian graveyard, rebuilt in the 11th and 14th c. and completely remodelled in the 18th c. However, the porch and Vasari's "corridor", connecting the Palazzo degli Uffizi (see entry) and the Palazzo Pitti (see entry), were retained.

Interior Inside the church, above the entrance, is the gallery for the Grand Dukes who attended services here. To the right of the entrance in the Cappella Capponi can be found the church's most important works of art, two masterpieces by Pontormo (1526–28), "Entombment of Christ" and "Annunciation". The chapel was built by Brunelleschi for the Barbadori family.

The **chapterhouse** in the church cloister is also a fine work of architecture.

Santa Lucia dei Magnoli   J/K7

Location
Via dei Bardi

Buses
B, C

The little **church** of Santa Lucia dei Magnoli is nicknamed "fra le rovinate" (among the ruins) because of the danger to the surrounding houses from the hillside boulders. The majolica version of St Lucia over the portal dates from 1520.

Interior Inside can be seen a beautiful panel of "Santa Lucia", by Lorenzetti, painted on a gold ground.

Santa Margherita a Montici

The partly medieval **church** of Santa Margherita a Montici, about 4 km (2½ mi.) south of Florence in the lovely Tuscan hills (towards Pian dei Giulari), has several fine works of art: the panels "Madonna" and "Santa Margherita" by the Master of St Cecilia (early 14th c.), "Madonna della cintola" by Piero del Pollaiolo (1450), an altar in the style of Michelozzo, and finely worked 15th c. liturgical vestments.

Location
Via Pian dei
Giulari

Bus
38

Santa Margherita in Santa Maria de'Ricci   K6

In the centre of the city stands the **church** of Santa Margherita in Santa Maria de'Ricci or della Madonna de'Ricci which owes its name and its existence (1508) to the miraculous picture of the "Madonna de'Ricci" (*c.* 1300) on the high altar.
   Santa Margherita was the parish church of some well-known Florentine families.

Location
Via del Corso 6

Buses
14, 23

Santa Maria del Carmine   G/H6

This large **church** stands in the Piazza of the same name, nowadays used for parking, in a busy working-class quarter of Florence. The church, begun in 1268, was not completed until 1476, as can be seen from the fact that there are both Romanesque and Gothic elements along the sides.
   Remodelled in the 16th and 17th c., it was so badly damaged by fire in 1771 that it had to be rebuilt (by Ruggieri and Mannaioni, until 1782). The ground plan of the church is a Latin cross with a single nave flanked by various chapels. Besides the Brancacci Chapel (see below) Santa Maria del Carmine also owes its fame to the Baroque Cappella Corsini by Pierfrancesco Silvani (1675–83; left arm of transept), with a fresco of the Apotheosis of St Andrea Corsini by Luca Giordano (1682) in the dome. The chapel contains the tombs of Neri and Pietro Corsini with three high-reliefs in marble by Giovanni Battista Foggini.

Location
Piazza del
Carmine

Bus
B

★ Cappella Brancacci

The entrance to the Cappella Brancacci is on the right of the church. Passing through the cloister added to the church in the early 17th c. we come to the chapel, which Felice Brancacci, a wealthy Florentine merchant, had decorated with frescoes in 1428. Mainly the work of Masaccio and Masolino, they represent an important stage in the development of European painting. In his frescoes Masaccio took art beyond the richness of form and colour of the medieval Gothic and developed the ideas initiated by Giotto. Following the tradition of Masaccio and Masolino, Filippino Lippi painted the five lower frescoes.

Location
Piazza del
Carmine

Open Mon.,
Wed.–Sat.
10am–5pm; Sun.,
pub. hols. 1–5pm

Major Renaissance artists studied the works in the Brancacci Chapel on.account of their confidence in the use of perspective, the austere realism of the characters depicted, the subtle characterisation of the faces, the freedom and intensity of expression. Sadly disfigured by previous attempts at restoration, the frescoes have recently been restored to their original colours.

The themes they represent, top row, from left to right, are: Adam and Eve being driven out of Eden, the Tribute Money (both by Masaccio), St Peter Preaching, Peter Baptising the Neophytes, Peter and John healing the Lame and raising Tabitha, the Temptation of Adam and Eve. Below, Peter visited by Paul in Prison, Peter raising the Son of Theophilus, Peter Preaching, Peter (with John) healing the Sick, Peter and John distributing Alms, Crucifixion of Peter, Peter and Paul before the Proconsul, Release of Peter from Prison.

Michelangelo is said to have become so enraged during an argument in front of these pictures that his nose was broken in the ensuing fracas.

"The Expulsion of Adam and Eve from Eden", a masterpiece by Masaccio

★Santa Maria Maddalena dei Pazzi K5

Location
Borgo Pinti 58

Buses
6, 31, 32

Maria Maddalena, a member of the famous Florentine Pazzi family, was canonised in 1669. The 13th c. complex of **church** and Benedictine convent, already remodelled two centuries earlier by Giuliano da Sangallo (1480–92), was enlarged in her honour, which is why the forecourt of the church is in the harmonious style of the second half of the 15th c. while other parts of the church and the convent have Baroque elements. The chapels contain precious works by such 15th and 16th c. Tuscan artists as Portelli and Giordano. The refectory is today part of a barracks for the Carabinieri, and Sangallo's cloisters belong to the Liceo Michelangelo.

Crocifissione del Perugino

Open 9am–noon,
5–7pm

In the chapterhouse of the adjoining convent are some of Perugino's finest frescoes (Crocifissione del Perugino), dating from between 1493 and 1496, his most creative period: Christ on the Cross and Mary Magdalene, St Bernard and Mary, St John and St Benedict, Christ on the Cross helping St Bernard. The landscape in the background is clearly Perugino's native Umbria (Perugia).

Santa Maria Maggiore   J5

Not far from the Baptistry (see Battistero), in Via de'Cerretani, is one of Florence's oldest churches, which was certainly built before the 11th c. and was rebuilt in the second half of the 13th c. (1912–13 carefully restored). The old bell-tower is still indicative of the lower level of the Romanesque **church**; high up in the wall can be seen "Bertha", a late-Romanesque bust of a woman. Above the church portal is the "Madonna and Child" of the 14th c. Pisan school (copy).

Location
Via de'Cerretani

Buses
1, 6, 7, 11, 13, 17, 33

The outstanding features of the aisled Gothic **interior** with its square pillars and fine paintings and statues are the "Madonna in Majesty with Child" (also known as "Madonna del Carmelo"), attributed to Coppo di Marcovaldo (1261), and a coloured gilded wooden relief. The original condition of the panel was considerably distorted by later overpainting, but a thorough restoration currently under way should remove all the later additions and also provide new information about painting techniques in the 13th c. The relief shows the artist's skill not only as a sculptor but also as a painter (possibly also Coppo di Marcovaldo).

★★Santa Maria Novella   H5

One of Florence's most important churches, the Dominican **church** of Santa Maria Novella was built in 1246 on the site of a 10th c. oratory (Santa Maria delle Vigne) and was basically completed around 1360, although it was slightly altered by various architects in the 14th/15th c.

Location
Piazza di Santa
Maria Novella

Closed for
restoration

Exterior Like the Franciscan church of Santa Croce (see entry), the approach to the main building is across a large square (see Piazza di

1 "Birth of Christ (Botticelli)
2 Marble pulpit
3 "Trinity" (Masaccio)
4 "Resurrection" (Vasari)
5 "Santa Caterina di Sienna" (Poccetti)
6 Sacristy
7 "San Giacinto" (Alessandro Allori)
8 Cappella Strozzi
9 Cappella Gaddi
10 Cappella Gondi
11 Main choir chapel
12 Cappella di Fillipo Strozzi
13 Cappella Bardi
14 Cappella Rucellai
15 Tomb of Joseph of Constantinople
16 Cappella della Pura
17 Tomb of Beata Villana
18 "Martyrdom of St Laurence" (Macchietti)
19 Exit to Museo di Santa Maria Novelle
20 Refectory
21 Cappellone degli Spagnoli
22 Chiostrino dei Morti (funerary chapel of the Strozzi family)

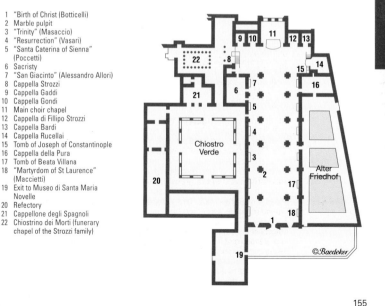

155

Santa Maria Novella). Here too the façade is articulated by coloured marble. It was added between 1456 and 1470 by Leon Battista Alberti commissioned by Giovanni Rucellai, whose family crest, the billowing sails, form the architrave halfway up. The architect gave it its distinctive shape by combining Romanesque-Gothic and Renaissance styles (portal, pillars on either side, design of the upper section with volutes).

There is an old cemetery to the right of the church.

The church **interior** displays a harmonious balance between soaring Gothic forms and the broad unified nave which appears even longer than it is (99.2 m (326 ft)) because the bays decrease in width from 15 m (50 ft) down to 11.4 m (38 ft) as they approach the altar. The width overall is 28.4 m (94 ft), and 61.4 m (202 ft) in the transept.

Internal façade In the lunette above the portal is a fresco of the "Nativity" (possibly an early Boticelli); the rose-window, the oldest in Florence, has the "Coronation of the Virgin".

Left aisle Against the second pillar is a marble pulpit designed by Brunelleschi in 1443 but the work of Buggiano. The fresco of the Trinity on the third altar is by Masaccio (1427) and considered one of his finest works on account of its intensity of expression and perfect perspective.

A door leads into the **sacristy** where there is a marble lavabo by Giovanni della Robbia, and, above the door, a "Crucifixion" by Giotto, an early work from about 1290.

Left ar of the transept Nardo di Cione painted the frescoes (themes from Dante's Divine Comedy, 1357) in the raised Cappella Strozzi, which also contains Andrea Orcagna's altarpiece "Redeemer and Saints".

A striking feature of the Cappella Gaddi is Bronzino's painting above the altar of "Christ raising the Daughter of Jairus". In the adjacent Cappella Gondi is the celebrated wooden crucifix by Brunelleschi (1410–25), the first representation of Christ without a loincloth, and the artist's equivalent of Donatello's realistic, peasant-like figure in Santa Croce (see entry).

The **apse** was completely covered in frescoes by Domenico Ghirlandaio and his assistants between 1486 and 1490 and these were commissioned by Giovanni Tornabuoni, They show scenes from the life of John the Baptist and the Virgin. Thanks to restoration at the end of the 1980s the last great cycle of 15th c. frescoes can now be seen in their soft luminous colours. The bronze crucifix is by Giambologna.

Right arm of the transept This also has two chapels on the left-hand side. The Cappella di Filippo Strozzi is decorated with frescoes by Filippino Lippi (1497–1502). The tomb of Filippo Strozzi is behind the altar, and is the work of Benedetto da Maiano (1491–93). The adjoining Cappella dei Bardi contains Vasari's "Rosary Madonna" (1570).

At the end of the transept is the Cappella Rucellai with a bronze memorial marking the grave of the Dominican-General Dati by Lorenzo Ghiberti (1423) and a marble statue of "Madonna and Child" by Nini Pisano. Nearby can be seen the tomb of Joseph, Patriarch of Constantinople, who died here in 1440 after the Council of Florence.

Right aisle Here a door leads into the Cappella della Pura with the miraculous picture of "Madonna and Child and St Catherine". Concerning this picture is a legend that in 1472 the Virgin, speaking from the picture, told two dirty children that they ought to have a wash, something much appreciated by Florentine mothers. The chapel leads into the old cemetery. Nearer the entrance are the tomb of the Beata Villana by Rossellino

(1451) and the side altar with Macchietti's "Martyrdom of St Laurence" (1573).

Museo di Santa Maria Novella

A visit to Santa Maria Novella should include the cloisters and the chapels of the former convent of Santa Maria Novella, now the Museo di Santa Maria Novella. The entrance is on the left of the church façade. Open Mon.–Thu., Sat. 9am–2pm; Sun., public holidays 8am–1pm.

The name "**Green Cloister**" (Chiostro Verde) refers to the green tones of frescoes by Paolo Uccello of scenes from the Old Testament, beginning with the creation of the animals and the Fall of Man (c. 1430); the compelling representation of the Flood was carried out twenty years later.

Refectory The liturgical vessels, the vestments embroidered with silver thread, and the golden reliquaries date from the 14th and 17th c.

The "**Spanish Chapel**" – its frescoes are among 14th c. Italy's greatest works of art – was built after 1340 by Jacopo Talenti as the chapterhouse of the Dominican monastery and assigned in 1540 by Eleonora of Toledo, wife of Cosimo I, to her Spanish retainers (hence the name) as a place of worship. Andrea da Firenze (Bonaiuti) was given the theme for his paintings – "the Dominican Order and the new open path to Salvation" – by Prior Jacopo Passavanti, and combined scenes from the scriptures, legends of saints and allegories of the medieval Humanities.

The tour ends with a visit to the "**Small Cloister of the Dead**" (Chiostrino de Morti) with the Strozzi funerary chapel (Cappella funeraria degli Strozzi).

Chiostrino de Morti

★ Santa Trinità   J6

The fondness of the Florentines for the **church** of Santa Trinità – on the square of the same name near the Arno – is due mainly to its great age. There was a church here as early as the 11th c., and this was rebuilt in the 13th c. (probably by Niccolò Pisano) as Florence's first Gothic church. It was rebuilt yet again in the late 14th c., this time by Neri di Fioravante. The façade, designed by Buontalenti, is from the late 16th c.

  The interior has the look of 14th c. Florentine Gothic, and has a nave, lined with side-chapels, and two aisles with a transept.

  A walk round the church will reveal many notable works of art (some of the chapels can be lit if money is put into the boxes provided for the purpose).

Location
Piazza Santa
Trinità

Buses
6, 11, 36, 37

Open 7.30am–
noon, 4–6pm

Left aisle In the third chapel there is an "Annunciation" on a gold ground by Neri di Bicci and the tomb of Giuliano Davanzati (d. 1444), an early Christian sarcophagus with high reliefs, and the fifth chapel holds the wooden Mary Magdelene by Desiderio da Settignano and Benedetto da Maiano (1464/1465).

In the **left arm of the transept** is the marble tomb of Bishop Benozzi Federighi (1455–56), one of Luca della Robbia's finest works.

The Cappella Sassetti, in the **right arm of the transept**, has celebrated frescoes by Domenico Ghirlandaio (1483–86) of the life of St Francis, including the famous "Confirmation of the Rule of the Order", into which the artist incorporated contemporary personalities and buildings such as Lorenzo the Magnificent, Ghirlandaio himself, hand on hip, and the Piazza della Signoria and Piazza della Trinità. The altarpiece "Adoration of the Shepherds" is also by Ghirlandaio (1485).

In the **sacristy** can be seen the tomb of Onofrio Strozzi by Piero di Niccolò Lamberti (1421).

Right aisle There is a cycle of frescoes by Lorenzo Monaco in the Cappella Salimbeni and a 14th c. panel of the Crucifixion in the chapel nearest the entrance.

★Santi Apostoli   J6

Location
Borgo Santi
Apostoli

Buses
6, 11, 36, 37

Open Mon.–Sat.
3.30–6.30pm, Sun.
9.30am–12.30pm

According to a Latin inscription on the left of the façade the Church of the Holy Apostles was founded by Charlemagne and dedicated by Archbishop Turpinus. All that is known for certain is that the **church** was in existence at the end of the 11th c. and was rebuilt in the 15th and 16th c. (restored between 1930 and 1938). Benedetto da Rovezzano added a fine portal to the Romanesque façade in the early 16th c.

The columns of green marble from Prato with composite capitals (the first two from the nearby Roman baths) which separate the aisles from the nave are a striking feature of the interior. The church and its works of art were badly damaged in the 1966 floods.

Particularly worth seeing are, in the left aisle, a large terracotta tabernacle by Giovanni della Robbia (presbytery) and the tomb of Oddo Altaviti by Benedetto da Rovezzano (1507); and, in the right aisle, a panel of the Immaculate Conception by Vasari (1541, third chapel).

★★Santissima Annunziata   K5

Location
Piazza della SS
Annunziata

Buses
6, 31, 32

Open 7am–
12.30pm,
4–6.30pm; Sun.
4–6.30pm

Whereas the religious centre of Florence is the Cathedral (see Duomo Santa Maria del Fiore), and the heart of its politics is the Palazzo Vecchio (see entry) and the Palazzo della Signoria, the intellectual life of the city is adjudged, quite rightly, to focus on the **church** of Santissima Annunziata (Church of the Annunciation) and its square, the Piazza della Santissima Annunziata (see entry).

The church of the Annunziata, founded about 1250 as an oratory for the Servite Order and completely rebuilt between 1444 and 1481 by Michelozzo, is an architectural masterpiece, not least because of the unusual ground plan for the church and its cloisters (nave with side chapels, fronted by a large round choir chapel, plus additions); it also contains many superb works of art.

Exterior The entrance is under a seven-arched portico (1559–61) supported by columns with elegant Corinthian capitals. Of the three doors, the one on the left leads into the Chiostro dei Morti (cloister of the dead), via the Sagrestia della Madonna. The right-hand door leads into the Cappella Pucci or di San Sebastiano, and the door in the middle to the Chiostrino dei Voti (little cloister of the votive offerings), so-called because of the votive offerings hung here by the faithful, and built by Manetti (1447) to designs by Michelozzo.

The frescoes in the **Chiostrino dei Voti** are famous. Beginning on the left, they include masterpieces by Andrea del Sarto (scenes from the life of St Filippo Benizzi"), Cosimo Rosselli ("Summoning and Robing of St Filippo Benizzi), Alesso Baldovinetto ("Nativity", 1460–62), another two by Andrea del Sarto ("Coming of the Magi" and, one of the artist's best works, "Birth of the Virgin", 1514) and Franciabigi's "Marriage of the Virgin", 1513 – the artist destroyed the Virgin's head because the monks

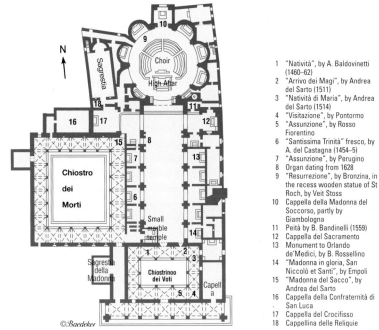

1 "Natività", by A. Baldovinetti (1460–62)
2 "Arrivo dei Magi", by Andrea del Sarto (1511)
3 "Natività di Maria", by Andrea del Sarto (1514)
4 "Visitazione", by Pontormo
5 "Assunzione", by Rosso Fiorentino
6 "Santissima Trinità" fresco, by A. del Castagna (1454–5)
7 "Assunzione", by Perugino
8 Organ dating from 1628
9 "Resurrezione", by Bronzina, in the recess wooden statue of St Roch, by Veit Stoss
10 Cappella della Madonna del Soccorso, partly by Giambologna
11 Peità by B. Bandinelli (1559)
12 Cappella del Sacramento
13 Monument to Orlando de'Medici, by B. Rossellino
14 "Madonna in gloria, San Niccolò et Santi", by Empoli
15 "Madonna del Sacco", by Andrea del Sarto
16 Cappella della Confraternità di San Luca
17 Cappella del Crocifisso
18 Cappellina delle Reliquie

looked at the picture before it was finished, and no-one was prepared to repair the damage. Finally, there are also great works by Pontormo ("Visitation of Mary", 1516) and Rosso Fiorentino ("Assumption of the Virgin", 1517).

The **interior** of the church itself consists of a nave lined by chapels, with the choir in the form of a rotunda. The walls are clad with marble dating from the complete refurbishment in the 17th and 18th c.

Close to the entrance, on the left, is a small marble temple, commissioned from Michelozzo by Piero de'Medici for the miraculous picture of the Annunciation, copies of which can be found throughout Italy. It is said that in the 13th c. the monk who was painting this fell asleep in a state of despair at his inability to create a truly beautiful Madonna, and an angel completed the Virgin's face as he slept. Florentine newly-weds still make their way here today for the bride to leave her bouquet with the Madonna.

Side-chapels On the left side of the nave is the Cappella Feroni containing a fresco by Andrea del Castagno, "Redeemer and St Julian" (1455).

There is another fresco by Castagno in the second chapel, his "Trinity", and one of his last highly realistic works. The fourth chapel has a panel by Perugino, "Ascension of Christ", which is worth seeing.

The **rotunda**, which is divided into nine chapels, was begun by Michelangelo (1444) and completed in a different style by Leon Battista Alberti. The fourth chapel from the left contains a painting by Angelo Bronzino, "Resurrection" (1550). The Cappella della Madonna del

The Church of Santissima Annunziata, in the Piazza of the same name

Soccorso (Madonna of Succour) was designed by Giambologna between 1594 and 1598 as his own tomb and is richly adorned with frescoes, statuary and reliefs.

In the **dome** is a fresco of the Coronation of the Virgin by Volterrano (1681–83).

Right arm of the transept Just inside the first chapel is a lovely "Pietà" by Baccio Bandinelli who is buried here with his wife.

★★Santo Spirito   H6

Location
Piazza Santo
Spirito

Bus
B

Open Thu.–Tue.
8.30am–noon,
4–5.30pm

Several wealthy Florentine families joined forces in the early years of the 15th c. to build a new **church** on the site of one that had been burned down. They commissioned Brunelleschi, the city's famous architect, to design it. At the time of his death (1446) building work had progressed as far as the vaulting, but then it practically came to a standstill under various architects (bell-tower: Baccio d'Agnolo, 1503–17) and was never completed wholly in accordance with the original plans. This is why the austere exterior of the building gives no hint of the fact that Santo Spirito inside is one of the purest Renaissance churches.

The façade of the church, which was consecrated in 1481, dates from the 18th c. and is totally without decoration, just bare plaster. Its principal feature is its outline and the large round window in the centre. There are three different-sized doors in the façade, one each for the nave and the two aisles.

The **interior** is on the plan of a Latin cross 97 m (318 ft) long, 32 m (108 ft) wide, 58 m (190 ft) in the transept, with a colonnaded central nave and

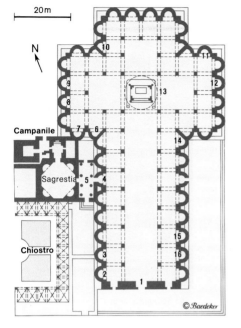

├─ 20m ─┤

N

Campanile

Sagrestia 5 4

Chiostro

© Baedeker

Santo Spirito

1 Window, "Discesa dello Spirito Santo", after Perugino
2 "Resurrezione", by di Jacopo
3 "Christo Risorto", by Landini, copy after Michelangelo
4 Access to the sacristy
5 Cronaca's vestibule, designed by G.da Sangallo
6 "Andata al Calvario", by M. Ghirlandaio
7 "Madonna col Bambino in trono e Santi", by dei Cari
8 "La Santissima Trinità adorata dalle Sante Caterina e Maddalena", by Granacci
9 Cappella Corbinelli, architecture and sculptures by Sansovino
10 "Presepio", by the school of Ghirlandaio
11 "Sposalizio della Vergine", by Sagrestani, and marble tomb of Neri di Gino Capponi
12 "Madonna col Bambino e San Giovannino", by F. Lippi
13 High altar by Caccini
14 "Raffaele e Tobiolo", marble panel, by Baratta (c. 1690)
15 San Nicola da Tolentino, wooden statue, by N. Unghero
16 Copy of Michelangelo's Pietà in Rome, by di Baccio Bigio (1549)

side aisles and forty semicircular side-chapels backing on to straight walls. Thanks to its many works of art, tombs and monuments, Santo Spirito resembles a very impressive museum.

The **side altars** are resplendent with paintings and statuary, reliefs and liturgical objects. The principal features of interest in a clockwise direction, starting at the entrance, are highlighted below.

The rose-window in the **internal façade** was designed by Perugino ("Descent of the Holy Ghost").

In the left aisle is the entrance to a beautiful vestibule built by Cronaca (1492–94) with a door leading into the **sacristy**, an octagonal chamber designed by Giuliano da Sangallo (1495/1496) and a masterpiece of European architecture.

Cloisters Another door in the vestibule leads into the first cloister, which is by Giulio and Alfonso Parigi (c. 1600). The second cloister, built by Ammanati between 1564 and 1569, is usually not open to the public because it is used for administrative purposes.

In the **crossing** is Caccini's early Baroque baldachin altar, richly ornamented with pietra dura.

Left arm of the transept In the first chapel Michele Ghirlandaio's "Ascent of Calvary" and the window are worth seeing. The adjoining chapel has Raffaele di Carli's panel "Madonna in Majesty" (1505). In the next but one chapel along there is another panel, "Trinity worshipped by St

Catherine and St Mary Magdalene", which is ascribed to Francesco Granacci.

Next comes the Cappella Corbinelli (sacramental chapel), exquisitely designed by Andrea Sansovino (1492), who was also responsible for the sculpture.

The **right arm of the transept** holds the altarpiece that is the most important work in the church, the "Madonna and Child with Saints and Donors" by Filippino Lippi (1490).

In the **apse**, on the left-hand side, can be seen an "Annunciation" (15th c. Florentine school) and a Nativity by the school of Ghirlandaio, while on the right there is a polyptych by Maso di Banco (c. 1340).

The Baroque altar by Caccini in Santo Spirito

Cenacolo di Santo Spirito

Open Tue.–Sat. 9am–2pm; Sun., pub. hols. 8am–1pm

The entrance to the Cenacolo di Santo Spirito is to the left of the church. This refectory is all that remains of the old Augustinian monastery, and it contains the great fresco of the Last Supper (c. 1360). This was attributed to Andrea Orcagna by Ghiberti, a view confirmed after considerable research and restoration. Although badly damaged, it is one of the sublimest 14th c. works of art in Florence.

The refectory also contains the fine sculpture of the Salvatore Romano Foundation.

★Santo Stefano al Ponte   J6

Location
Piazetta Santo Stefano

Bus 23

In course of restoration

In a small traffic-free square, mentioned in documents as early as 1116, stands the **church** of Santo Stefano al Ponte (or Santi Stefano e Cecilia), displaying architectural features from a number of different centuries (13th c. façade, 16th c. altars, 17th c. works in the nave).

The bronze relief "The Stoning of St Stephen" is by Ferdinando Tocca (1656). Buontalenti's impressive marble stairs (1574) to the presbytery were formerly in the church of Santa Trinità (see entry).

Settignano

Excursion
8 km (5 mi.) E

The little town of Settignano is a delightful destination for a trip a few miles out of Florence to the east. The 15th c. parish church of the "Assunta" in the town centre has undergone many renovations.

In the Tuscan hills around Settignano nestle many magnificent villas, with grand gardens. These include the I Tatti Villa, at Ponte a Ménsola, which became Harvard University's Centre for the History of the Renaissance after the death of American art critic Bernard Berenson (1865–1959), whose "Collezione Berenson" contains important works of art.

Villa "I Tatti"

Not far from Settignano is the famous Villa Gamberaia (72 Via del Rossellino), one of the finest of the 16th c. villas and gardens. It was badly damaged in the Second World War but then restored to its former glory. Today it stands in what still looks like a typical Renaissance garden, with geometrically trimmed box hedges, a classically quartered parterre garden and a fountain in the middle, traversed by a great walk from one end to the other (viewing by appointment, tel. 0 55603251).

Villa Gamberaia

Tempio Israelitico   L5

The monumental Tempio Israelitico is one of the supreme examples of 19th c. European **synagogue** building. Financed by an endowment, the centrally-planned, domed building was constructed in 1874–82 by three architects on the model of the Hagia Sophia in Istanbul. The Moorish style is preserved in some elements of the architecture and interior furnishings. Other particularly noteworthy features are the murals and the stained glass windows.

Location
Via Luigi Carlo
Farini 6

Buses
6, 31, 32

Adjoining is the **Museo Ebraico** ("Jewish Museum"; open Thu.–Sun. 11am–1pm and 2–5pm) where documents relating to the history of the Florentine Jews, and ritual accessories from various different centuries can be seen.

The portico leads to the church of **Santa Maria degli Innocenti** and beyond that, through a door connecting it with the church, to a cloister designed by Brunelleschi. In the lunette is a glazed terracotta "Annunciation" by Andrea della Robbia.

Besides the Galleria dello Spedale degli Innocenti's own works of art there is also a collection of **frescoes** on the first floor that have been brought here from their original sites. They are by such Florentine artists as Poccetti, Bicci di Lorenzo, Lorenzo Monaco, Allori, Rosselli, Ghirlandaio, Fra Bartolomeo, Perugino and della Robbia.

★Galleria dello Spedale degli Innocenti

The Galleria dello Spedale degli Innocenti has pictures, sculpture, miniatures and furniture from the 14th to 18th c. Outstanding exhibits include works by Giovanni del Biondo, Rossellino, Benedetto da Maiano and, in particular, Domenico Ghirlandaio and Andrea del Sarto, as well as Luca della Robbia's terracotta Madonna. Open Mon., Tue., Thu.–Sat. 8.30am–2pm; Sun., pub. hols. 8.30am–1pm.

Via dei Tornabuoni   J6

The Via dei Tornabuoni is one of the most elegant (on account of its shops), most beautiful (due to 19th c. planning) and most interesting (because of the 15th to 19th c. palazzi) streets in Florence. It is like a history book come to life, where the story of the city is told in magnificent buildings. In the shopping streets can be found well-known names in the

Location
between Ponte
Santa Trinità and
Piazza Antinori

fashion world – Gucci, Versace and Ferragamo, the jewellers Buccellati and the famous Café Giacosa.

Also of interest are the palazzi of Larderei-Giacomini (early 16th c.) and Corsi-Tornabuoni (1875, by Michelozzo where the Palazzo Tornabuoni once stood), the Logetta dei Tornaquinci (early 16th c.) and the 17th c. Palazzo Strozzi (see entry).

Villa Romana   G8

Location
Via Senese 68

Buses
11, 36

The Villa Romana stands on the south side of the Arno, outside the medieval town walls, and was acquired in 1905 by Max Klinger with the aid of the German Artists' Federation to serve as artists' studios and living quarters, as well as a venue for temporary exhibitions.

Ville Medicee

Some members of the many branches of the Medici family built themselves, as their summer homes, imposing villas in large grounds in the beautiful Tuscan hills close to the city. Here, in the buildings and gardens, the architects could give free rein to their talents and their imagination, albeit initially within the constraints of the Renaissance. Artists, painters and sculptors were presented with plenty of opportunities to show the lighter side of their art. Some of the finest of these villas, which can be visited, are described below.

Villa la Petraia: formerly the summer residence of the kings of Italy

The lack of signing makes it difficult to find the Villa la Petraia which is on the right, above the road between Florence and Sesto. Ferdinando de'Medici acquired the estate in 1575 and had it remodelled by Buontalenti, but kept the old tower. In the 19th c. the villa was a summer residence for the Kings of Italy, and can be visited since it is still in state ownership. It has lovely grounds which provide a good view of Florence.

★Villa la Petraia

The park is open Tuesday to Sunday 9am to 7.30pm (in winter 4.30pm, and in spring and autumn 5.30 and 6.30pm); the villa closes half an hour earlier.

The Villa Medicea di Castello, its grounds dating back to the 16th c., is just a few hundred yards west of the Villa la Petraia. The villa contains the Accademia della Crusca and is therefore not open to the public but the grounds are, with their magnificent fountains, grottos and statuary. The figures in the central fountain are of Hercules locked in combat with the giant Antaus (Tribolo).

Villa di Castello

The gardens are open Tuesday to Sunday 9am to 7.30pm (4.30pm in winter, 5.30pm and 6.30pm in spring and autumn).

About 18 km (12 mi.) north-west of Florence on the main road to Pistoia, in the village of Poggio a Caiano, is what is generally considered to be the Medici's finest and most splendid summer residence. It was built by Giuliano da Sangallo for Lorenzo the Magnificent, and much altered and extended by the Medici in later years. Their artistic tastes are reflected in such details as the entrance loggia, the terracotta reliefs in the entrance hall, the large drawing room with its frescoes by Andrea del Sarto, Pontormo, Franciabigio and Allori ("Cicero's Return from Exile", "Caesar accepting Tribute from Egypt", "Vertunno and Pomona"). There are also furnishings, etc. left by King Victor Emmanuel II, who lived here with his morganatic wife the Contessa di Mirafiori.

★Villa di Poggio a Caiano

Although the villa alone merits a visit, it is also worth taking a pleasant stroll through the grounds with their ancient trees.

The park is open April to October, Monday to Saturday 9am to 6.30pm; Sunday 9am–1.30pm. November to March, Monday to Saturday 9am to 4.30pm; Sunday 9am–1.30pm; the villa is open daily 9am to 1.30pm, Sunday 9am to 12.30pm. Closed 2nd and 3rd Monday of each month.

**Practical
Information
from A–Z**

Practical Information from A–Z

Accommodation

See Hotels, Camping, Youth Hostels

Advance bookings

Whenever possible it is a good idea to obtain tickets for cultural events from the hotel porter who will usually be found to have some – albeit a bit more expensive – even when other sources are completely sold out. Theatre tickets are best purchased from the advanced booking office of the theatre in question or from one of the following agencies:
Globus Viaggi, Piazza Santa Trinità 2r, tel. (055) 214992, Fax (055) 2381258

Festival tickets

Festival ticket applications should be made as early as possible to:
Maggio Musicale, Via Solferino 15, I-50123 Firenze, tel. (055) 21158, Fax (055) 2779410 (open Tue.–Sat. 9am–1pm)
Estate Fiesolana Fond, Toscana Spettacola, Via Alamanni 41, I-50123 Firenze, tel. (055) 219851, Fax 219853

Air Travel

Airport

Florence airport, Amerigo Vespucci, is at Peretola, 5 km (3 mi.) north-west of the city centre. It is a scheduled destination for Alitalia and other major airlines. A bus shuttle service to the airport runs every fifteen minutes from the main station.

Airlines

Alitalia
Lungarno Acciaiuoli 10/12r; tel. (055) 27881, Fax (055) 2788400

British Airways
Via della Vigna Nuova 36/38r; tel. 218655

TWA
Piazza S. Trinità 2r; tel. 284691

Antiques

See Shopping

Banks

See Currency

◀ *Reflections in the water: the Ponte Vecchio by night*

Business Hours

See Opening Times

Cafés

Cafés rich in tradition line the Piazza della Repubblica, making it in summer one great open-air café where visitors can sit under awnings or large sunshades in areas fenced off by tubs of flowers. Most of the cafés are open late into the night and thus continue as favourite after-dinner meeting places or somewhere to go after a concert or show.

Piazza della Repubblica

Cibreo, Via Verrocchio 5, tel. (055) 2345853 (opposite the famous restaurant of the same name; comfortable café offering excellent fare)
Giacosa (closed Mon.), Via Tornabuoni 83, tel. (055) 296226 (substantially built, elegant café, meeting place for prosperous Florentines; the cappucchino is first class)
Gilli (closed Tue.), Piazza della Repubblica 39r, tel. (055) 2396310 (spacious, elegant café founded in 1733 and still endowed with turn of the century charm; the pastries and marrons glacés can be highly recommended)
Giubbe Rosse (closed Thu.), Piazza della Repubblica 13r, tel. (055) 212280 (also boasts a long history; at the turn of the century was the haunt of artists and writers)
Kaffeehaus, in the Giardino di Boboli (on the "Kaffeehaus terrace", given its German name by the Italians; a haven of peace with an incomparable view over Florence)

The Café Rivoire in the Piazza della Signora

Florentine Festivals

While the Florentines are perhaps not widely known for their gaiety – they did after all choose the ascetic desert preacher John the Baptist to be patron saint of their city – in their own way they know how to celebrate.

The year's season of popular festivals gets under way on Easter Sunday at twelve noon with **Lo Scoppio del Carro**, an intriguing pyrotechnic ritual held on the square between the Cathedral and the Baptistery, emphatically proclaiming the resurrection of Christ amidst a cacophony of noise. Following Easter mass in the Cathedral, a rocket (known as "la colombina", the dove) is sent fizzing along a rope stretching from above the high altar into the square, igniting the hearse-like carro ("cart") which, festooned with firecrackers, has earlier crossed the Arno, pulled by two white oxen, to its position in front of the Duomo. The more violent the explosion and the greater the amount of smoke, the more can farmers and tradespeople look forward to a prosperous year.

From about May onwards the sun shines down onto squares and gardens and people's spirits rise too. On Ascension Day many Florentines gather on the grass in the Parco delle Cascine for a traditional picnic snack, enjoying all manner of sweatmeats such as nougat, strings of hazelnuts and candied fruit to the accompaniment of the chirping of the crickets which give the festival its name – **Festa del Grillo** ("cricket"). Originally people caught the crickets for themselves but today they are sold in pretty little cages. After the fun is over the custom is to let the insects fly free again.

June 24th, Saint John the Baptist's Day, witnesses far noisier and more energetic celebrations in honour of the city's patron saint. Young and old gather on the Piazza Santa Croce to cheer on their teams in the **Calcio in Costume**, a traditional ball game played in period costume, dating back to 1530 when the Florentines used it as a way of demonstrating to those beseiging them their resilience and strength. A wonderfully colourful procession with about 500 participants drawn from all districts of the city makes its way from Santa Maria Novella to the Piazza Santa Croce. The game, involving four teams identified by the distinctive colours of their districts, is played according to abstruse rules more akin to those of rugby football, with hands and

The historic "Calcio in Costume"

elbows much in evidence. The festival ends with the splendid St John's firework display on the Piazzale Michelangelo.

At the **Festa delle Rificolone** (Nativity of the Virgin) on the eve of September 8th, the Piazza SS Annunziata is transformed into a colourful sea of light by children carrying lanterns.

Paszkowski (closed Mon.), Piazza della Repubblica 6, tel. (055) 210236
(another of Florence's famous old cafés; open-air music in summer)
Rivoire (closed Mon.), Piazza della Signoria 5r, tel. (055) 214412 (picturesque old café by the Palazzo Vecchio, famous for its chocolate; no
better place to watch the hustle and bustle of the always busy Piazza
della Signoria)

Cavini, Piazza delle Cure 22r (long established; immense variety of ice-
creams)
Veneta, Piazza Beccaria 7 (homemade ice-creams)
Vivoli, Via Isola delle Stinche 7r (Florence's best-known ice-cream
parlour; excellent ices)

Ice-cream
parlours

Calendar of Events

Florence Trade Fair (leather goods and clothes)

January

Pitti Mode Fair (fashion fair): outer clothing and underwear; materials
and gifts

January/February

Aurea Trade (goldsmiths' fair)

February

Furniture Fair
March 25th (the Annunciation): festival in the Piazza della SS Annunziata

March

Easter Sunday: Scoppio del Carro (see Baedeker Special p. 170)

March/April

International Craft Fair (until May)

April

Ascension Day: Festa del Grillo (see Baedeker Special p. 170)

May

Maggio Musicale Fiorentino: international music festival, particularly in
the Teatro Comunale and Teatro della Pergola also in the open air in
Piazza della Signoria and Boboli Gardens

May/June

June 24th: Festival of St John the Baptist (patron saint of Florence) with
fireworks on the Piazzale Michelangelo.
   Calcio Storico Fiorentino (see Baedeker Special p. 170)

June

Estate Musicale Fiesolana (summer in Fiesole): music and cultural festival, often with open-air performances in venues such as Fiesole's Teatro
Romano

July/August

August 10th: concert and street festival in the Piazza San Lorenzo
Pitti Bimbo (children's fashion fair)
International leather goods fair

August

Festa dell'Unità in the Cascine Park
Festa dell'Avanti in the Piazza della Libertà
Festa del'Amicizia in the Fortezza da Basso
Pitt-Uomo (men's fashion fair)
Pitti-Filati (knitwear and embroidery fair)
Casual (leisurewear fashion show)
September 7th: Festa delle rificolone (see Baedeker Special p. 170)
Oltrarno di Firenze (September Festival)
September 28th: (mornings) Fiera degli Uccelli (birdmarket in the Allee
von der Porta Romana at Poggio Reale)

September

Antiques Fair (every two years)
Pitti Donna (women's fashion fair)

October

November   Start of the opera, theatre and concert season (to end April)
            Italian spectacles fair

December   Christmas cribs in many places

Camping

Italian campsites, like hotels, are classified by stars. These are in ascending order, from one to five, and indicate the level of charges, amenities and services.

Florence   ★★Camping Michelangelo
            Viale Michelangelo 80; tel. (055) 6811977, Fax 689348
            Closed: November to March; 320 pitches

            ★Camping Villa di Camerata
            Viale A. Righi 2/4; tel. (055) 600315, Fax (055) 610300
            Closed: November to March; 55 pitches

Barberino di   ★★Camping Sergente
Mugello   Via S. Lucia 26, Monte di Fò; tel. (055) 8423018
                80 pitches

Barberino Val   ★★Camping Semifonte
d'Elsa   Bustecca; tel. (055) 8075454, Fax (055) 8075454
                 Closed: November 6th to March 14th; 90 pitches

Calenzano   ★★Campeggio Autosole
             Spazzavento; tel/Fax (055) 8825576
             70 pitches

Fiesole   ★★★Camping Panoramico
           Via Peramonda; tel. (055) 599069, Fax (055) 59186
           190 pitches

Figline Valdarno   ★★★Camping Norcenni Girasole Club
                    Via di Norcenni 7; tel. (055) 959666, Fax (055) 959337
                    Closed Nov. 1st to Mar. 19th; 300 pitches

San Piero a Sieve   ★★★Camping Mugello Verde
                     La Fortezza: tel. (055) 848511, Fax (055) 8486910
                     180 pitches

Car Parking

Florence city centre is mostly closed to private vehicles. Visitors can only drive to hotels to load and unload. Nearly all the parking in the centre is for residents only, which means that visitors have to use the multi-storey car parks. Hotels without their own parking will recommended a nearby car park. Space is at a premium, and often keys have to be left so that the car can be moved.

Car Rental

Via Guiseppe Tartini 13, tel. (055) 367898
Via Arturo Chiara 27, tel. (055) 3024321

Airport Amerigo Vespucci, tel. (055) 315588

Via Attilio Manotti 7, tel. (055) 691216
Airport Amerigo Vespucci, tel. (055) 317543

Via Maso Finiguerra 33, tel. (055) 2398205
Via di Novoli 75, tel. (055) 4362560

Via Maso Finiguerra 11, tel. (055) 210238
Airport Amerigo Vespucci, tel. (055) 311256

Chemists

Mon.–Fri. 8.30am–12.30pm and 3.30–7.30pm; in summer 4–8pm

Opening times

Farmacia Comunale No. 13
in Santa Maria Novella station; tel. (055) 289435

Open 24 hours a day

Farmacia Molteni
Via Calzaioli 7r; tel. (055) 289490

Farmacia Taverna
Piazza S. Giovanni 20r; tel. (055) 211343

Every district of the city has a chemist that is open day and night. The name of the chemist on duty can be found in the daily newspapers or by telephoning 192.

Night service

City Sightseeing

Tourist guides can be obtained for 3 or 6 hours through the Ufficio Guide Turistiche (Via Ugo Corsi 25, tel/Fax (055) 4220901.

Tourist guides

Universalturismo organises a three-hour tour of the city (starting from Piazza della Stazione. Information from Universalturismo (Via Cavour 18r, tel. (055) 50391, Fax (055) 5039211) and SITA (Via S. Caterina di Siena 15r, tel. (055) 211487, Sat., Sun.; tel. (055) 483651, Mon.–Fri.). Both organisations offer excursions in the surroundings and to Pisa, San Gimignano and Sienna.

Tours of the city

Conference and Exhibition Centres

Fortezza da Basso
Viale Filippo Strozzi; tel. (055) 49721
See A to Z, Fortezza da Basso

Palazzo degli Affari
Via Cennini 5; tel. (055) 27731

Palazzo dei Congressi
Pratello Orsini 1 (Via Valfonda); tel. (055) 26025

Consulates

Palazzo Castelbarco, Lungarno Corsini 2; tel. (055) 284133

United Kingdom

United States   Lungarno Amerigo Vespucci 38; tel. (055) 2398276

Currency

The Italian unit of currency is the lira (plural lire). There are banknotes for 1000, 2000, 5000, 10,000, 50,000 and 100,000 lire and coins in denominations of 20, 50, 100, 200 and 500 lire.

Euro

On January 1st 1999 the euro became the official currency of Italy, and the Italian lira became a denomination of the euro. Italian lira notes and coins continue to be legal tender during a transitional period. Euro bank notes and coins are likely to be introduced by January 1st 2002.

Import and export

There are no restrictions on the import of lire or foreign currency into Italy, but in view of the strict controls on departure it is advisable to declare any currency brought in on the appropriate form – modulo V2 – at the frontier.

Foreign currency can be exported up to a value of 20,000,000 lire per person except where a larger sum has been declared on entry.

Credit cards

Banks, the larger hotels and restaurants, car rental firms and many shops accept most international credit cards.

Banks

See also Opening Times.

Changing money

Outside normal opening times money can be changed in the bank at Santa Maria Novella station which is open Mon.–Sat., 8.20am–7pm (Eurocheques not accepted). Money can also be changed 24 hours a day at various bank self-service cash machines in the city centre.

Customs Regulations

EU

Within the European Union the import and export of goods for private use is to a large extent free of customs duties. In order to distinguish between private and commercial use the following maximum amounts apply: 800 cigarettes, 400 cigarillos, 200 cigars, 1 kg pipe tobacco, 10 litres of spirits, 20 litres of fortified wines, 90 litres of table wines (max. 60 litres of sparkling wines) and 110 litres of beer. In the event of spot checks, it is important to be able to show that the goods are essentially for private use.

The import of arms, imitation weapons, gas pistols, sheath knives, multi-purpose knives and tear-gas sprays is forbidden. Carrying any quantity of reserve fuel or filling fuel containers at petrol stations is also forbidden.

If it is necessary to import large amounts of money in the form of cash into Italy, the visitor is recommended to declare these sums on entry.

Outside the EU

Travellers to Italy from outside the EU aged 17 and over may bring in duty-free 200 cigarettes or 100 cigarillos or 50 cigars or 250g pipe tobacco, 2 litres each of table and sparkling wine, or 1 litre of spirits with more than 22% vol. of alcohol, 500g of coffee or 200g of coffee extract, 100g of tea or 40g of tea extract, 50g of perfume or 0.25 litre of toilet water.

Electricity

The current is 220 volts AC. Since British plugs will not fit Italian sockets an adaptor, which is easily available, is necessary.

Emergencies

Police, fire and ambulance: tel. 113
Police headquarters (for thefts, passport
problems, etc.): tel: 055 49771

See entry

Medical
assistance

Excursions

Excursions in the immediate vicinity of Florence (multi-lingual guides) can be booked at most travel agents and also at C.I.T., the State tourist agency (Via Cavour 54r; tel. 2760382, and Piazza Stazione 51r; tel. 284145).

Bus tours

There are many Medici villas, with magnificent grounds, around Florence, and an account of the finest of them can be found in the A to Z section under Ville Medicee.

Medici Villas

It is worth combining a trip to the Certosa del Galluzzo monastery and the little town of Impruneta (see A to Z) with a drive through the Chianti district (see Monti del Chianti).

Certosa del
Galluzzo, Chianti

The little town of Fiesole (see A to Z) near to Florence is worth a visit on account of its attractions and beautiful view; it is easy to get to by public transport.
    If travelling by private car the return to Florence can be made the pretty way via Settignano (see A to Z).

Fiesole,
Settignano

On the old Roman road, 35 km (22 mi.) south of Florence, is Barberino Val d'Elsa. Its defensive walls served the citizens of Florence in their war against Siena. The Porta Senese, the only gate in the encircling ramparts, dates from the 14th c. The Palazzo Pretorio and the parish church of San Bartolomeo are also worth seeing.

Barberino Val
d'Elsa

Certaldo, 30 km (19 mi.) south-west of Florence, boasts some well-preserved medieval houses and palaces.

Certaldo

Castelfiorentino is 40 km (25 mi.) south-west of Florence in the valley of the river Elsa. The town, founded as a bastion against the Sienese, has two attractive churches and a small picture gallery.

Castelfiorentino

The modern industrial town of Empoli lies 35 km (22 mi.) along the Pisa road. Of interest are the collegiate Church of St Andrew, the church of Santo Stefano and the collegiate museum.
    Some 10 km (6 mi.) north of Empoli is Vinci, the birthplace of the great artist Leonardo da Vinci (museum and house where he was born).

Empoli, Vinci

Borgo San Lorenzo, 30 km (19 mi.) north of Florence, is worth visiting to see the church dedicated to St Laurence, the town's patron saint.
    The chief features of Scarperia, 10 km (6 mi.) north-west of Borgo San Lorenzo, are the Palazzo Pretorio and the Protestant church.

Borgo San
Lorenzo,
Scarperia

For further information about the above places and other sights in the surroundings of Florence see Baedeker Guide to Tuscany.

Exhibition Centres

See Conference and Exhibition Centres

There are several ways of getting to Italy, but entry will most probably be by way of France or Switzerland. The major passes, which are closed in winter, are served by road or rail tunnels. The distance to Florence from the Channel ports is approximately 1370–1430 km (850–890 mi.), requiring one or two night stops. Car-sleeper services operate during the summer from Boulogne, Brussels or Paris to Milan and Boulogne to Bologna.

The major frontier crossings are: France/Italy, open 24 hours, Mont Blanc Tunnel (Chamonix-Aosta) and Fréjus Tunnel (Chambéry-Turin); Switzerland/Italy, open 24 hours, St Bernard (road tunnel, Lausanne-Aosta – the pass itself is usually closed from October to June) and Simplon Pass (the pass is occasionally closed during the winter; alternative rail tunnel available but not 24-hour, Brig-Milan); Chiasso (Lugano-Como-Milan) and Castasegna/Chiavenna, the Maloja Pass (St Moritz-Milan); Austria/Italy, open 24 hours, Brenner Pass (Innsbruck-Bolzano), Résia (Reschen) Pass (Landeck-Merano-Bolzano), Arnback/Prato alla Drave (Lienz-Dobbiaco-Cortina) and Tarvisio (Villack-Udine-Venice).

By coach

There are numerous package tours by coach, either direct to Florence or including Florence in a longer circuit. For information apply to any travel agent.

There are also various scheduled bus services between Britain or northern Europe and Florence.

By rail

The fastest route from London to Florence takes just about 17 hours, leaving London (Victoria) at 10am, crossing the Channel by hovercraft and changing in Paris, or by Eurostar through the channel tunnel. An alternative route, via Hook of Holland to Florence, leaves London (Liverpool Street) at 9.45am (9.20 Sundays), changing at Cologne and arriving at Florence at 3.20pm the next day (see also Rail Travel).

Hotels

Categories

Hotels are officially classified in five categories, from de luxe (five stars) to modest (one star).

The following list accords with this classification. The address, telephone and facsimile numbers are followed by the number of rooms (r); P indicates that the hotel has its own garage or parking, SP a swimming pool.

Reservations

Consorzio Informazioni Turistiche Alberghiere (I.T.A.)
Santa Maria Novella Railway Station
Tel. (055) 282893, Fax (055) 288429
Open daily 8.30am–9pm

Consorzio Regionale Aziende Turistiche
della Toscana (C.R.A.T.), c/o F.I.V.E.T.
Via Martelli 5
Tel. 294900
(requests for reservations must be in writing)

Tariffs

Tariffs vary considerably according to time of year. The rates given in the following table are for a single or double room with bath in the peak season. They are in lire and based on information in the 1998 index of Florentine hotels published by apt (azienda di promozione turistica firenze).

The Hotel Excelsior

	Single	Double
★★★★★	440,000–650,000	770,000–1100,000
★★★★	220,000–400,000	270,000–700,000
★★★	70,000–290,000	130,000–320,000
★★	60,000–210,000	95,000–250,000
★	35,000–140,000	52,000–200,000

Excelsior, Piazza Ognissanti 3, tel. (055) 264201, Fax (055) 210278, 192r,　★★★★★
P (old style luxury hotel in a splendid 19th c. building by the Arno; magnificent roof-top view)

Grand Hotel, Piazza Ognissanti 1, tel. (055) 288781, Fax (055)
2396097, 107r (old-established luxury hotel with old world atmosphere)

★Helvetia & Bristol, Via dei Pescioni 2, tel. (055) 287814, Fax (055)
288353, 49r, P (facing the Palazzo Strozzi; fabulous, smart hotel belonging to the Charming group. Built at the end of the 19th c., it quickly
gained a reputation as one of the best in Florence. Pirandello,
Stravinsky, de Chirico and Elonora Duse were among its distinguished
guests. Following extensive renovation the magnificent rooms, their
Florentine-English style preserved, are once again restored to their
former glory. The Bristol Restaurant offers exquisite gourmet menus
based on traditional Tuscan recipes)

Regency, Piazza M. d'Azeglio, tel. (055) 245247, Fax (055) 2346735, 33r,
P (small villa with English style décor; pretty garden and excellent
cuisine)

The Grand Hotel, overlooking the Arno

★Villa Cora, Viale Machiavelli 18, tel. (055) 298451, Fax (055) 229086, 48r, SP (noblesse oblige in this fashionable 19th c. Neo-Classical villa; Napoleon's widow Eugenie chose the house for her receptions attended by a galaxy of celebrated musicians and writers; grandiose stucco ceilings, an excess of Carrara marble and expensive antiques adorn the lounges, restaurant and bedrooms; swimming pool set in a spacious park)

Villa Medici, Via il Prato 42, tel. (055) 2381331, Fax (055) 2381336, 108r, P, SP (elegant, historic 18th c. palazzo in an oasis of greenery; valuable antique furnishings and unparalleled views over the city from the bedrooms)

★★★★   Albani, Via Fiune 12, tel. (055) 26030, Fax (055) 211045, 75r (a few steps from the station; luxury hotel opened in 1993 in a former palazzo; rooms with lovely fabric wall-coverings, stucco-work, mahogany beds and marble baths; restaurant offering the finest Italian cuisine and a large selection of first-class wines)

Bernini Palace, Piazza S. Firenze 29, tel. (055) 288621, Fax (055) 268272, 86r, P (delightful hotel behind the Palazzo Vecchio; between 1865 and 1871, when Florence was the capital of Italy, parliament met in what is now the breakfast room)

Brunelleschi, Piazza S. Elisabetta 3, tel. (055) 562068, Fax (055) 219653, 96r, P (beautiful position near the Cathedral; 6th c. tower and small museum)

De la Ville, Piazza Antinori 1, tel. (055) 2381805, Fax (055) 2381809, 73r, P (tranquil and very comfortable high amenity hotel)

J and J, Via di Mezzo 20, tel. (055) 2345005, Fax (055) 240282, 18r, P (stylish small hotel in a 16th c. building adorned with frescoes)

Lungarno, Borgo San Jacopo 14, tel. (055) 2642111, Fax (055) 268437, 66r, P (on the south bank of the Arno, some rooms looking out over the river; collection of modern art)

Monna Lisa, Borgo Pinti 27, tel. (055) 2479751, Fax (055) 2479755, 30r, P (old palazzo with many antiques; refined atmosphere and lovely garden)

Montebello Splendid, Via Montebello 60, tel. (055) 2398051, Fax (055) 211867, 45r (elegant 14th c. villa in the city centre; meals in the glassed-in veranda overlooking the garden)

Rivoli, Via della Scala 33, tel. (055) 282853, Fax (055) 294041, 60r, P (former Franciscan monastery dating from the 15th c., with courtyard garden)

Torre di Bellosguardo, Via Rotti Michelozzi, tel. (055) 2298145, Fax (055) 229008, 16r, P, SP (delightful Renaissance palazzo with 12th c. tower; lovely view of the city)

Villa Carlotta, Via M. di Lando 3, tel. (055) 2336134, Fax (055) 2336147, 32r, P (patrician villa near the Palazzo Pitti; beautiful garden)

Ville Sull'Arno, Lungarno C. Colombo 1/3/5, tel. (055) 670971, Fax (055) 678244, 47r, P, SP (by the Arno; hospitality delivered with style)

Beacci Tornabuoni, Via dei Tornabuoni 3, tel. (055) 212645, Fax (055) 283594, 29r (well-kept pension centrally located in the celebrated shopping mile; very popular with Americans) ★★★

Hermitage, Vicolo Marzi 1, tel. (055) 287216, Fax (055) 212208, 28r (small hotel near the Ponte Vecchio; fine view of the city from the roof terrace; some rooms noisy)

Pendini, Via Strozzi 2, tel. (055) 211170, Fax (055) 281807, 42r (centrally situated pension more than a hundred years old; comfortable rooms but some noisy)

Porta Rossa, Via Porta Rossa 19, tel. (055) 287551, Fax (055) 282179, 81r, P (the city's oldest hotel, dating from the 14th c.)

La Scaletta, Via Guiciardini 13, tel. (055) 283028, Fax (055) 289562, 11r (very tasteful; terrace with fine view of the city; but many of the rooms noisy) ★★

Liana, Via V. Alfieri 18, tel. (055) 245303/4, Fax (055) 2344596, 18r (in the former British embassy; terrace and small garden; elegant rooms)

Information

The first place to go for information when planning a trip to Florence is the Italian State Tourist Office (ENIT).

Italian State Tourist Office (ENIT)

1 Princes Street, London W1R 8AY
Tel. (0207) 4081254

United Kingdom

500 North Michigan Avenue, Chicago, IL 60611
Tel. (312) 6440990-1
630 Fifth Avenue, Suite 1565, New York, NY 10111

United States of America

Tel. (212) 2454822-4
360 Post Street, Suite 801, San Francisco, CA 94108
Tel. (415) 3926206-7

Canada

c/o Alitalia, 85 Richmond Street, Toronto
Tel. (416) 3631348

Information in
Florence

Azienda di Promozione Turistica (apt)
Via Menzoni 16
Tel. (055) 23320, Fax (055) 2346286
Open: Mon.–Sat. 8.30am–1.30pm

Azienda di Promozione Turistica Firenze – Provincia di Firenze – Comune
di Firenze
Via Cavour 1r, tel. (055) 290832/3, Fax (055) 2760381

Comune di Firenze
Borgo Santa Croce 29r, tel. (055) 23404444, (055) 2264524
Piazza Stazione, tel. (055) 212245, Fax (055) 2381226

Consorzio Informazioni Turistiche Alberghiere Interno (I.T.A.),
Stazione Santa Maria Novella, tel. (055) 282893, Fax (055) 288429
(only for hotel rooms)

Ufficio Informazioni Turistiche
Aeroporto A Vespucci, tel. (055) 315874, Fax (055) 318609

Telephone
information

Information and advice can be obtained throughout Italy by ringing 116,
which is staffed by multilingual personnel.

Insurance

Car

It is very desirable to have an international insurance certificate ("green
card"), although this is not a legal requirement for citizens of EU countries. It is important to have fully comprehensive cover, and it is desirable
to take out short-term insurance against legal costs if these are not already
covered. Italian insurance companies tend to be slow in settling claims.

Health

British visitors to Italy, like other EU citizens, are entitled to receive
health care on the same basis as Italians (including free medical treatment, etc.); they should apply to their local Departments of Health, well
before their date of departure, for a certificate of entitlement (form
E111). Fuller cover can be obtained for the duration of your stay by
taking out insurance against medical expenses if you are in a private
health insurance scheme; and non-EU citizens will, of course, be well
advised to take out appropriate insurance cover.

Baggage

In view of the risk of theft it is desirable to have adequate insurance
against loss of, or damage to, baggage.

Language

The Italian language is a direct descendant of Latin, and is closer to it
than any of the other Romance languages. Owing to Italy's earlier political fragmentation it developed as several dialects, and of these Tuscan
came to be the standard language, as it is today, thanks to the great
writers of the 13th and 14th c. and Dante in particular. The language of
the Florentine is considered Italian at its purest.

Although English is understood and spoken in the larger hotels and restaurants, it is still useful to be able to help out with a few Italian words and phrases.

The stress is usually on the second last syllable. Where it falls on the last syllable this is always indicated by an accent (perché, città). Where the stress is on the third from last syllable an accent is not officially required, except in certain doubtful cases. However it is often shown as an aid to pronunciation (chilòmetro, sènapa), with é and ó indicating the closed vowel and è and ò the open vowel. The vowels in a dipthong are pronounced separately (ca-usa, se-i), and e is never silent.

C or cc before e or i is pronounced ch, otherwise like k; g before e or i is pronounced like j, otherwise hard (as in "go"); gn and gl are like n and l followed by a consontantal y (roughly as in "onion" and "million"); h is silent, qu as in English; r is rolled; s is unvoiced (as in "so") at the beginning of a word before a vowel, but has the sound of z between vowels and before b, d, g, l, m, n, and vv; sc before e or i is pronounced sh, z is either like ts or ds.

0 zero	19 diciannove	
1 uno, una, un, un´	20 venti	
2 due	21 ventuno	
3 tre	22 ventidue	
4 quattro	30 trenta	
5 cinque	31 trentuno	
6 sei	40 quaranta	
7 sette	50 cinquanta	
8 otto	60 sessanta	
9 nove	70 settanta	
10 dieci	80 ottanta	
11 undici	90 novanta	
12 dodici	100 cento	
13 tredici	101 cento uno	
14 quattordici	153 centocinquantatre	
15 quindici	200 duecento	
16 sedici	1000 mille	
17 diciasette	5000 cinque mila	
18 diciotto	1 million un milione	

1st primo (prima)	7th settimo
2nd secondo	8th ottavo
3rd terzo	9th nono
4th quarto	10th decimo
5th quinto	20th ventesimo/vigesimo
6th sesto	100th centesimo

½ un mezzo (mezza)	⅒ un decimo
¼ un quarto	

Good morning, good day	Buon giorno
Good evening	Buona sera
Goodbye	Arrivederci
Yes, no	Si, no
I beg your pardon	Scusi
Please	Per favore
Thank you (very much)	(Molte) grazie
You're welcome	Prego
Excuse me (when passing in front of someone)	Con permesso
Do you speak English	Parla inglese?
A little, not much	Un poco, non molto
I don't understand	Non capisco
What is the Italian for ...	Come si dice ... in italiano

Language

What is the name of this church?	Come si chiama questa chiesa?
cathedral	il duomo
square	la piazza
palace	il palazzo
theatre	il teatro
Where is the Via ...?	Dov'è la via X?
Where is the road (motorway) to ...?	Dov'è (l'autostrada) per ...?
left, right	a sinistra, a destra
straight ahead	sempre diritto
above, below	sopra, sotto
When is (it) open?	Quando è aperto?
How far is it?	Quanto è distante?
today	oggi
yesterday	ieri
the day before yesterday	l'altro ieri
tomorrow	domani
Have you any rooms?	Ci sono camere libere?
I should like ...	Vorrei avere ...
a room with bath (shower)	una camera con bagno (doccia)
with full board	con pensione complete
What does it cost?	Qual'è il prezzo? Quanto costa?
all-in (price)	totto compreso
That is too dear	E troppo caro
Bill, please (to a waiter)	Cameriere, il conto!
Where are the lavatories?	Dove si trovano i gabinetti? (il servizi, la ritirata)
Wake me at six	Può svegliarmi alle sei!
Where is there a doctor (dentist)?	Dove sta un mèdico (un dentista)?

At the post office	address	indirizzo
	airmail	posta aerea
	express	espresso
	letter	léttera
	post box	buca delle lettere
	postcard	cartolina
	Poste Restante	Fermo posta
	postman	postino
	stamp	francobollo
	registered letter	léttera raccomandata
	telegram	telegramma
	telephone	telefono

Travelling	aircraft	aeroplano
	airport	aeroporto
	arrival	arrivo
	baggage (luggage)	bagagli
	booking office	sportello
	bus (tram) stop	fermata
	change (trains)	cambiare treno
	departure (air)	partenza (Decollo)
	departure (rail)	partenza
	fare	prezzo di biglietto, tariffa
	flight	volo
	guard	capotreno
	No smoking	Vietato fumare
	platform	marciapiede
	porter	portabagagli, facchino
	station	stazione
	stop	sosta
	ticket collector	conduttore

timetable	orario	
track	binario	
waiting room	sala d'aspetto	
Monday	Lunedi	Days of the week
Tuesday	Martedi	
Wednesday	Mercoledi	
Thursday	Giovedi	
Friday	Venerdi	
Saturday	Sabato	
Sunday	Domenica	
day	giorno	
weekday	giorno feriale	
holiday	giorno festivo	
week	settimana	
New Year	Capo d'anno	Holidays
Easter	Pasqua	
Whitsun	Pentecoste	
Christmas	Natale	
January	Gennaio	Months
February	Febbraio	
March	Marzo	
April	Aprile	
May	Maggio	
June	Giugno	
July	Luglio	
August	Agosto	
September	Settembre	
October	Ottobre	
November	Novembre	
December	Dicembre	

Language Courses

Florence has a number of institutes where courses in the Italian language are held. They cater for different levels of proficiency, starting with beginners, and the courses last for two to four weeks, depending on how intensive they are. There are also special holiday courses which include hotel accommodation and a social programme.

Centro Koinè
Via Pandolfini 27; tel. (055) 213881

Language schools

Centro Pontevecchio
Piazza del Mercato Nuovo 1; tel. (055) 2396887

Macchiavelli
Piazza S. Spirito 4; tel. (055) 2396966

Lost Property

Ufficio Oggetti Smarriti
Via Circondaria 19; tel. (055) 367943

Lost Property
Office

Markets

Provision markets	**Mercato Centrale** Piazza del Mercato Centrale, near San Lorenzo Open Mon.–Fri. 7am–2pm (in winter 7.30am–1pm); Sat. and before public holidays also 4–8pm. Fish, meat, cheese and delicatessen are all on the ground floor of the market hall – one of the best in Italy – and fruit and vegetables are sold on the upper floor. There are also some stalls selling snacks and drinks. **Mercato Sant'Ambrogio** Piazza Ghiberti; open Mon.–Sat. mornings
Flea market	**Mercato della Pulci** Piazza dei Ciompi; open Tue.–Sat. all day
Weekly market	**Mercato delle Cascine** Parco delle Cascine; open Tuesday morning This market, which starts at the Ponte delle Vittoria, sells clothes (including some amazingly cheap designer models), shoes, fabrics, and household goods as well as food and plants.
Leather goods, souvenirs, clothing	**Mercato Nuovo** Loggia di Mercato Nuovo, Piazza del Porcellino Open Tue.–Sat. 9am–5pm The market is known for the straw handicrafts sold here, but also for china, knitwear, etc. **Mercato di San Lorenzo** Piazza San Lorenzo; open Mon.–Sat. 8am–7pm The mass of market stalls around the Church of San Lorenzo sell almost everything, including clothes, shoes, bags, belts, jewellery, toys, etc.

Medical Assistance

The emergency number throughout Italy is 112.

First Aid	**Croce Rossa Italiana (Red Cross)** Lungarno Soderini 11; tel. (055) 215381 **Pubblica Assistenza Humanitas** Viale Talenti 160; tel. (055) 713961
Emergency doctor	Emergency 24-hour service for tourists (house calls): tel. (055) 475411; public holidays and at night: tel. (055) 477891.
Accidents	Tel. 118
Hospitals	**Generale di Careggi** Viale Morgagni 85; tel. (055) 4277111 **Ospedale Nuovo di S. Giovanni di Dio** Via Torregalli 3; tel. (055) 27661 **Ospedale di Santa Maria Nuova** Piazza Santa Maria Nuova 1; tel. (055) 27581 **Policlinico Universitario** Viale Morgagni; tel. (055) 43991

The Mercato Centrale, one of the best covered markets in Italy

Pediatrico Mayer (children's hospital)
Via Luca Giordano 13; tel. (055) 43991

Istituto Ortopedico Toscana "Piero Palagi" (orthopaedic clinic)
Viale Michelangelo 41; tel. (055) 27691

Ospedale Oftalmico Fiorentino (eye clinic)
Via Masaccio 213; tel. (055) 578444

EU citizens are entitled to receive health care on the same basis as Italians, provided they can produce their E111 form, which they should obtain before departure from their home country (see Insurance). For routine cases other than emergencies anyone in need of treatment should apply to "Unit Sanitaria Locale". These local health units can be found in, for example, the Ospedale di Santa Maria Nuova and the Ospedale Nuovo di S. Giovanni di Dio, where treatment is then free of charge.

Health insurance

Motoring

Diesel apart, the cost of motor fuel in Italy is considerably above the European average, and since January 1992 the petrol coupons that entitled visitors to cheaper fuel have been discontinued. Lead-free petrol (benzina senza piombo) can now be obtained at most filling stations in northern Italy (opening times see entry). For safety reasons spare cans of petrol may not be carried in vehicles in Italy.

Fuel

In general traffic regulations in Italy do not differ essentially from those

Traffic regulations

Motoring

in other European countries where vehicles drive on the right. Traffic signs are the standard international ones.

City centre parking

Most of Florence city centre is closed to non-commercial traffic (see Car Parking).

Speed limits

The speed limit in built-up areas is 50 kph (31 mph), and on main roads 90 kph (56 mph)

On motorways the speed limit is 110 kph (68 mph) for cars up to 1.1 litre and 130 kph (81 mph) for cars of 1.1 litre and above. Speed limits for motorbikes depend on engine size: under 349 cc the speed limit is 110 kph (68 mph) and from 350 cc it is 130 kph (81 mph). Cars towing trailers or caravans are limited to 80 kph (50 mph) on motorways and 70 kph (43 mph) on main roads.

Other regulations

The minimum age at which a visitor may drive a temporarily imported car is 18. Motorists should carry their driving licence and car registration document. A translation of the licence, obtainable from motoring clubs or the ENIT (Italian State Tourist Office), is normally required but not for the "pink" EU-type licence. An international insurance certificate ("green card") is not obligatory but is advisable (see Insurance). The car should have a nationality plate, and a warning triangle must be carried.

Motorbikes

Motorbikes under 150 cc are not allowed on motorways. There is an age limit of 21 before anyone is allowed on a motorbike over 350 cc. Motorbikes are not allowed to tow trailers.

Seat belts

The wearing of seat belts is compulsory for everyone in the car over fourteen. Children under four can only travel in special car seats.

Priority

Traffic on main roads has priority where the road is marked with the priority sign (a square with the corner pointing downwards, coloured white, with a red border or yellow with a black and white border). Otherwise, even on roundabouts, the rule is "right before left", and motorists give way to vehicles coming from their right. On narrow mountain roads uphill traffic has priority. Vehicles that run on rails always have priority.

Overtaking

Drivers must signal with their indicators before and after overtaking. The horn should also be sounded before overtaking outside built-up areas in daylight, and lights flashed at night.

No hooting

Drivers may not sound their horns if there is a "no hooting" sign (a horn with a stroke through it) or, in towns, it says "zona di silenzio". If necessary, outside a built-up area the horn may be sounded at cross-roads, junctions, blind curves and in other dangerous situations.

Lights

Sidelights only are permitted on well-lit roads, but dipped headlights must be used at all times in tunnels and galleries.

Drinking and driving

Drinking and driving is against the law.

Towing away

Illegally parked vehicles will be towed away by the "rimozione forzata". If this happens contact the city police (vigili urbani, see Police) or the towed-away vehicle compound (Via Dell'Arcovata 6; tel. 355231).

Accidents

In the event of an accident make sure to get the names and addresses of all the drivers involved and the registration numbers of the vehicles, as well as the other parties' insurers; this can be taken from the square

sticker on Italian car windscreens. It is also wise to get the name and address of witnesses and take a photograph of the accident site. If the accident involves personal injury it must be reported to the police. The driver's insurance company should be notified as soon as possible; if the driver is in any way responsible the Italian insurers whose address is given on your green card should be informed. They can help with advice and supply the name of a lawyer if there is a possibility of a prosecution.

If the car is a total write-off the Italian customs authorities must be told immediately, otherwise the full import duty on the vehicle may be demanded.

Total write-off

Autombil Club d'Italia (ACI)
Viale Amendola 36; tel. 24861
ACI breakdown service throughout Italy: tel. 116
ACI assistance in Florence: also tel. 678156

Italian Automobile Club

Assistance with breakdowns is free for members of a motoring organis- ation that is affiliated to the Autombil Club d'Italia (ACI). However, cars that have been abandoned on the Italian motorway can only be towed away by the Italian breakdown service, and the police can fine anyone not using that service. A fine can also be imposed for failing to use a warning triangle. This should be placed not less than 50 m (165 ft) behind the vehicle. (See also Emergencies.)

Breakdown assistance

A report on the state of the roads in Tuscany can be obtained by tele- phoning 1941.

State of the roads

See Travel Documents

Driving documents

Museums

Admission to museums and other attractions in Florence is expensive. Reductions for EU citizens under 18 and over 60 can be obtained by presentation of an identity card. For the state museums (Galleria degli Uffizi, Galleria dell'Accademia, Palazzo Pitti, Capelle Medicee, Museo di San Marco, Museo Nazionale del Bargello, Museo Archeologico, Opificio dell Pietre Dure) reservations for the same day can be made by telephoning (055) 294883.

Appartamenti Monumentali
See A to Z, Palazzo Pitti

Casa Buonarroti (Michelangelo Museum). See A to Z

Casa di Dante (Dante Museum). See A to Z

Collezione Contini Bonacossi (Contini Bonacossi Collection)
Palazzina della Meridiana
(access via Galleria d'Arte Moderna in Palazzo Pitti)
See A to Z, Giardino di Boboli

Corridoio Vasariano (Vasari corridor)
See A to Z, Palazzo degli Uffizi

Galleria dell'Accademia (Academy Gallery). See A to Z

Galleria d'Arte Moderna (Gallery of Modern Art)
See A to Z, Palazzo Pitti

Galleria Carnielo (sculpture collection)
Piazza Savonarola 18; open: Sat. 9am–1pm

Galleria Corsini. See A to Z, Palazzo Corsini

Galleria del Costume (costume from the 18th c. to the First World War)
See A to Z, Giardino di Boboli

Galleria Palatina/Galleria Pitti
See A to Z, Palazzo Pitti

Galleria dello degli Innocenti
See A to Z, Ospedale degli Innocenti

Galleria Strozzina. See A to Z, Palazzo Strozzi

Galleria degli Uffizi
See A to Z, Palazzo degli Uffizi

Museo della Casa Fiorentina Antica (old Florentine house museum)
See A to Z, Palazzo Davanzati

Museo di Antropologia ed Etnologia (Museum of Mankind)
See A to Z

Museo Archeologico Centrale dell'Etruria (archaeological museum)
See A to Z

Museo degli Argenti (silver collection)
See A to Z, Palazzo Pitti

Museo Bardini. See A to Z

Museo del Bigallo
See A to Z, Piazza San Giovanni

Museo Botanico (botanical museum)
See A to Z, Orto Botanico

Museo delle Carrozze (collection of coaches)
See A to Z, Palazzo Pitti

Museo Ebraico (Jewish museum), Via Farini 4
See A to Z, Tempio Israelitico

Museo della Fondazione Horne (Horne Foundation Museum)
See A to Z

Museo di Geologia e Paleontologia (geological and paleontological museum)
Via La Pira 4; open Mon. 2–6pm, Tue., Wed., Thu., Sat. 9am–1pm and every 1st Sun. in the month 9.30am–12.30pm (closed July–September)

Museo Marino Marini. See A to Z

Museo di Mineralogia e Litologia (mineralogy museum)
Via La Pira 4; open Mon.–Sat. 9am–1pm, every 1st Sunday in the month 9.30am–12.30pm (closed August)

Museo Nazionale del Bargello
See A to Z

Museo dell'Opera del Duomo (cathedral museum). See A to Z

Museo dell'Opera di Santa Croce
See A to Z, Santa Croce

Museo delle Porcellane (porcelain museum)
See A to Z, Giardino di Boboli

Museo di Preistoria (prehistory museum)
Via S. Egidio 21; open Mon.–Sat. 9.30am–12.30pm

Museo Salvatore Ferragamo
See A to Z, Palazzo Spini-Ferroni

Museo di San Marco. See A to Z, San Marco

Museo Santa Croce
See A to Z, Piazza di Santa Croce

Museo di Santa Maria Novella
See A to Z, Santa Maria Novella

Museo Stibbert. See A to Z

Museo di Storia della Fotografia "Fratelli Alinari" (photography
museum)
See A to Z, Palazzo Rucellai

Museo di Storia della Scienza (history of science museum)
See A to Z

Museo Storico Topgrafico "Firenze com'era"
("Florence as it was" historical museum). See A to Z

Museo degli Strumenti Musicali Antichi
(collection of old musical instruments)
See A to Z, Conservatorio Musicale Luigi Cherubini

Museo Zoologica "La Specola" (zoological museum). See A to Z

Opificio e Museo delle Pietre Dure (mosaic museum and workshops)
See A to Z

Raccolta di Arte Moderna "Alberto della Ragione"
(Alberto della Ragione modern art collection)
Piazza della Signoria 5; open Mon.–Sat. 9am–2pm, Sun. 8am–1pm

Music

See Theatres, Concerts

Nightlife

Florence is not particularly noted for its night life. In summer, however,
the streets are crowded until well into the night, especially around the
Piazza della Repubblica, where it only starts quietening down after midnight. Anyone then in search of further distraction can make for the hotel

bars or one of the following discos or bars with music (usually open from 10pm; many of them are closed on Mondays).

Discos

Andromeda, Piazza Cerci 7, tel. (055) 292002
Videos, dance floor with lasers

Central Park, Via Fosso delle Macinate 13, tel. (055) 356723
Entrance from the Cascine Park; in summer also open-air disco

Meccanno, Viale degli Olmi 1, tel. (055) 331371
Best known and most popular disco in Florence

Space Electronic, Via Palazzuolo 37, tel. (055) 293082
Avant-garde disco with laser shows and maxi-videos; mostly for young people.

Tenax, Via Pratese 46a, tel. (055) 308160
Live music

Yab Yum, via Sassetti 5r, tel. (055) 290608
Popular elegant disco with live music up until 1am; not only for the young.

Bars with music

Dolce Vita, Piazza del Carmine 12, tel. (055) 284595
Jazz

Genesi, Piazza del Duomo 20r, tel. (055) 287247
Live jazz and blues

Piansa, Borgo Pinti 18r, tel. (055) 2342362
Live jazz

Opening Hours

Banks

Mon.–Fri. 8.20am–1.20pm and 2.45–3.45pm; the bank in Santa Maria Novella station is open Mon.–Sat. 8.20am–6.20pm. (See also Currency.)

Chemists

Summer: Mon.–Fri. 8.30am–12.30pm and 4–8pm; winter Mon.–Fri. 8.30am–12.30pm and 3.30–7.30pm.

Churches

The larger churches are usually open until noon and from 4 until 7pm; some of the major churches are open all day.

Filling stations

Mon.–Sat. 7.30am–noon and 3–7.30pm; some filling stations are open round the clock (see Fuel).

Museums

The opening times are given under the entry for each museum (see Practical Information A to Z and Museums). Most museums are closed on public holidays as well as one day a week, usually a Monday.

Because of frequent changes in opening times and unforeseen closures due to staff shortages, strikes, renovation, etc. it is wise to check museum opening times before making a visit.

Post offices

Mon.–Fri. 8.15am–1.30pm, Sat. 8.15am–12.30pm; head post office (Via Pellicceria) Mon.–Fri. 8.15am–6pm, Sat. 8.15am–12.30pm

Restaurants

Most restaurants are open in summer from noon to 3pm and from 5 or 6pm to midnight. In winter they are not usually open for so long in the evening (7–11pm).

Mon.–Sat. 8.30/9am–1pm and 3.30/4pm–7.30pm. Many shops are closed on Monday morning and most food shops on Wednesday afternoon.

Shops

Police

Tel. 113

Emergency

Questura, Via Zara 2; tel. 49771

Police headquarters

Carabinieri, Borgognissanti 48; tel. 112

Flying squad

Vigili Urbani, Piazzale di Porta al Prato 6; tel. 32831

Urban police

Polizia stradale; tel. 577777

Traffic police

Post

Letters and postcards within Italy and to EU countries (up to 20 grams) 850 lire

Postal rates

Italian letter boxes are red.

Letter boxes

Stamps (francobolli) can be bought at tobacconists (with a "T" over the entrance) as well as post offices.

Stamps

Opening times: see entry

Post offices

Telegrams can be sent from the main post office between 8am and 11.30pm or by telephone: 186.

Telegrams

See entry

Telephone

Public Holidays

January 1st	New Year's Day
January 6th	Epiphany
March/April	Easter Monday
April 25th	Liberation Day (1945)
May 1st	Labour Day
August 15th	Ferragosto (Assumption)
November 1st	All Saints
December 8th	Immaculate Conception
December 25th/26th	Christmas

Public Transport

The ATAF is the only company to provide a public bus service in Florence. Single tickets are available valid for 1, 2 or 24 hours, also season tickets and special tourist tickets allowing unlimited same-day travel. In addition the Carta Arancio buys a week's travel on all forms of public transport. Tickets can be purchased from authorised sales outlets, ticket machines, tobacconists and bars displaying the sign "biglietti ATAF". Tickets must be cancelled once on the bus.

City transport (see bus map pages)

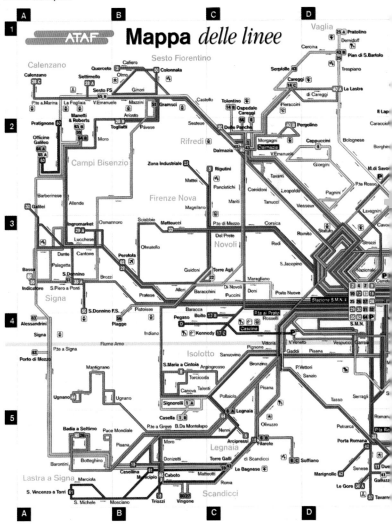

An ATAF town plan showing all the bus routes can be obtained from Piazza Stazione, tel. (055) 5650222.

Environs of Florence

SITA and other companies operate buses in the area around Florence. Details of timetables are provided in four languages by a computerised information service at the bus station in the Via S. Caterina da Siena (15r), near the railway station.

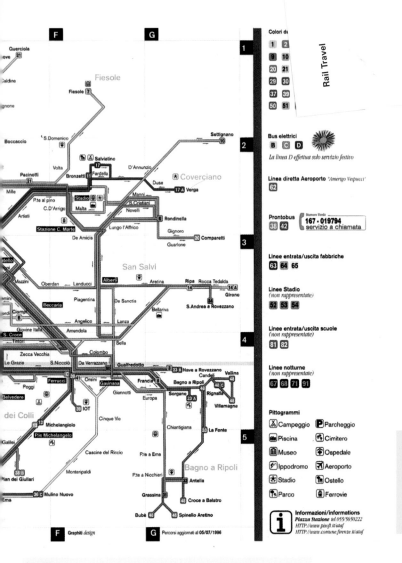

Radio

During the tourist season RAI, the Italian radio service, broadcasts news, etc. for foreign visitors in various languages.

Radio Uno O.M. (medium wave) transmits a daily programme of messages for tourists and information on traffic conditions – Green Wave-Euroradio – at 1.56pm in four languages. Emergency messages to tourists are also broadcast in English and Italian at various times throughout the day.

Information on overseas radio transmissions can be obtained from BBC External Services, P.O. Box 76, Bush House, London WC2B 4PH.

Rail Travel

Ferrovie dello Stato (FS)

The Italian rail network covers a total of 16,000 km (10,000 mi.), most of it run by Italian State Railways (Ferrovie dello Stato).

Tickets

Tickets for the Italian rail network vary according to the length of the journey, and can range in validity from one day (for up to 250 km (155 mi.)) to six days (for over 1000 km (620 mi.)).

Children accompanied by an adult travel free up to the age of four; between four and twelve they go for half fare.

Special tickets

Tourist Tickets, either first or second class, are valid for an unlimited number of journeys on the entire Italian rail network for periods of 8, 15, 21 or 30 days.

Inter-Rail tickets (for young people up to the age of 26), Rail-Europe Family Tickets (for families of at least three) and Rail-Europe Senior Tickets (with a Senior Citizens' rail card) entitle the holders to fare reductions in Italy.

Information and reservations

Further detailed information and tickets can be obtained from travel agents or direct from CIT, the Italian State Tourist Offices.

United Kingdom

CIT Offices:
Marco Polo House, 3–5 Lansdown Road, Croydon, CR9 ILL; tel. (0891) 715151

United States

765 Route 83, Suite 105, Chicago, Ill.
5670 Wilshire Boulevard, Los Angeles, Cal.
668 Fifth Avenue, New York, NY

Canada

2055 Peel Street, Suite 102, Montreal
111 Richmond Street West, Suite 419, Toronto

Telephone information in Italy

A central information service for rail travel in Italy is 1478-88088 (7am to 9pm)

Railway Station

The terminal for both national and international passenger traffic is the Stazione Centrale Santa Maria Novella.

Trains

For information: tel. 166/105050

Lost property

Ufficio Oggetti Rinvenuti, Zentrale; tel. (055) 2767-2190

Railway police

Tel. (055) 212296

Restaurants

Visitors to Florence must expect to pay relatively high prices for food. Charges additional to the basic cost of the meal include pane e coperto (cover charge and a charge for bread) and a service charge (servizio) of anything between 10 and 15%. In bars it is usually rather more expensive to eat at a table than at the counter.

Besides the often relatively lavish and expensive *ristoranti* Ital
many generally more modest but good quality eating places. The
the *osterie* (originally country hostelries providing wine and plain
and *trattorie* (urban versions of osterie, mostly serving regional dis
For quick service try a *pizzeria*, or a *tavola calda* or *rosticceria*, the l
two being types of snack bar.

★Cibreo (closed Sun. and Mon.), Via dei Macci 118, tel. (055) 234
(gourmet establishment with restaurant, café, taverna and delicates
the little room behind the kitchen is cosier than the antiques-furnished
dining-room; exquisite cuisine – try the stuffed chicken neck)

★Enoteca Pinchiorri (closed Mon.), Via Ghibellina 87, tel. (055) 242777
(elegant restaurant in a former 16th c. palazzo with lovely inner courtyard; superlative culinary experience at a price to match; the wine cellar,
stocked with more than 150,000 bottles of the best vintages from all over
the world, is already legendary)

★Sabatini, Via de'Panzani 9a, tel. (055) 211559 (luxurious restaurant,
long renowned)

Alle Murate (open evenings, closed Mon.), Via Ghibellina 52r, tel. (055)
240618 (imaginative cuisine based on Italian regional recipes)

Dino (closed Sun. and Mon.), Via Ghibellina 51r, tel. (055) 241452 (very
good yet not over-expensive; exceptionally pleasant atmosphere,
ancient recipes)

Don Chisciotte (closed Sun. and Mon.), Via Cosimo Ridolfi 4/6r, tel. (055)
475430 (elegant restaurant, creative Tuscan cooking)

La Capannina di Sante (closed Sun. and Mon. lunchtime), Piazza Ravenna,
tel. (055) 688345 (wooden building by the Arno; excellent for fish)

Coco Lezzone (closed Tue. and Sun. evenings), Via del Parioncino 26r,
tel. (055) 287178 (unsophisticated Tuscan-style restaurant serving good
Tuscan food at agreeable prices; special tip: ribollita)

Osterie

Benvenuto (closed Wed. and Sun.), Via della Mosca 16, tel. (055) 214833
(good value Tuscan cuisine)

Trattorie
(See Baedeker
Special p. 198)

Cammillo (closed Wed. and Thu.), Borgo Sant'Jacopo 57r, tel. (055)
212427 (typical Florentine trattoria; rather expensive)

Garga (closed Mon.), Via del Moro 48, tel. (055) 2398898 (homely trattoria with art-covered walls; delicious Florentine specialities)

La Baraonda (closed Sun.), Via Ghibellina 67r, tel. (055) 2341171 (traditional Tuscan dishes and good quality Tuscan wine)

Sostanza (Il Troia), Via del Porcellana 25r, tel. (055) 212691 (Chagall and
Steinbeck ate at this historic Florentine inn; special tip: the bistecca alla
fiorentina)

Zà Zà (closed Sun.), Piazza Mercato Centrale 26r, tel. (055) 215411 (very
good Florentine cooking, wide-ranging clientele)

Shopping

Florence is famous for its fabulous choice of fashion stores – all the big

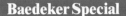

Feasting the Tuscan way

Whether served in a wine vault or a Renaissance palace, the good plain tasty cooking which for centuries in Tuscany has nourished city merchants and farmers alike, can still be found. A splendid time can be had at **Il Cantinone del Gallo Nero** (Via Santo Spirito 6r, tel. 218898, closed Mon.), a restaurant in an old wine vault where guests are seated at scrubbed wooden tables and proceedings open, naturally, with a glass of Chianti Classico, which has the black cockerel (gallo nero) on the label signifying red wine of outstanding quality. Perhaps to start with choose an antipasto misto with a few slices of prosciutto toscano, an aromatic farmhouse ham, and finocchiona, salami flavoured with fennel, accompanied by a few crostini di fegato, slices of white bread with poultry liver paté. Purists are sent into raptures by the simple but heavenly toasted slices of farmhouse bread known as fettunta, spread just with garlic and olive oil. Panzanella, a kind of bread salad with a subtle mixture of farm-baked bread, tomatoes, cucumber or celery, basil, onions or extra virgin olive oil, is another well-known appetizer. After that a plate of fagioli all'uccelletto, white beans seasoned with sage and lightly smoked pork sausage makes a satisfying and tasty dish. The trippe alla fiorentina on the other hand, tripe steamed in wine and tomatoes and garnished with a piquant sheep's cheese called pecorino, will perhaps not be to everyone's taste. To finish with, what about a little bit of pecorino – which could be anything from mild to very strong – or a handful of biscotti di mandorle, rock-hard almond kernels dipped in Vin Santo to bring out their full flavour.

A more elegant and dearer setting altogether for enjoying Tuscan specialities is the **Cantinetta Antinori** (Piazza degli Antinori 3, tel. 292234, closed Sat. and Sun.). The old aristocratic Antinori family serve produce from their estate, beautifully prepared and presented in their Renaissance palazzo. In anticipation of the delights to follow, try a glass of San Gioconda as an aperitif, or a sparkling spumante secco. Among the generously proportioned yet easily digested dishes are pappa al pomodoro and minestrone di pane, hot bread-soups prepared with tomatoes or beans. The estate-reared chicken, in whatever guise – pollo alla diavola for example, served with rosemary, sage and lemon – retains its real poultry flavour. The beef and pork also come from home-bred herds, making dishes such as spezzatino alla casalingha or stracotto di manzo that little bit special. Mild-flavoured ricotto, not unlike curd cheese, offers an alternative to pecorino in the cheese course. For something sweet to finish with, what better than castagnaccio, a cake made from chestnuts flavoured with rosemary, pine kernels and raisins. And of course no meal is complete without a glass, or better still a bottle, of the superlative red or white Antinori wine.

Should these two establishments be fully booked or closed, alternative suggestions can be found under the heading "Restaurants" in this Guide. So that none give up disappointed, here are three more tips, albeit somewhat heavy on the purse. Typically Tuscan starters such as ribollita and pappardelle alla lepre, well-known main courses such as arista and bistecca alla fiorentina, and sweet torta della nonna and other dishes can be enjoyed in pleasant surroundings at **Buca Mario** (Piazza Ottaviani 16r, tel. 214179, closed Wed.), the **Taverna del Bronzino** (Via della Ruote 25/17r, tel. 495220, closed Sun.) and the rustic **Il Latini** (Via Palchetti 6r, tel. 495220, closed Sun.).

names are represented here – but there are also many shops selling jewellery, leather goods, fine fabrics and gourmet fare, all of which are however expensive.

Bartolazzi, Via Maggio 18r
Ugo Camiciotti, Via di Santo Spirito 9r

Antiques

There are many small antique shops in and around the Borgo Ognissanti, Via Maggio, Via Fossi, Via di Santo Spirito and Via della Vigna Nuova

Emilio Paoli, Via della Vigna Nuova 26r (in addition to the once famous Florentine hats, this old family firm still sells baskets and a range of wickerwork, straw and rattan)

Basketwork

Alinari, Via della Vigna 46 (old photographs)
Feltrinelli, Via Cavour
Salimbeni, Via Palmieri 14r (antiquarian books)
Seeber, Via dei Tornabuoni 70r (international publications)

Books

Galleria Machiavelli, Lungarno Guicciardini 104r
Sbigoli Terracotte, Via Sant'Egidio 4r (own studio)

Ceramics

Armando Poggi, Via dei Calzaiuoli 105 and 116r (huge selection of china, glass and silver tableware)

China

Pegna, Via dello Studio 8 (old-established shop with a huge selection and wide range of prices)
Procacci, Via dei Tornabuoni 64r (rare delicacies, gourmet corner)

Delicatessen

Nencioni, Via della Condotta 36r (large selection of embroideries of different periods)

Embroidery

Antico Seticio, Via della Vigna Nuova 97 (lovely silks adorned with patterns used in antiquity; expensive but also exclusive)
Casa dei Tessuti, Via dei Pecori 20–24r (designer fabrics)
Haas, Via dei Tornabuoni 53
Lisio, Via dei Fossi 45r (precious brocades and silks)

Fabrics

Alex, Via della Vigna Nuova 19r (ladies' fashions)
Armani, Piazza Strozzi 16r
Enrico Coveri, Via della Vigna Nuova 27–29r (ladies' and gentlemen's fashions)
Ermano Daelli, Via Roma 12r (ladies' and gentlemen's fashions and accessories)
Fendi, Via dei Tornabuoni 27r (ladies' fashions)
Ferragamo, Via dei Tornabuoni 16r (ladies's fashions and accessories)
Gabbanini, Via Porta Rossa 31 (menswear)
Laura Biagotti, Via Calimale 27r (ladies' fashions)
Luisa via Roma, Via Roma 19–21r (all the famous designers and own creations)
Principe, Via Strozzi 21
Pucci, Via de'Pucci 6
Ugolini, Via dei Tornabuoni 22r
Valentino, Via dei Tornabuoni 67r (ladies' and gentlemen's fashions)
Zanobetti, Via Calimala 20 (ladies' fashions)
Via Calimali 22 (exceptionally elegant gentlemen's outfitters in the Palazzo della Lana; salesrooms embellished with 14th c. frescoes)
Zegna, Piazza Rucellai 4–7r (clothing and accessories for the fashion-conscious male)

Fashions

Bijoux Cascio, Via Por San Maria 1r (exclusive and original)

Fashion jewellery

Shopping

Gloves, ties	Ugolini's Gloves, Via dei Tornabuoni 20–22
Jewellery	Bucellati, Via dei Tornabuoni Fratelli Coppini, Via Por S. Maria 78r Meli, Ponte-Vecchio 44–48r (lovely old jewellery and wonderful silver) Torrini, Piazza del Duomo 9r Ylang Ylang, Via dei Tornabuoni 54 (unusual designs) A large selection of precious gold- and silverwork is available from more than 30 shops on the Ponte Vecchio.
Leather goods	Cellerini, Via del Sole 37r (suitcases and bags still made by hand here) Gucci, Via dei Tornabuoni 57–59r Il Bisonte, Via del Parione 35 Ottino, Via de'Cerretani 60–62r Scuolo dei Cuoio, Piazza Santa Croce 16 (the "Leather School", housed in the cloisters of Santa Croce; handmade leather goods)
Lingerie	Loretta Caponi, Borgo Ognissanti 12r (underwear and fine lingerie)
Paper	Edizioni & C, Via della Vigna Nuova 82r Il Papiro, Via Cavour 55, Piazza Duomo 24 (typical Florentine handmade paper)
Shoes	Beltrami, Via dei Pecori 1 and 16r Dominici, Via Calimala 23 Ferragamo, Via dei Tornabuoni 16r (classically elegant ladies' shoes from the "king of shoemakers", supplier of shoes to the Hollywood stars) Mario Valentino, Via dei Tornabuoni 67 Pollini, Via Calimala 12

Jewellery shops on the Ponte Vecchio

Raspini, Via Roma 25–29 (the latest in Italian fashion shoes at not too outrageous prices)
Romano, Via Porta Rossa 14
Vitali, Via Panzani 20

Naj Oleari, Via della Vigna Nuova 35r (unusual gifts and superb fabrics)   Souvenirs

Bonati, Via Gioberti 66 (fine wines from Chianti, Trentino and Friuli)   Wine

Value added tax in Italy on, for example, jewellery and other luxury goods,   Value added tax
can be as high as 38% and thus more than in other European countries. It
therefore pays to obtain receipts for expensive items and on departure to
get the Italian customs to confirm export of the item against production
of the bill. This proof of export can then be sent to the Italian establishment concerned who should refund the value added tax accordingly.

Sport

Stadio Comunale, Viale Manfredo Fanti   Stadium
Capacity 55,000; swimming pool

Galoppo Ippodromo del Visarno   Horse racing
Trotto Ippodromo delle Muline Cascine
See A to Z, Cascine

Golf dell'Ugolino   Golf
Grassina, Strade Chiantigiana 2

Circolo del Tennis, Cascine, Viale Visarno 1   Tennis
Club Sportivo Firenze, Via Fosso Macinante 13

Piscina Comunale Bellariva, Lungarno Colombo 6   Outdoor
swimming pools

Piscina Costoli, Viale Paoli

Piscina Il Poggetto, Via Michele Mercati 24b

Piscina Le Pavoniere, Via delle Cascine

Taxis

There is a minimum tariff for taxi journeys independent of the number
of passengers. Between 10pm and 6am, as well as on Sundays and
public holidays, a surcharge is added to the fare. This can be stopped in
the street but not in the vicinity of a taxi rank. When a taxi has been
booked for a journey ask the driver for a "ricevuta" (receipt).

Via Steccuto 12; tel. 4390 and 4798   Radio-cars

A list of taxi ranks can be found under "Taxi" in the Yellow Pages (pagine   Taxi ranks
gialle).

Telephone

To the United Kingdom: 00 44   International
To Canada and the United States: 00 1   dialling code from
Florence

International dialling code to Florence	From the United Kingdom: 00 39 55 From Canada and the United States: 011 39 55
Pay phones	Public pay phones take both tokens (gettoni, worth 200 lire) and 100, 200 and 500 lire coins. Calls can also be made from most public phones with phone cards (carta telefonica). These can be bought in bars and tobacconists, or from the Telecom Italia SpA for 5000, 1000 or 1500 lire. Long-distance calls can also be made for cash from the Telecom exchanges. Most bars also have pay phones (indicated by the yellow disc over the entrance), operated by tokens or 100 and 200 lire coins, for local calls. If the yellow disc contains the words "teleselezione" or "interurbana" international calls also can be made.
Tariff	The Italian telephone tariff system is very complex. The cheapest rate is between 10pm and 8am.

Theatres, Concerts

Opera, concerts	Theatro Comunale, Corso Italia 12; tel. (055) 27791 Theatro della Pergola, Via della Pergola 12; tel. (055) 2479651/2
Concerts	Sala Bianca, Palazzo Pitti, Piazza Pitti Sala del Conservatorio di Musica, Piazza Belle Arti 2
Drama	Teatro dell'Oriuolo, Via Dell'Oriuolo 31; tel. (055) 2340507 Teatro Niccolini, Via Ricasoli 3; tel. (055) 13282
Revue	Teatro Verdi, Via Ghibellina 101; tel. (055) 396242
Festivals	Particularly in the summer Florence has a full programme of cultural events (see Calendar of Events).

Time

Italy observes Central European Time (one hour ahead of Greenwich Mean Time; six hours ahead of New York time). From April to October Central European Summer Time (two hours ahead of GMT and seven hours ahead of New York time) is in force.

Tipping

In hotels and restaurants service is included, but 5–10% of the bill is still expected as a tip. In bars and cafés service is often not included and then it is usual to tip between 12 and 15%. For taxis round up the fare.

Traffic Regulations

See Motoring

Travel Documents

Since January 1st 1993 passport control does not apply to EU citizens. Nevertheless spot checks can still be carried out.

British and US citizens require only a passport (or the one-year British visitor's passport). This also applies to citizens of Canada, Ireland and many other countries.

It is a good idea to take photocopies of passports, etc. since this makes it easier to get replacements in the event of loss. The British, US, Canadian, etc. consulates can issue a substitute document.

British, US and other national driving licences are valid in Italy but should be accompanied by an Italian translation (obtainable free of charge from automobile clubs). No translation is required for pink EU-type licences. Motorists should also take their vehicle registration papers. The international green card will be demanded in the event of damage, and anyone who does not have one will have to get relatively expensive insurance at the frontier (see Insurance).

Foreign cars must display the oval nationality plate.

Viewpoints

Florence, set amid the Tuscan hills, has a number of impressive viewpoints:

Campanile
Views in every direction; no lift; admission charge.
See A to Z, Duomo Santa Maria del Fiore

Duomo Santa Maria del Fiore
The cathedral dome offers a magnificent view (no lift; admission charge). The best time to photograph the Campanile from here is early in the day. See A to Z, Duomo Santa Maria del Fiore

Fiesole
On a clear day there is a good distant view of Florence from the terrace below the church of Sant'Alessandro in Fiesole.
See A to Z, Fiesole

Forte di Belvedere
From the ramparts around the Forte di Belvedere there is a view similar to that from the Piazzale Michelangelo. Here, however, it is usually much quieter but there is a fairly high admission charge if the Forte di Belvedere palace is hosting an exhibition.
See A to Z

Giardino di Boboli
Florence may have more spectacular viewpoints, but here the visitor can overlook the city from the terrace of the Kaffeehaus in the Boboli Gardens in relative tranquillity.
See A to Z

Piazza di Bellosguardo
The Piazza di Bellosguardo, some way from the centre, also provides a lovely view.
See A to Z

Piazzale Michelangelo
The classic view of Florence is from the Piazzale Michelangelo, but it is usually crowded with visitors. The gardens below the Piazzale tend to be somewhat quieter. The best time for taking photographs is in the morning.
See A to Z

San Miniato al Monte
There is a good distant view of Florence from the square in front of the
church of San Miniato al Monte.
See A to Z

When to Go

The best times to visit Florence are from April to June, and September
to October, when average temperatures are between 15° and 20° C.
Easter and Whitsun, however, should be avoided as the city is very
crowded.

Climate Table

	Temperatures °C				
	Average maximum	Average minimum	Hours of sunshine per day	Days with rain	Rainfall mm
January	8.7	2.1	4.0	7.0	60.5
February	10.5	2.7	4.5	7.0	58.0
March	14.3	5.4	5.2	9.0	72.5
April	18.0	8.3	6.8	8.0	66.5
May	23.3	12.1	8.8	7.5	61.0
June	27.5	15.6	9.3	6.5	69.5
July	30.3	18.0	10.7	3.0	25.5
August	30.2	18.0	9.4	3.5	35.5
September	25.6	15.0	7.5	5.5	68.5
October	19.6	11.0	6.0	8.5	97.0
November	13.6	6.5	3.5	9.5	101.5
December	10.0	3.8	3.0	9.0	78.0
Year	19.3	9.8	6.7	84	795

In July and August, at the height of the summer season, when many
Italians take their holidays, it can be difficult to find a hotel room unless
a reservation is made well in advance.

November to March sees Florence at its most undisturbed and many
visitors are happy to endure the unsettled weather for this privilege.

Wine

Italy has been making wine from time immemorial, and today it leads
the world in the total amount produced – almost a quarter of the world's
wine comes from Italy, and Tuscany is one of Italy's best organised wine-
producing regions.

Quality
designations

Introduced in 1992, Italy's current wine laws lay down a compulsory
system of labelling for wines of different qualities. At the bottom end of the
scale are table wines labelled simply vino rosso or vino bianco with no
indication of year or place of origin. Above them in the hierarchy come
table wines of designated origin, e.g. vino rosso Toscano, while at the top,
representing the highest grades, are the DOC- and DOCG wines
("Denominazione di Origine Contrallata e Garentita") signifying they come
from an officially recognised wine producing area and that their quality is
controlled and guaranteed. DOC and DOCG wines are always analysed
and tasted before sale. The new laws also control and where appropriate
require a guaranteed declaration on the label of the region, province, district, sub-district, species of grape and vinyard. The more specific the
details of origin, the more severe the quality requirements met.

Red

Tuscany produces probably the world's best-known wine, Chianti. It is
made from the dark Sangiovese grape together with Canaiolo and the

paler Trebbiano and Malvasia grapes. Chianti colli Fiorentini, produced in the hills around Florence, is a fresh ruby-red wine that makes a good table wine. Chianti Classico comes from the countryside between Florence and Siena; this soft, slightly sharp wine generally matures after two to five years, and good vintages can keep for over a decade. This "classic" Chianti can be identified by the black cockerel on the label, and is virtually matched in quality by Chianti Putto, which has a cherub as its trademark. The increasing sales resistance that Chianti has been meeting with of late may be due to its highly variable quality. The mass production that has gone on, especially outside the actual true Chianti region, has tended to make many Chiantis less acceptable in the eyes of the connoisseur.

An outstanding, if expensive, red wine is Brunello di Montalcino. Good vintages mature very well indeed, acquiring a distinguished bouquet as they do so. Rosso dei Vigneti di Brunello comes from the same region and the same grape, but from years that are not so good and grapes that are less ripe. Dry and velvety, it is drunk young, and has a rich bouquet.

Vino Nobile di Montepulciano is another excellent wine and is from the south-east of Tuscany. The colour of brick, or pomegranate, it is dry and has a bouquet reminiscent of violets. Only the very best vintages are put down for longer periods.

A growing demand has led to the resurgence of the Tuscan white wines. Although officially only red wine can be sold under the Chianti appellation, white Chianti from Trebbiano and Malvasia grapes is increasingly being produced in this region. It is generally dry and light, but can also be made fruity. These table wines go under a variety of names. Galestro, which has a maximum alcohol content of 10.5% and is dry, fresh and fruity, is a good, above-average wine. Bianco della Lega has similar qualities.

White

Monte Carlo, from east of Lucca, is one of Tuscany's best white wines. It is made from a blend of different grape varieties, so its characteristics vary according to the producer. It is usually drunk young. Vernaccia di San Gimignano is a white wine with its own tradition – rich and dark if fermented with the grapeskins, or light and fresh, with a flowery bouquet, if the skins are left out. It too is seldom kept for long.

Those who prefer a rosé should try Brolio Rosé, a very fragrant wine, or Ros, di Bolgheri, from the Sangiovese and Canaiolo grapes.

Rosé

The terms in general use on Italian wine labels are only a very limited indication of the nature of the wine in question. They can refer to places or varieties of grape, but are often simply brand names or figments of the imagination. It is by no means unusual for red and white wines widely differing in characteristics and quality to be sold under one and the same name. The 1963 Italian Wine Law established three quality appellations.

Labels

"Denominazione Semplice" indicates an ordinary table wine of no prescribed quality.

"Denominazione di Origine Controllata", DOC, the appellation of controlled origin, can be applied for by any group of producers wanting to register their wine as "DOC". This then indicates that it comes from an officially recognised wine-producing region, and is made in accordance with pre-determined methods and from specific varieties of grapes. The producers in a DOC district prescribe their own specifications. DOC wines are subject to quality control, and must carry a DOC label in addition to their own.

"Denominazione di Origine Contrallata e Garantita", DOCG, the appellation of controlled and guaranteed origin, is only awarded to select wines from individual producers, who usually bottle their wine themselves and guarantee the fact with an official seal.

Terms

amabile	smooth
annata	year
azienda agricola (agraria)	estate, vineyard
barbera	full-bodied grape from Piedmont
bianco	white
cantina	winery
cantina sociale	wine co-operative
classico	from the centre and best part of the region
frizzante	slightly sparkling
gradazione alcoolica	alcohol content
metodo champenois	champagne method
nero	dark red
riserva	wine laid down for a prescribed period, usually three years
rosato	rosé
rosso	red
secco	dry
spumante	sparkling
superiore	superior quality DOC wines
tenementi	estate or vineyard
uva	grape
vendemmia	vintage
vigna	vineyard
vino ordinario	"ordinary" wine, usually bottled else where
vino di tavola	table wine

Youth Hostels

Ostello "Villa Camerata"
Viale Augusto Righi 2/4; tel. 601451

Ostello Santa Monica
Via Santa Monica 6; tel. 268338

Villa Favard
Via Rocca Tedalda; tel. 690847
(free overnight sleeping outdoors in summer)

Index

Index

Principal Sights of Tourist Interest

Imprint

83 illustrations, 18 maps and plans
1 large city plan at the end of the book

German text: Heinz-Joachim Fischer, Linda Fischer, Reinhard Strüber

Editorial work: Baedeker Redaktion (Carmen Galenschovski)

General direction: Rainer Eisenschmid, Baedeker Ostfinden

English translation: Babel Translations, Norwich, Wendy Bell

Cartography: Huber, Munich
Mairs Geographischer Verlag GmbH & Co., Osfilden (large city plan)

Source of Illustrations:
Archiv (3), Galenschovski (6), HB Verlags- und Vertriebsgesellschaft mbH (5), Historia-Foto (9), Lade, Fotoagentur (3), Mader (1), Reincke (3), Schapowalow, Fotoagentur (1), Schuster, Fotoagentur (1), Strüber (1), Uffisien (4)

Front cover: Tony Stone Images. Back cover: AA Photo Library (J. Edmanson)

5th English edition 2000

© Baedeker Osfilden
Original German edition 2000

© 2000 The Automobile Association
English language edition worldwide

Published by AA Publishing (a trading name of Automobile Association Developments Limited, whose registered office is Norfolk House, Priestley Road, Basingstoke, Hampshire RG24 9NY. Registered number 1878835).

Distributed in the United States and Canada by:
Fodor's Travel Publications, Inc.
201 East 50th Street
New York, NY 10022

A CIP catalogue record of this book is available from the British Library.

Licensed user:
Mairs Geographischer Verlag GmbH & Co.
Osfilden

Printed in Italy by G. Canale & C. S.p.A, Turin

ISBN 0 7495 2265 8